Claiming the Future

Choosing Prosperity

in the Middle East and North Africa

The World Bank
Washington, D.C.

Manufactured in the United States of America
First printing October 1995

Contents

This report was prepared by a team led by Nemat Shafik and is based on background papers prepared by Bob Anderson, Jon Avins, Sue Berryman, Milan Brahmbhatt, Uri Dadush, Fred Golladay, Bernard Hoekman, Jalal Jalali, Bjorn Larsen, Albert Martinez, John Page, E. Mick Riordan, Shane Streifel, Kazue Takagaki, Willem van Eeghen, John Waterbury, and Lawrence Wolff. The team was assisted by Jesmin Rahman and Soumaya Tohamy. Many others in and outside the Bank, especially in the Middle East and North Africa region, provided valuable contributions and comments (see the preface and bibliography). Bruce Ross-Larson served as the principal editor, working with Kim Bieler, Mark Bock, and Paul Holtz from American Writing Corporation. Jan-Marie Hopkins and Azeb Yideru provided administrative and production support. The report was initiated by Caio Koch-Weser and was carried out under the general direction of John Page.

Foreword

The countries of the Middle East and North Africa (MENA) region face unprecedented challenges. The pace of change in the global economy has never been faster, prompting the need for new economic strategies to participate successfully in it. Meanwhile, the end of the cold war, the aftermath of the Gulf conflict, the evolving Middle East peace process, and the rise of fundamentalism call into question traditional political assumptions and structures. Navigating these turbulent waters requires a coherent and purposeful vision of the way ahead among the region's leaders, business people, and citizens.

This study is intended to contribute to such a vision. It is the product of considerable work at the World Bank on long-term issues in the Middle East and North Africa. Its findings—sometimes troubling, often surprising—are ultimately hopeful. The troubling and surprising aspects lie in the region's poor economic performance during the past decade, despite its former favorable record and considerable underlying economic advantages. The explanation lies in the region's policies and in the dramatic recent changes in the international economic environment, including lower oil prices, greater competition, and increasingly mobile capital. But the study also offers cause for hope. Many MENA countries have clearly demonstrated that they can dramatically reduce poverty, educate unprecedentedly large numbers of their citizens, and accumulate substantial capital assets. The region's economic future lies in making productive use of these resources—human, financial, and physical—to take advantage of the opportunities that globalization brings.

Ultimately, the well-being of all MENA's people will depend on realizing a development paradigm of growth that is rapid, widely shared throughout societies, and environmentally sustainable. This study focuses on the "rapid" and "shared" components of the paradigm. Issues of environmental sustainability are addressed in other Bank studies—*Middle East and North Africa Environmental Strategy: Toward Sustainable Development* and *A Strategy for Managing Water in the Middle East and*

North Africa—which complement this one. While the decisions that will shape the future of the region lie in the hands of MENA governments and peoples, we hope that this work will contribute to the formulation of economic policy in the region. And we at the World Bank stand ready to work with our partners in the region in facing the challenges ahead and realizing the vision of a more prosperous future.

Caio Koch-Weser
Vice President
Middle East and North Africa Region

Preface

This report is the product of a collaborative effort both in the World Bank and with scholars and policymakers from the Middle East and North Africa region. Throughout the process we have consulted a wide variety of individuals knowledgeable about the region. None of our collaborators, however, is responsible for the findings of this report, which are the views of World Bank staff.

To get feedback on the report's emerging messages, the Bank cosponsored a workshop with the Economic Research Forum for the Arab Countries, Iran, and Turkey in Tunis in June 1995. Papers were also commissioned from scholars in the region about local perspectives on long-term strategic issues and presented at the Tunis workshop. A group of distinguished thinkers in the region participated in reviewing the final draft report and served as advisers before publication. Valuable contributions were made by these regional "friends" (Dr. Jassim Al-Mannai, Director General and Chairman of the Board of the Arab Monetary Fund; Dr. Abdullah El-Kuwaiz, Associate Secretary General for Economic Affairs of the Gulf Cooperation Council; Professor Said El-Naggar, Cairo University; Dr. Ziad Fariz, Chairman of the Jordan Trade Association; Dr. Attila Karaosmanoglu, former Deputy Prime Minister of Turkey and World Bank Managing Director; Mr. Ismail Khelil, former Minister and Ambassador for Tunisia; Dr. Ghassan Salame, Professor at the Institute of Political Studies in Paris; and Dr. Yusif Sayigh, Economic Consultant).

The report draws on much of the ongoing economic and sectoral work prepared on the MENA region by Bank staff. Further details and supporting analysis for the results in this report can be found in the background papers prepared for this study. In addition, a series of seminars based on the background papers were held in the Bank, and comments from participants were very helpful in shaping the messages in the report. In particular, valuable contributions were made by the seminar discussants: Ishac Diwan, William Easterly, Mohamed El-Erian, Ahmed Galal,

Elizabeth King, Barbara Nunberg, Lant Pritchett, Julian Schweitzer, David Tarr, Dominique van der Walle, and Michael Walton. In addition to the MENA regional staff, a group of senior "friends" throughout the World Bank advised on the content of the report at the final stages: Masood Ahmed, Abdallah Bouhabib, Magdi Iskander, Emmanuel Jimenez, Jagannathan Murli, Daniel Ritchie, Joanne Salop, Anil Sood, Lyn Squire, Inder Sud, William Tyler, and John Underwood.

Executive Summary

A vision for a prosperous Middle East and North Africa

By 2010 the countries of the Middle East and North Africa have the potential to double incomes, increase life expectancy by close to ten years, and cut illiteracy and infant mortality by almost half (figure 1). They could also become full partners in the global economy, using integration with Europe and within the region as a stepping stone to international competitiveness. Peace, macroeconomic stability, and an attractive investment environment could attract billions of dollars of capital from nationals and foreign investors. The faster economic growth would reduce poverty and bring down unemployment, restoring hope to millions.

FIGURE 1

Major economic and social improvements are possible

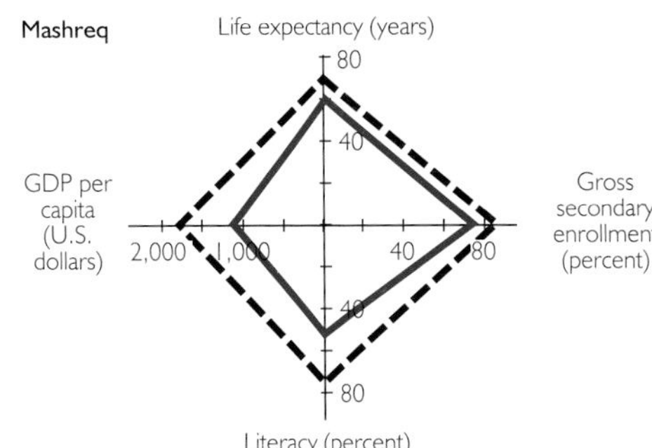

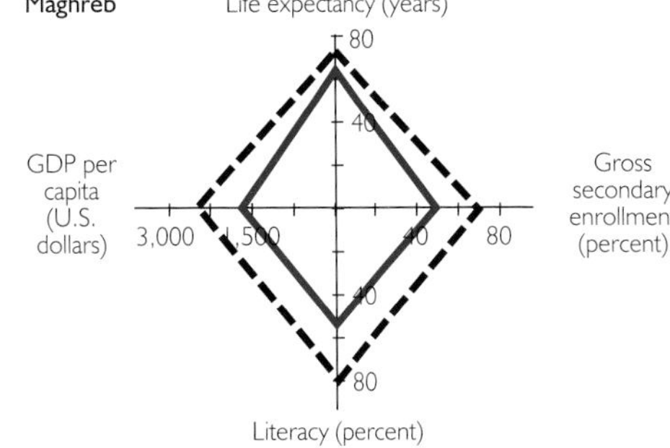

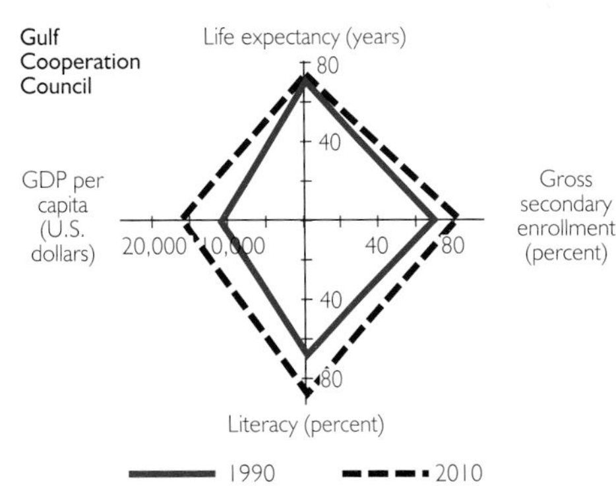

Note: GDP per capita for 2010 has been projected using the 2.5% growth rate from the base case scenario.
Source: Diwan and Squire 1992; World Bank staff estimates.

From vision to reality

Making this vision a reality is within the grasp of today's policymakers. Perhaps the greatest feature of today's global economy is that no country is destined to be poor because of a bad endowment of natural resources, an isolated location, or a concentration on certain products. Production, finance, and trade have changed to make human talent more important than natural endowment, agility more crucial than location, and quality and innovation more important than mass production. The implication is that countries can choose, through their policies, to be rich—or to be poor.

For too long, countries in the Middle East and North Africa (MENA) region have squandered their potential. The MENA region is vast—spanning from Morocco in the west to Iran in the north and east and as far south as Yemen. And while the region is very heterogeneous, some common themes characterize many countries' development experience. Political energy has sometimes focused on regional conflicts and rivalries rather than on economic development. Oil wealth often went for activities with low social returns. Major investments in education and health often helped the privileged rather than the disadvantaged. And natural resources were mined to fuel this process.

That era is waning. Peace, with all its vicissitudes, is bound to reduce the political risks in the region and make space for more determined efforts at economic reform over the long run. The domestic voices for change are growing more numerous. The region's governments are under greater pressure to be accountable to their citizens and transparent in their actions. To attract private investment, all countries will have strong incentives to offer access through association agreements to the vast European market as well as to the numerous regional markets. But realizing the vision will mean that the economies of the region will have to look quite different from the way they do today.

Realizing the vision will mean that economies of the region will look quite different from today

Yesterday's achievements, today's predicament

MENA countries were "high performers"

During 1960–85 the MENA region outperformed all other regions except East Asia in income growth and the equality of income distribution (figure 2).

FIGURE 2

Past growth was rapid . . . but not sustained

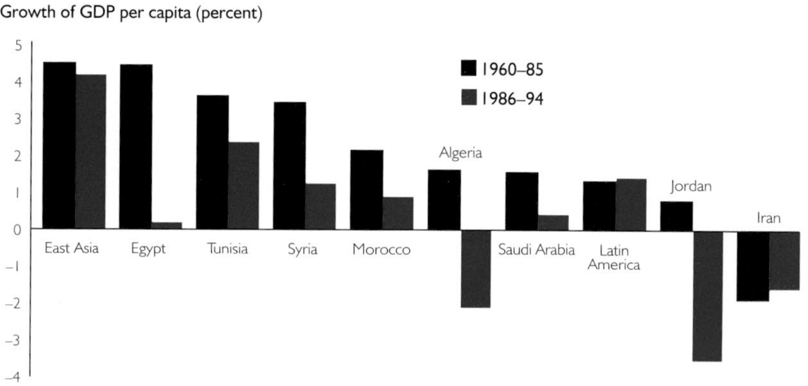

Note: East Asia includes China, Hong Kong, Indonesia, Republic of Korea, Malaysia, the Philippines, Singapore, and Thailand. Latin America includes Argentina, Bolivia, Brazil, Chile, Colombia, Ecuador, Paraguay, Peru, Uruguay, and Venezuela. GDP growth rates are calculated as

$$\left[\frac{\text{end year per capita GDP}}{\text{beginning year per capita GDP}}\right]^{1/\text{number of years}} - 1.$$

Source: World Bank data.

The social payoffs have been enormous. Infant mortality more than halved, and life expectancy rose by more than ten years. Primary school enrollment shot up from 61% in 1965 to 98% in 1991. And adult literacy improved from 34% in 1970 to 53% in 1990, with particular progress made in the oil-exporting countries.

The region's governments were also effective at reducing poverty (figures 3 and 4). By 1990 only 5.6% of the population in MENA lived on less than $1 a day—the global benchmark for absolute poverty—compared with 14.7% in East Asia and 28.8% in Latin America. And whatever the wealth, poverty was lower in MENA countries than elsewhere. These achievements were the result of rapid growth in the 1970s and early 1980s and generous transfers to large parts of the population.

FIGURE 3

Poverty in MENA has been low . . .

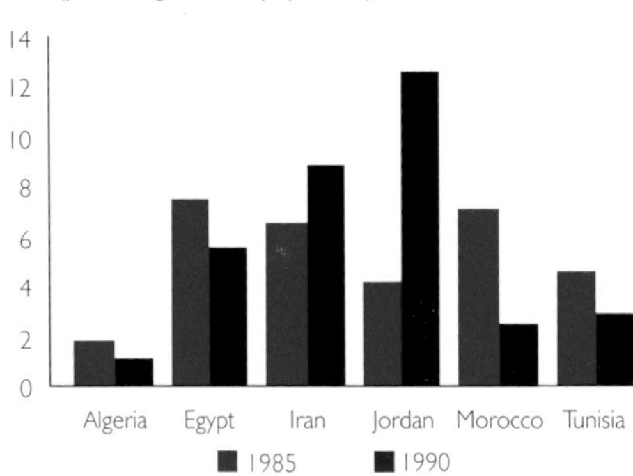

Note: Poor is defined as average spending of less than $1 a day at 1985 purchasing power parity.
Source: van Eeghen 1995.

Past achievements were the outcome of easier circumstances

The era of statism coincided with a far more accommodating international context for MENA countries. Oil prices were high. The world economy was buoyant. Industrialization was still in the easy stages. And the world was a less competitive place. Times have since changed, and many of the policies and institutions that seemed to serve MENA countries well have become the stumbling blocks to the future.

The economic crisis of the past ten years is the product of two fundamental factors—collapsing oil prices and deteriorating productivity. Since 1986 real per capita incomes have fallen by 2% a year—the largest decline in any developing region. For oil exporters, the fall in output per capita of 4% a year between 1980 and 1991 closely paralleled oil prices. Even the non–oil exporters in the region (such as Jordan, Morocco, and Tunisia) grew by less than 1% because oil revenues had strong "ripple effects" through regional labor and capital markets. Investment in MENA countries also declined in the 1980s, but output declined even more, implying that productivity was falling, too (figure 5).

FIGURE 4

. . . compared with the rest of the world

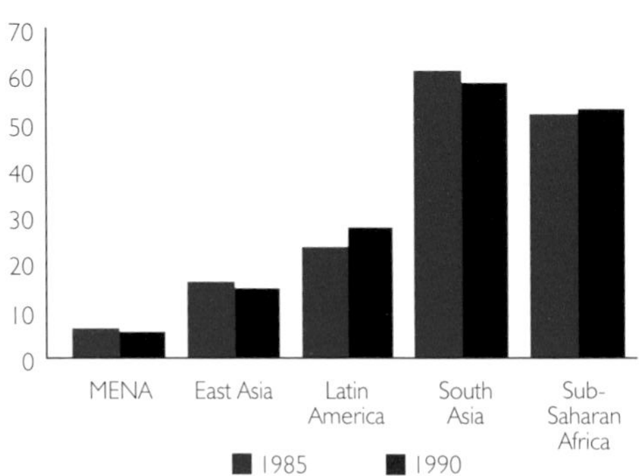

Note: Poor is defined as average spending of less than $1 a day at 1985 purchasing power parity. MENA includes Algeria, Egypt, Iran, Jordan, Morocco, and Tunisia.
Source: Chen, Datt, and Ravallion 1993; van Eeghen 1995.

Past investments are the nub of today's reform predicament

The huge investments in state-owned enterprises and human skills unsuited to today's marketplace are the nub of the adjustment problem facing most MENA economies. Overall productivity, though accelerating rapidly in other parts of the world, has been declining steadily by about 0.2% a year (figure 6). High investment rates yielded lower than expected returns under policies that thwarted competition.

Competitive pressures from the world economy—along with domestic pressures for new and better job opportunities—are the most likely forces to trigger change. Until recently, oil and other revenues (such as aid and remittances) enabled many countries to postpone reforms. It is no accident that the countries most integrated with the world economy—Jordan, Morocco, and Tunisia—lacked substantial natural resources on which to rely.

The postponement of reform has meant that interest groups profiting from the old regime are deeply entrenched. Firms that have benefited from protection and cheap credit and a middle class accustomed to subsidized commodities and services are reluctant to see their privileges eroded. And governments often have been slow to respond with better policies, effective services, and more transparent procedures.

FIGURE 5

Output fell more than investment—so productivity fell

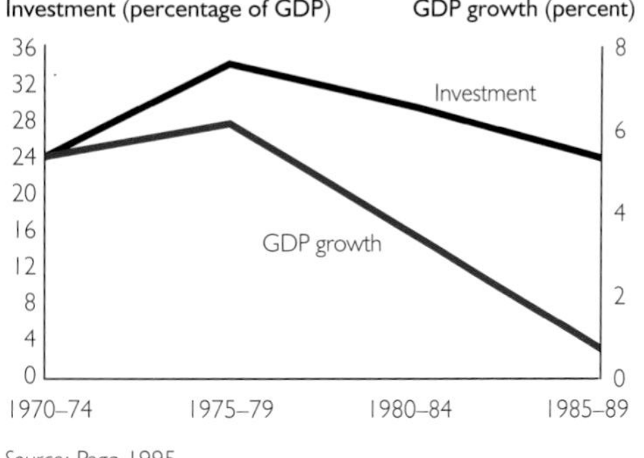

Source: Page 1995.

FIGURE 6

MENA is losing competitiveness

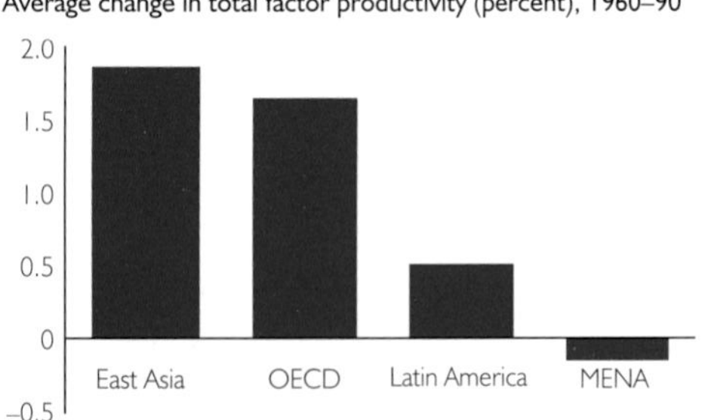

Source: World Bank 1993.

Choosing to prosper

How can governments overcome the troublesome nexus of state-owned enterprises, resistance to trade liberalization and privatization, and the labor elite in the public sector? What direction should reforms take to ensure a prosperous future for the region? In addition to maintaining macroeconomic stability, four measures are essential: promoting non-oil exports, making the private sector more efficient, producing more skilled and flexible workers, and reducing poverty through faster growth (box 1).

Promoting non-oil exports

MENA's non-oil exports (with 260 million people) are less than Finland's (with 5 million people). Meeting future import requirements (such as food) means that exports will have to grow, and non-oil merchandise exports offer the biggest opportunity for the future if there is progress in trade liberalization and competition policies. Manufacturing

BOX 1

Getting from here to there: A reformer's checklist

For now . . . / **. . . and tomorrow**

Credible and consistent trade liberalization must lead the way

For now:

- Use international signaling mechanisms, such as the World Trade Organization and the association agreements with the EU, to lock in reforms and gain credibility.
- Support non-oil exports through assistance in financing and market penetration.

And tomorrow:

- Move toward free trade or uniform tariffs not in excess of 5% by 2010.

Create a high return, nimble investment environment

For now:

- Abolish burdensome licensing requirements, excessive customs fees, and protracted conflict resolution.
- Encourage competition in the financial sector to reduce financing costs for producers and develop securities markets, payment and trading systems, and regulatory capacity.

And tomorrow:

- Reduce the costs of doing business by upgrading infrastructure services with private sector financing.

Make privatization a priority

For now:

- Centralize the management of the program under a high-level privatization "champion."
- Decentralize the implementation of privatization transactions by using consultants and managers who are paid fees based on the price at which they sell the firm.
- Sell privatization to the public through information campaigns.

And tomorrow:

- Use simple, transparent rules for enterprise sales and for regulating private investment in infrastructure.
- Reward managers for successfully implementing privatization.

Get on the international financial map

For now:

- Provide clear, simple, and credible rules for foreign investors.

And tomorrow:

- Put information in the international arena by publishing economic data, issuing international paper, and obtaining internationally recognized credit ratings.

Integrate education and the economy

For now:

- Increase student flexibility by focusing on basic skills and reducing early specialization.
- Make vocational training demand-driven through joint public-private management, governance, and financing.
- Liberalize labor markets to increase the productivity of educational investments.

And tomorrow:

- Raise access targets by level and increase quality through various feedback mechanisms to test the educational system's performance with national and international standards.

Use natural resources sustainably

For now:

- Eliminate remaining subsidies to natural resources (energy and water) and environmental services (municipal water and sanitation).

And tomorrow:

- Impose environmental taxes to ensure that polluters pay.

Rely on growth and targeted interventions to reduce poverty

For now:

- Aim for rapid growth and keep real wages in check.
- Reassess regulations that discourage job creation for the poor (such as minimum wages and restrictions on firing and temporary contracts).

And tomorrow:

- Rely on self-targeted interventions where possible, such as differential qualities of goods or public works programs.
- Provide cash transfers for the chronic poor, but monitor closely to ensure maximum benefits to the truly needy.

FIGURE 7

Manufacturing exports are not growing

Manufacturing exports per capita (U.S. dollars)

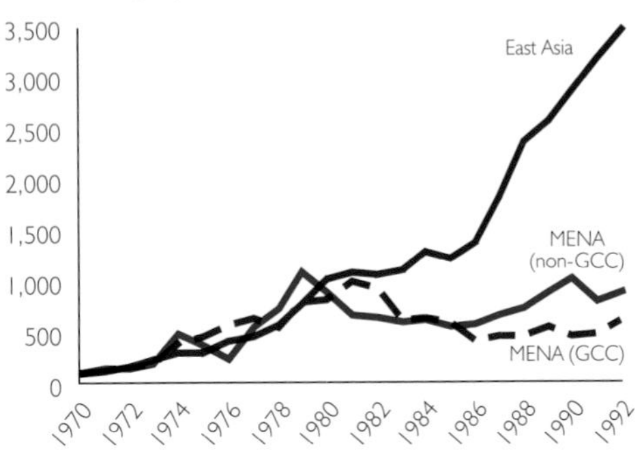

Source: World Bank data.

FIGURE 8

The average tariff burden on trade is high

Collected tax/value of imports, 1993

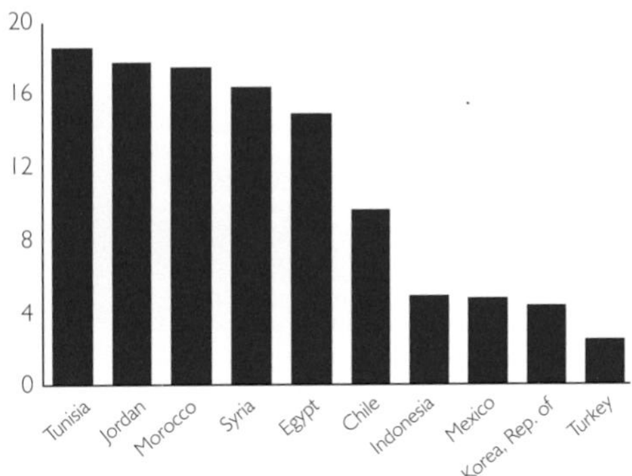

Source: IMF 1994b and 1994c.

FIGURE 9

Clothing and chemicals have been MENA's largest exports, 1992–93

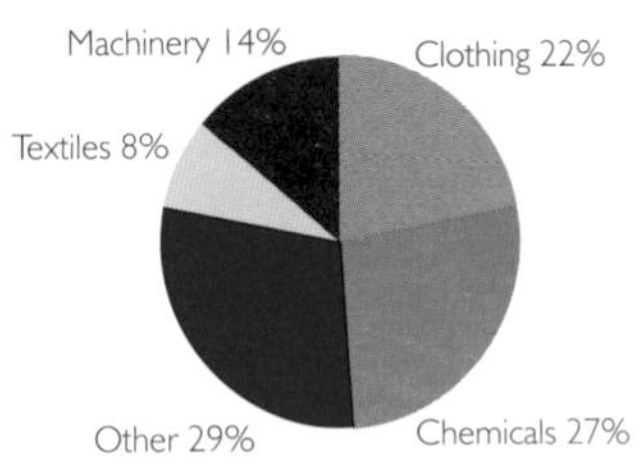

Note: Excludes Israel.
Source: Riordan and others 1995.

exports, usually a major source of productivity gains, have grown slowly (figure 7). And the openness of MENA economies lags behind their competitors (figure 8). For some countries in the region—such as Jordan, Morocco, and Tunisia—the required growth in exports is attainable given their recent performance. But for many oil-dependent economies, the improvement in non-oil exports needed to maintain living standards is massive—and difficult without fundamental changes in policy.

What should governments do to promote non-oil exports? Successful exporters in East Asia used four key elements—access for exporters to imports at world prices, export financing, assistance in market penetration, and policy flexibility in response to changing circumstances (World Bank 1993). What sectors are likely to fuel the growth in exports? The main export growth so far has been in chemicals, clothing, machinery, textiles, and other manufactures, such as carpets, gold, silver, and jewelry (figure 9). Building competitive advantage on this existing export capacity is the most promising approach in the immediate future.

Making the private sector more efficient

All countries compete for the attention of the private capital so critical for growth. But with its increased mobility, private capital has become fickle. It follows high rates of return and leaves when the environment sours. MENA countries have been unable to keep national capital home (capital from the region held abroad is about $350 billion), and they generally have been unsuccessful at attracting foreign investors (figure 10). About half the capital held abroad is from the GCC, for whom investing abroad is economically optimal given their need to diversify.

Why has investment lagged? The business environment is plagued by burdensome regulations. Privatization has been slow. Infrastructure quality is inadequate and financial markets remain underdeveloped. For example, Egyptian entrepreneurs spend about 30% of their time resolving problems with regulatory compliance. Even in Morocco, where the investment regime has been substantially liberalized, as many as 20 documents and six months are needed to register a business. The percentage of unsuccessful telephone calls is 34% in Tunisia, 46% in Yemen, 50% in Lebanon, 57% in Morocco, and 60% in Jordan. Intermediation margins—the difference between banks' lending and deposit rates—averaged about 9% for non–Gulf Cooperation Council (GCC) MENA countries in 1991–93, compared with about 3–4% in Asia and the OECD. Profitable for banks—unappealing for businesses.

Dismantling burdensome regulations while simultaneously building a system that addresses the needs of a more global economy is essential in most MENA countries. First, privatization needs to be a priority. Countries with large and inefficient public sectors (such as Algeria and Egypt) will have to focus simultaneously on selling off state-owned enterprises and trying to attract private investment in infrastructure. Countries with less burdensome public enterprise sectors (such as Jordan, Lebanon, Morocco, Tunisia, and many Gulf countries) will be able to focus on attracting investment in infrastructure and other services that are crucial to long-term competitiveness. Second, the MENA region needs to get on the international financial map by clarifying regulations and putting information into the international arena to attract investors. Given the investment requirements into the next century, governments will need to bring in the private sector as serious partners.

FIGURE 10

Foreign investment is low, 1993

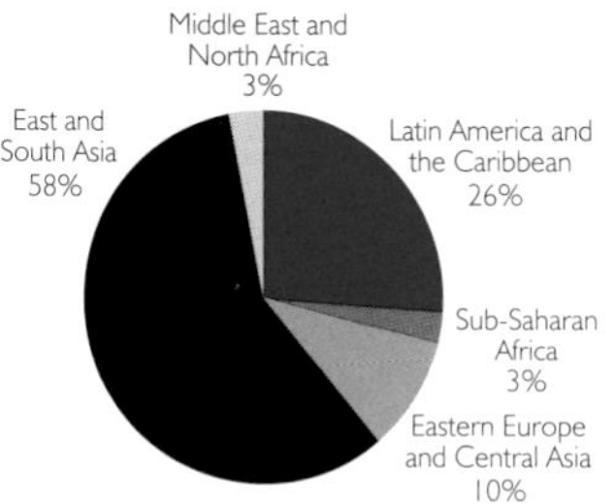

Source: Saba 1995.

Producing more skilled and flexible workers

To create the human capital for international competition, labor markets will have to be liberalized (to ensure investments in human capital have high payoffs) and access to education will have to increase. MENA countries have to set a goal of nine years of basic education for all children. By 2010 minimum enrollment rates should be 100% for primary school in all countries, 70% for secondary school, and 25% for higher education. Increasing enrollments, demographic pressures, and the need to improve quality will put severe financing pressure on the education sector. The annual cost of achieving this expansion (adjusted for population growth, higher teacher salaries, and modest quality improvements) would be about $17.5 billion in Egypt, Iran, Jordan, Morocco, and Tunisia in 2010, three times their spending in 1990. Such an increase in spending can only be achieved if the region's economies are growing rapidly.

Vocational training programs, now often "warehouses" for unemployed youth, will have to become flexible systems that respond to the changing skill requirements of labor markets. In Egypt 61% of secondary students attend vocational and technical schools, despite their higher costs, often to divert the numbers seeking admission to higher education. The result: the vocational training system supplies five to seven times the number of technical workers needed in the economy. In Morocco a payroll tax on employers goes solely to publicly provided vocational training, often divorced from the needs of the private market. In most MENA countries training programs need to be linked to employers through joint private and public financing, management, and goal-setting—as is starting to happen in Iran, Jordan, Tunisia, and Yemen.

With reform, abject poverty could be dramatically reduced

Public financing should go for universal literacy, numeracy, and coherent social and cultural values through high participation rates in primary, lower secondary, and eventually upper secondary education. Economic growth's higher incomes will enable private financing of higher levels of education. This is already happening in Lebanon (where private higher education predominates), Iran (where half the university enrollments are in one private university), and Jordan (where 20% of higher education enrollments are in the private sector).

Reducing poverty through faster growth

Higher growth is essential for reducing poverty and for providing sustainable social spending and safety nets. Moving from zero growth to 1% annual growth in the MENA region would reduce the number of poor in the region by 8 million over the next decade. Without the higher growth that reform can bring, the number of poor (those living on less than $1 a day) would rise to about 15 million by 2010 (figure 11). Because many people in the MENA region are close to the poverty line, faster economic growth can greatly reduce their vulnerability. With reform, abject poverty could be dramatically reduced, although at higher incomes the definition of poverty would have to change.

Additional GDP growth has less impact—a percentage point increase in the average rate of growth from 5% to 6% would reduce the number of poor people by only 1.5 million over the next decade. Policies have to become much more specific, targeted to address the needs of the chronic poor. The amounts needed to eliminate poverty are small, but some leakages are inevitable, and targeting can be costly, both politically and administratively. Tunisia's subsidy program, which includes some targeting, still costs three times as much as would be needed to give all the poor the equivalent of the poverty line income each year. Egypt's social assistance program provides very small payments (about 5% of the poverty line) to 2.7 million beneficiaries, but administrative costs consume 12% of total costs.

Jordan, Morocco, and Tunisia are beginning to reap the rewards of reform

A few countries have made important strides in their reform efforts—with Jordan, Morocco, and Tunisia as notable examples. They began their adjustment programs in the 1980s with macroeconomic stabilization, deficit reduction, trade liberalization, and structural reforms in pricing, regulation, and financial market development. All three instituted reforms gradually. But unlike many of their neighbors, they have been fairly consistent in the direction of reform, building up credibility over time. None of the three was an oil exporter, and, except for phosphates in Jordan and Morocco, they could not draw on rents to finance the public sector. Remittances were important to all three, but because of profitable opportunities for the private sector at home, capital flight was very low.

Incomes, exports, and jobs are growing faster among reformers

The new policies are starting to pay off (table 1). All three countries—Jordan, Morocco, and Tunisia—have higher growth in incomes, exports, and jobs than do other countries in the region. Jordan and Tunisia are exceptional performers on virtually every indicator of human development—life expectancy, enrollment rates, and infant mortality.

FIGURE 11

Reform will bring down poverty

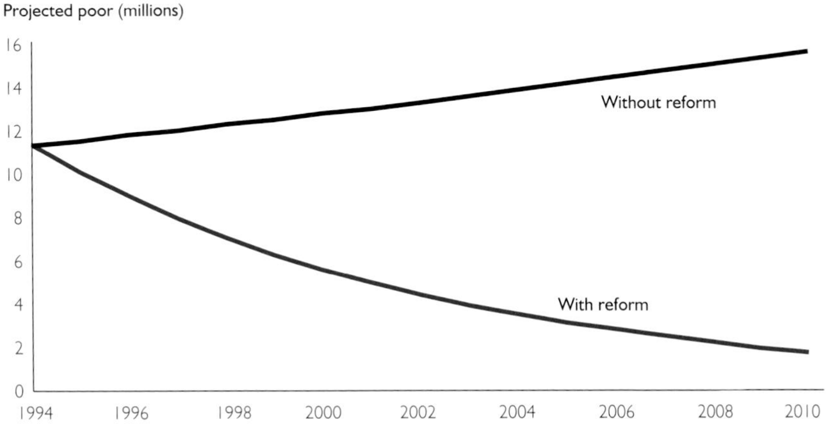

Note: Poor is defined as average spending of less than $1 a day at 1985 purchasing power parity. The growth elasticitiy of poverty used here is –4.48. Without reform, GDP per capita grows at –0.46% for MENA. With reform, GDP per capita grows at 2.5%. Includes Algeria, Egypt, Iran, Jordan, Lebanon, Morocco, Syria, Tunisia, and Yemen.
Source: van Eeghen 1995.

Many low-wage jobs, crucial to reducing poverty, were created in export-oriented industries in Morocco and Tunisia. And unlike other countries in the region, where labor market policies have encouraged investors to substitute capital for labor (figure 12), both Morocco and Tunisia have given investors incentives to create jobs and have kept capital-labor ratios low. And both have cut poverty in half (table 2).

The payoff to reforms is considerable

What would the payoff to reforms be for other countries in the region? Considerable. An ambitious reform scenario of 3.5% per capita growth to 1999 and 5.0% thereafter would result in a doubling of per capita incomes by 2010. Even under a more probable scenario of 2.5%

TABLE 1

Jordan, Morocco, and Tunisia have had better economic results
(percent, unless otherwise indicated)

Country	Per capita GDP growth rate, 1990–94	Non-oil exports growth rate, 1980–93	Average annual inflation rate,[a] 1984–94	FDI inflows/ GDP, 1993	Mean years of schooling, 1987	Population spending less than $1 a day, 1990
Jordan	0.39	4.3	5.33	–0.65	5	12.60[b]
Morocco	0.70	3.8	5.73	2.00	2	2.49
Tunisia	2.10	10.5	6.00	1.63	5	2.89
Algeria	–2.33	4.5	18.00	0.03	4	1.16
Egypt	–0.72	0.5	14.80	1.20	5	5.60
Iran	–1.04	–1.0	20.50	–0.05	4	8.94

a. Using GDP deflator.
b. This estimate was done at the time of the Gulf war. Higher growth rates since then have probably reduced poverty in Jordan.
Source: World Bank data; van Eeghen 1995.

FIGURE 12

Morocco and Tunisia have created more jobs with lower capital-labor ratios

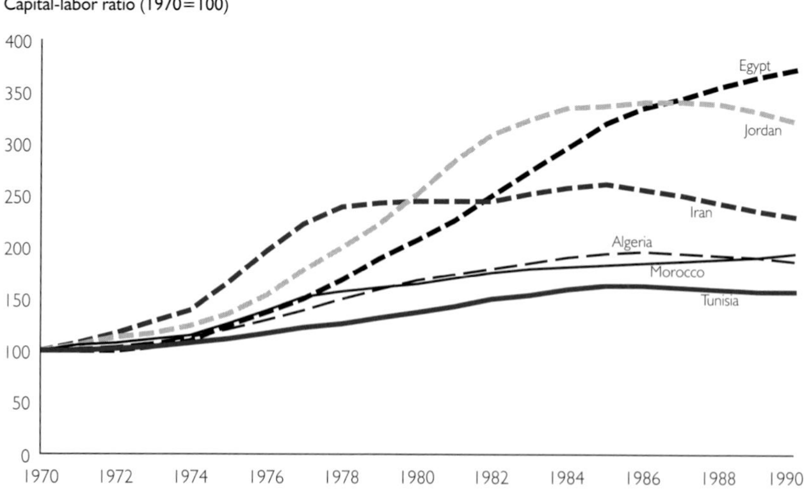

Source: World Bank staff estimates based on data from Nehru and Dhareshwar 1993.

TABLE 2
Morocco and Tunisia have reduced poverty substantially

	Morocco		Tunisia	
	1984/85	1991	1985	1990
Head-count index	6.06	1.64	4.63	2.89
Poverty-gap index[a]	1.62	0.23	0.89	0.64
Squared poverty gap index[b]	0.82	0.06	0.31	0.28

Note: Poverty is defined as average spending of less than $1 a day at 1985 purchasing power parity.
a. The shortfall in expenditure from the poverty line of the average poor person, expressed as a percentage of the poverty line.
b. A measure of the distribution of income of those below the poverty line.
Source: World Bank 1995e; Chen, Datt, and Ravallion 1993.

per capita growth, incomes would be 50% higher by 2010. Instead of having rising unemployment and domestic tension, reforming economies will grow fast enough to absorb their expanding labor forces while experiencing a gradual rise in real wages. With reform, all countries can realize positive growth rates in per capita incomes. Without reform, all countries that have not already initiated reforms experience falling per capita incomes.

Now is the time for action

Pressures for reform are mounting

Potential winners from reform outnumber the losers

In today's fast-paced world economy, the gradualist strategies of the past may mean no growth (given the mobility of capital) if policies lack credibility. And half-hearted or stop-go approaches to reform are a sure way to lose credibility. While the region's population is growing at 2.7% a year, the labor force is growing at 3.3%. Jobs for 47 million new entrants to the labor force will have to be found by 2010. The number of unemployed, now about 9 million, will rise to 15 million by 2010 at today's high rates. Attracting investors to create jobs will require credible public institutions with a clear long-term reform strategy.

Just as the number of "losers" from the lack of reform is growing, so is the cost of inaction. In many MENA countries those interested in new job creation (the unemployed and those entering the labor force) now outnumber those interested in the preservation of old jobs (those employed in the state sector). Even under conservative assumptions about overstaffing in the public sector, the potential winners always outnumber the potential losers by at least three times. In Egypt the poor number 3.2 million and the unemployed number 1.7 million, compared with about 1 million with protected jobs in public enterprises.

Experience elsewhere shows that structural reforms involve some job destruction, but that it is more than offset by the new jobs created through efficient investment and faster growth.

Reform costs

Economic reform has costs in the short run. A substantial share of existing capital—both human and physical—must be retrained, converted, or simply retired to allow for the accumulation of more appropriate types of capital. These costs translate into higher unemployment and lower consumption (to allow for greater investment) during the transition, conservatively estimated to be about five years. Without additional external support, estimates of these adjustment costs in MENA countries are a 1–2% loss in per capita consumption and a 3% rise in unemployment relative to the no-reform scenario. Where population growth rates are high (as in Algeria, Jordan, Syria, and Yemen) or economies are dominated by inefficient public enterprises (Algeria and Egypt), the development of a dynamic private sector will require more sacrifices in consumption (to enable greater investment) and will take longer than for the more advanced reformers.

The absolute costs of implementing reforms are fairly small

But the absolute costs of implementing some of the reforms outlined in this report are fairly small. Providing a package of basic health care interventions would cost less than 0.5% of the region's GDP. Paying every poor person enough to bring them to the poverty line is less than 1% of GDP in most countries. And eliminating the gender gap in education would cost less than 1% of the region's GDP. Economic growth is central to making such higher spending on the social sectors politically viable. For example, with no growth, maintaining per student expenditures on education in Jordan would require doubling the education budget's share of total spending over the decade—unlikely. But with faster growth, higher social expenditures can easily be accommodated.

Partners can share the burden

The costs of reform can be shared—with the private sector and with donors—and there is no shortage of financing to cushion the costs of adjustment in the MENA region. The approximately $350 billion in assets held abroad is just one source of potential financing for the massive investments in new industries, new infrastructure, and new commercial and social services outlined in this report. The $158 billion in private capital flows to developing countries in 1993 is another potential source of financing. Donor funds are also sizable—the European Union's Mediterranean Initiative alone could increase official resource flows to the region by more than half. With such additional external support, the costs of reform in terms of lower consumption and higher unemployment can be significantly reduced.

With external support, the costs of reform can be significantly reduced

The key is for international support to reinforce rather than replace the reform process. Private financing will not materialize unless the conditions are right—and that means serious progress on structural reforms to create a competitive business environment. And donors are willing to finance the political costs of reform—such as severance payments or targeted transfers—to ease the short-run difficulties for reform-minded governments. The central issue for governments is to have a credible long-term strategy and to sequence and set priorities in the interim to realize the vision of a prosperous future.

CHAPTER 1

Disengagement from the Changing Global Economy

MENA's policies are ill-suited to the global economy

The economies of the Middle East and North Africa (MENA) have been unable to deliver improved living standards to their populations over the past decade.[1] Comparing the performance of MENA countries with others indicates that they are lagging behind in exports, private investment, labor productivity, and in managing their natural resources sustainably. The reason: policies are ill-suited to a world economy that is fundamentally different from that in the past.

Despite fairly high rates of investment in both human and physical capital, growth rates were abysmal in the 1980s as productivity stagnated. Real per capita GDP fell by 2% a year over the past decade—the largest such decline in any developing region (figure 1.1). Meanwhile, many countries in Asia witnessed the best economic performance in recent memory. The downturn was particularly severe among MENA's oil-exporting countries (their GDP per capita fell by 4% a year between 1980–91), but even the non–oil exporters in the region grew by less than 1% a year (Riordan and others 1995). The early 1990s have seen some improvement in growth performance, especially in Bahrain, Oman, Saudi Arabia, Syria, and Tunisia, but in most countries there were minimal or negative gains in per capita incomes.

For the non-oil countries in MENA (such as Jordan, Lebanon, Morocco, and Tunisia), oil has strong "ripple effects." Links between regional labor and capital markets amplify the impact of oil markets. Worker remittances have been the most important link—with a 10% increase in oil prices associated with a 6% rise in remittance income for MENA countries. For Egypt, Jordan, and Yemen, remittances amounted to $90 per capita, 40% of exports, and 10% of GDP in 1993. In the Maghreb, where workers tend to migrate to Europe, the link to oil markets is weaker, but the importance of remittances for foreign exchange revenues is still significant. Aid from the oil economies to others in the

FIGURE 1.1

Annual income growth has been the world's worst, 1980–91

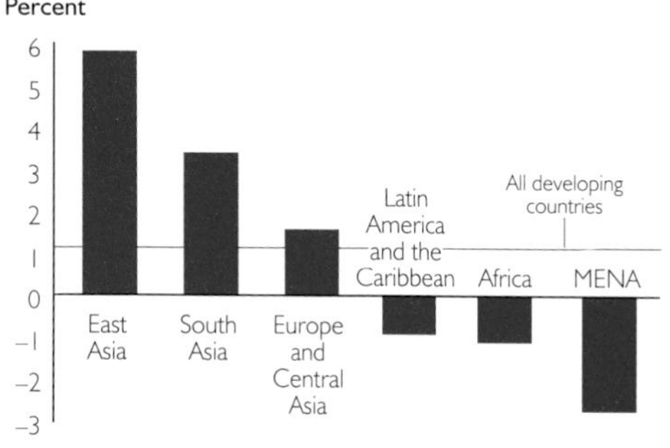

Source: Riordan and others 1995.

FIGURE 1.2

OPEC aid has fallen with oil prices

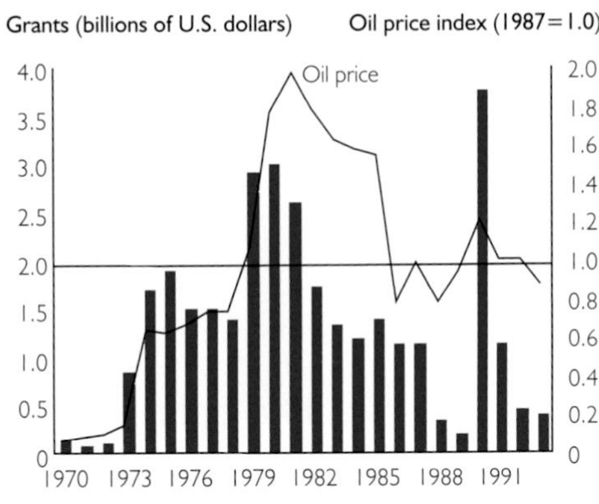

Source: World Bank data; Riordan and others 1995.

region has been another important link—closely following developments in oil markets. Official grants from the oil exporters to their MENA neighbors peaked at about $3 billion a year during 1979–81 (with the exception of a peak in 1990 during the Gulf war), but with falling oil prices grants have averaged only about $500 million a year more recently (figure 1.2). In 1993, 80% of OPEC official grants went to the Mashreq, with only 10% to the Maghreb.[2]

Missing out on globalization

Perhaps most striking is that MENA countries have not used integration with the world economy as an engine of growth. They are less integrated today than 30 years ago, with trade as a share of output having declined, in contrast to all other regions except Sub-Saharan Africa (figure 1.3). The Gulf Cooperation Council (GCC) countries are perhaps the most integrated, with a high ratio of trade to GDP and intraregional trade equivalent to about 7% of total trade. Yet despite decades of emphasis on diversification and industrialization policies in the region, primary exports, especially fuel, remain the most important link to the global economy. Oil constitutes 80% of total exports for the region—and for some countries petroleum products are virtually the only source of foreign exchange (table 1.1). That MENA countries trade so

FIGURE 1.3

MENA's trade integration has actually declined

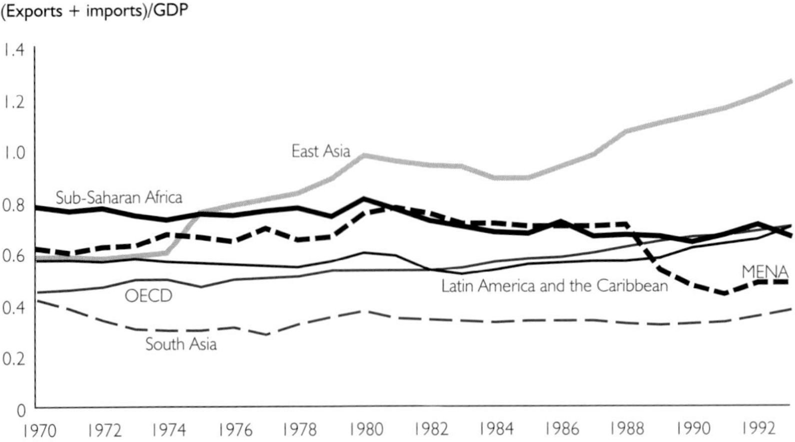

Note: MENA does not include Jordan, Lebanon, Oman, Qatar, and Yemen.
Source: Riordan and others 1995.

TABLE 1.1
Oil continues to dominate many MENA economies
(percent)

Oil exporter	Trade in fuels as a share of GDP[a] 1970	1974	1984	1993[b]	Share of total exports 1993
Gulf Cooperation Council	50	85	35	35	95
Bahrain	140	105	72	67	90
Kuwait	62	80	47	40	80
Oman	78	70	47	30	95
Saudi Arabia	46	90	37	33	99
United Arab Emirates	40	78	3	40	95
Other exporters	10	30	10	10	85
Algeria	15	30	22	20	85
Egypt	5	2	6	7	45
Iran	20	47	7	15	90
Iraq	3	2	9	2	35
Syria	6	8	7	14	42
Total	25	60	20	30	90
MENA exports (billions of US$)	10	90	100	110	80

a. Mineral fuels (including petroleum and products, natural gas, and natural gas liquids).
b. Estimate.
Source: Riordan and others 1995.

little with each other (intraregional trade is only 7–8% of total trade) is a reflection more that they trade very little at all, not that there are no regional trading opportunities.[3]

Export prospects are bleak and more volatile than in any other region

More worrisome is that the region's real export earnings per capita are highly volatile and on a gradual decline. Oil prices are projected to remain flat, with growth in MENA's real oil export earnings increasing by only 2–3% a year through 2010 (figure 1.4). The prospects for oil markets are subject to large uncertainties. Some are on the demand side, because of potential energy conservation. Others are on the supply side—with the eventual return of Iraq to the market, uncertainty about output from the former Soviet Union, and possible technological advances. Over the long run, the floor for oil prices is about $5 a barrel (equal to the long-run competitive costs of production) and the ceiling is about $25 a barrel (the price of the closest alternative energy source). But even at $25 a barrel, the region's real export revenues per capita would be less than half those achieved during the boom years of 1975–85.

FIGURE 1.4
Oil prices will probably be flat

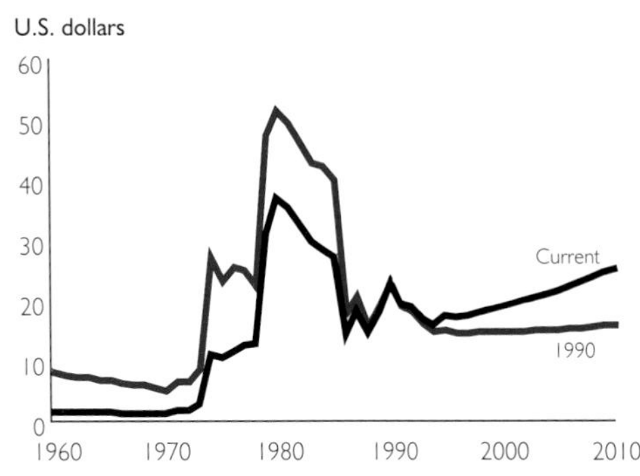

Source: Riordan and others 1995.

Transfers and income flows to the region (remittances, aid, and income from assets abroad) also are expected to remain flat. Remittances are expected to stabilize as European demand for immigrant labor continues to decline. The Gulf countries will try to encourage greater labor force participation of nationals while meeting a portion of imported labor requirements through lower-wage Asian workers. Interest and dividend earnings also are likely to decline, especially for the GCC countries, as foreign assets have been depleted, especially during the Gulf war. Aid flows to the region are expected to remain stable in real terms as increased assistance from the European Union offsets declining support from the United States and the GCC.

Tourism revenues are a bright spot—the entire MENA region's revenues were less than Mexico's and about equal to Thailand's in the 1990s—implying substantial potential for growth given the region's geography and wealth of destinations. But the size of the sector is too small to offset other adverse trends, and regional stability will be a key factor since tourists are unlikely to visit destinations with high perceived risks.

While export prospects are bleak, needed imports (such as food) will absorb up to half the export revenues in the Mashreq. The recent surge in international food prices will increase the region's food import bill by $4–5 billion a year (figure 1.5). In the medium term, as the Uruguay Round reduces the breadth and depth of the industrial countries' intervention in agricultural markets, world food prices are expected to rise. But the agricultural liberalization under the Uruguay Round is limited, and the net effect will be relatively small—a 1–4% increase in prices over six years. In the longer term, with continuing gains in worldwide crop yields, the international prices of staples such as cereals are expected to decline in real terms.

FIGURE 1.5
The food deficit is growing

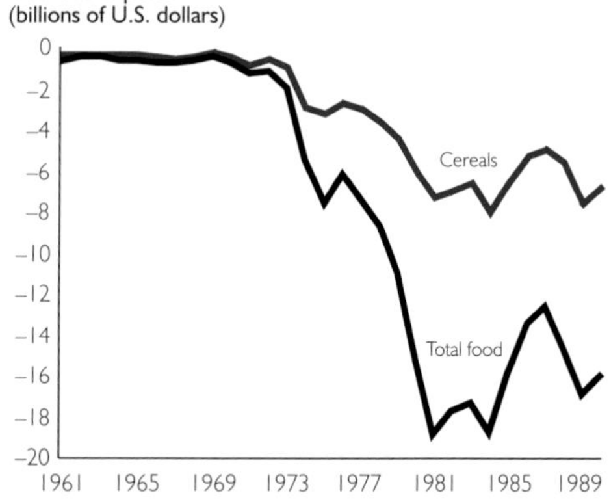

Source: Riordan and others 1995.

Financing the region's deficits will get harder

The MENA region was once the only capital exporter among all developing regions, but its resource deficit (on goods and non-factor service trade) became the largest of all developing regions in the 1990s. This was driven largely by rising external deficits in the Gulf countries (particularly Iran, Iraq, and Saudi Arabia) as a result of falling oil prices and uneven macroeconomic adjustment to this new reality. Resource deficits in the Maghreb and the Mashreq have shrunk because of policy adjustments to reduce imbalances and as external financing from both private and official sources has been harder to attract.

Relative to its GDP, the region's financing requirements are the largest for any developing region. The situation is particularly extreme in the Mashreq countries, where the financing requirements as a share of GDP are three times those in Africa or South Asia. Moreover, interest payments on foreign debt relative to GDP are now as high as in Sub-Saharan Africa in the early 1990s or as in Latin America in the 1980s. Debt to GDP ratios averaged 62% in the Maghreb between 1990–93 and 114% in the Mashreq—comparable to the Sub-Saharan ratio of 70% of GDP in the same period. In the GCC countries declining overseas assets have meant a halving in net interest income—from more than 10% of GDP in 1985–89 to less than 5% in 1990–93.

The region has not featured in the upsurge of private capital to developing countries

Moreover, the region has not featured in the upsurge of private capital flows to developing countries—attracting less than 1% of the total (El-Erian and Kumar 1995). In 1990–93 MENA countries attracted less than $1 billion in private capital (comprising private debt, foreign direct investment, and portfolio equity). In countries like Egypt, Jordan, and Lebanon, much of the flow ended up in government reserves (which often needed bolstering) rather than in new investment. Explanations for poor performance include political tensions, slow progress on structural reforms, and lower oil prices.

Foreign direct investment showed more variation—with flows into Morocco increasing from $122 million a year in 1985–89 to $407 million a year in 1990–93 while those in Tunisia more than doubled to about $200 million a year in 1990–93.[4] In contrast, stagnation in the reform process and mounting political tensions resulted in a sharp drop in foreign direct investment in Egypt—from $1.1 billion a year in 1985–89 to less than $500 million a year in 1990–93 (World Bank 1994c).

Domestic policies are ill-suited to new global realities

Unlike the past, when the accumulation of capital was the key to efficient mass production, today's market demands more flexible production that takes advantage of the plummeting costs of international communications and transport. Competitive advantage no longer solely means producing a uniform product efficiently in one location. It means being able to organize and coordinate production of goods and services among multiple suppliers to respond quickly to the demands of various niche markets.

Globalization also sharpens the differences in performance among different policy regimes. As Mexico's recent experience shows, increasing integration in the world market brings important benefits, but it also requires stricter discipline in economic management, since policy errors are punished swiftly. For most countries in the MENA region, the policy regime has lagged behind one that would enable producers to take advantage of globalization's opportunities.

Ease of communications is the main driver of globalization

Technological innovations imply "the end of geography"

Communications are ever cheaper and easier, and competition forces companies to seek the lowest cost location for production. The cost of an international phone call fell by a factor of six between 1930 and 1950 and by a factor of ten since. The average number of international air-passenger miles traveled per person increased by 15 times in the past 20 years. Innovations of the past ten years appear to spell yet another revolution, "the end of geography." The advent of the fax machine and of computer networks such as the Internet put offices in Paris and Washington next door. In Western Europe between 1987 and 1992, the number of fax machines per person increased from 1:1,000 to 120:1,000, but most developing countries in 1992 were still at 1:1,000.

The implication of the "end of geography" for many companies, small and large, can be summarized in two words: specialize and globalize. Narrow the business focus, and aim for the world market. Increasingly, there is international specialization of functions within companies—software development in India, airline tickets cleared in the Caribbean, and car design in Italy.

Ease of communications allows trade to extend to a wide array of service activities, often not properly reported. Even with underreporting, the share of services in world trade rose from 17% in 1980 to 22% in 1993, and it looks set to accelerate due to the growth of long-distance services. Swissair recently decided to move parts of its back office from Zurich to India—taking advantage of the fact that the salary of a bank clerk in Bombay is a fortieth of that in Zurich. The World Bank estimates that long-distance services of this kind could double commercial service exports by developing countries in the long run from the current level of $180 billion (World Bank 1995b). For many developing countries, becoming part of these highly complex networks at a stage other than the production of primary commodities or simple components represents a new challenge.

Just as producers of goods and services have to become more responsive to changes in consumers' tastes and demands, the skills demanded of workers must change dramatically. Flexible production requires flatter organizational hierarchies, decentralized responsibility, and workers with broader job skills, more initiative, and better problem-solving skills. The impact of such changes is fewer low-skill jobs, restructuring some less-skilled jobs to require higher-level skills, and changing what workers need to know. Ensuring that the educational systems in MENA countries produce workers with the needed skills will require redefining the social contract governing both access to and the quality of schooling.

Trade liberalization is lagging

Distortions that thwart competitiveness need to be eliminated

An open trade regime is the channel for transmitting the benefits of integration and the signals for needed reforms. But MENA countries are currently ill-prepared to take advantage of the potential benefits that the Uruguay Round could bring (box 1.1). To take advantage of new market opportunities (which most MENA countries had access to before), domestic distortions that thwart competitiveness need to be eliminated. These distortions reside both in policies (such as tariffs and quotas) and institutions (bureaucratic hassles, lack of internationally accepted standards, and costly transport and communications services).

MENA countries' average tariffs were fairly typical of other developing countries in the 1980s. While quantitative restrictions have been reduced, average collected tariffs in MENA (with the exception of the GCC economies, which are quite open) are now higher than those in most Latin American and East Asian economies (table 1.2). Imports too are often subject to additional taxes. In Jordan these additional taxes included a 5% import license fee, a 4% tax earmarked for universities, a 2% tax for municipalities, a consolidated fee of 6%, a customs fee of 0.2%, and a surcharge of 3–5%. Morocco imposes an import levy of 12.5–15.0%. Tunisia imposes surcharges on a range of products. And Egypt maintains service fees of 3–6%. The cumulative effect of such trade distortions is higher prices for consumers and less competition for domestic producers. The bureaucratization of trade also has increased costs and reduced competitiveness (box 1.2).

BOX 1.1

Benefiting from the Uruguay Round begins at home

The Uruguay Round achieved substantial liberalization in many areas. Industrial country tariffs on manufactured goods will be lowered by 40% (from approximately 4% to 2.4%), although the cuts are lower than average for products of major importance to developing countries (such as textiles, clothing, footwear, and some machinery). Tariffs on natural resource–based products (such as metals, minerals, and fish) will be cut by 38%. Although agricultural trade was not substantially liberalized, tariff equivalents were agreed to, facilitating future liberalization.

What are the implications for MENA exports? Estimates from a recent study indicate that they should increase by $800–$900 million. This is equivalent to an annual expansion of less than 1%. Why is the impact so small?

- Average tariffs facing Middle Eastern exporters before the Uruguay Round already were generally low—0.4% into the European Union, 3% into Japan, and 1.1% into the United States. In part this is because oil, the region's major export, is generally imported duty free or faces very low tariff barriers.
- MENA countries did not offer to liberalize their markets by very much under the Round and therefore their exports will not become more competitive.
- Many preferential arrangements that benefited Middle Eastern exporters (such as distortions from the Multi-Fibre Agreement) are being phased out under the Round. So, the region's exporters will face greater competition.

Without changes in policies, the overall impact of the Uruguay Round on MENA countries will be negative. Despite the modest export gains, the net effect is adverse as preferences are eroded and food import prices rise. Estimates reveal that social welfare in the region will fall by about $2.6 billion a year (0.45% of 1992 GDP) with the implementation of the Round.

These welfare loss estimates are based on the current policy stance in MENA countries. But the dynamic effects could be far more beneficial if MENA countries unilaterally liberalized their trade policies so that domestic firms would become more competitive and take advantage of the enhanced market access opportunities that the Uruguay Round can offer. Achieving these dynamic gains will depend mainly on the policy decisions in MENA countries.

Source: Yeats 1995; Diwan, Yang, and Wang 1995.

TABLE 1.2

Trade taxes shelter domestic producers from competition, 1993

(percent)

Country	Average collected tariff (revenue/imports)	Share of import duties in total government revenue	Share of "other" taxes in total import tax revenue
India	29.9	23.6	0.8
Yemen	19.1	20.2	3
Pakistan	19.0	10.0	0
Tunisia	18.7	28.3	46
Jordan	17.8	35.9	40
Morocco	17.5	17.7	52
Syria	16.4	10.0	25
Egypt	14.9	10.0	8
Chile	9.7	9.9	..
Indonesia	4.9	5.2	..
Mexico (1990)	4.8	5.1	..
Korea, Rep. of	4.4	4.8	..
Bahrain	4.0	9.2	..
Oman	3.0	3.2	..
Turkey	2.5	4.4	78
Israel	1.2	1.0	..

.. Not available.

Source: Hoekman 1995.

BOX 1.2

Costs of trading in Egypt

Egypt provides a good example of how complex trade regulations and poor trading facilities reduce competitiveness. A plethora of government entities regulate trade—the Customs Authority, Ministry of Health, Ministry of Supply, General Organization for Veterinary Services, General Organization for Quarantine, Atomic Energy Association, Industrial Control Authority, and General Organization for Export and Import Control—with the objective of protecting consumers from low-quality goods.

But because Egypt does not recognize international certification bodies, the General Organization for Export and Import Control must inspect a sample of every consignment of goods that is on a list of products subject to quality control. Some 1,550 tariff lines, or 25% of the tariff schedule, are subject to quality control. The process is time-consuming for importers, who face additional uncertainty about when products will be cleared. Firms also have no incentive to employ the services of certification entities and increase their awareness of the quality standards needed in international trade.

Poor infrastructure also raises trading costs. The costs per ton of handling a container in the port of Alexandria is two to three times that in other Mediterranean ports. Insurance premiums charged for trade coverage are higher than those confronting Egypt's competitors on world markets. Unlike the tariffs on intermediate inputs, the extra costs associated with customs clearance, quality control, customs valuation, and the monopoly service providers in the ports cannot be recovered through a duty drawback scheme. They constitute, therefore, a major disadvantage for firms producing for export—and a major disincentive for foreign firms that might invest in export-oriented activities.

Source: Hoekman 1995.

Savings rates are below where they should be

Government revenues come from rents, not production

Most countries in the MENA region are relatively advanced in macroeconomic stabilization and, except those at war, have managed to avoid the bouts of high inflation observed in several countries in Latin America, Africa, and Eastern Europe. But in the long run, there will have to be a fundamental reorientation in MENA countries' fiscal stances as revenues from oil and aid decline. This is true not only for major oil exporters, but also for Egypt, Jordan, and Yemen, which benefit from oil revenues indirectly.

Savings rates remain below where they should be, especially given the rates of natural resource depletion. MENA countries' gross savings rates are about 10 percentage points of GDP lower than in Indonesia, Malaysia, or Thailand. Adjusting for the depletion in natural resources, the estimated net savings rate has been negative for many countries in the MENA region. In contrast, several natural resource extractors in East Asia have dramatically improved their net savings performance (figure 1.6).

FIGURE 1.6

Savings rates are well below optimal levels

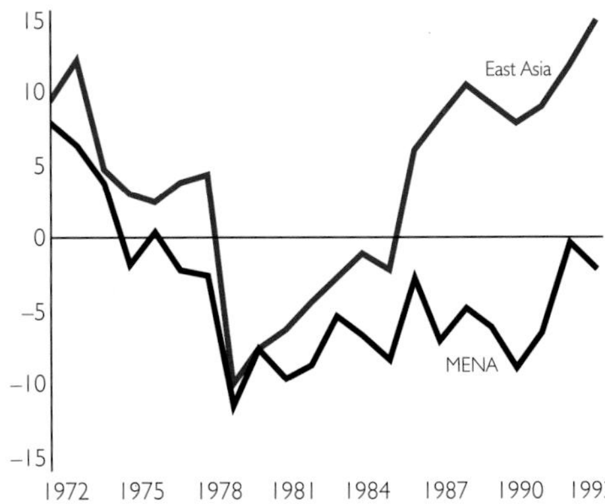

Note: Net national savings rate is defined as (gross national savings rate – depreciation of capital stock – depletion of nonrenewable resources)/GNP. East Asia includes China, Indonesia, and Malaysia. MENA includes Algeria, Egypt, Iran, Syria, and Tunisia.
Source: Larsen 1995.

The situation is particularly severe in Algeria, Egypt, Oman, and Syria, which are expected to deplete their reserves of oil and gas in 15–40 years. The major oil and gas exporters in the Gulf have more time to adjust their savings rates to ensure that they will be able to maintain consumption levels.

A major feature of the required fiscal adjustment will be greater reliance on taxation to finance the government. At present, governments rely excessively on rents and indirect taxes. Heavy reliance on customs duties will have to diminish if progress on trade liberalization is to be achieved (see table 1.2). Future reliance on income and consumption taxes are likely to coincide with increased pressure for greater accountability and more efficient use of public resources.

The investment regime is not seductive

All countries are now competing for the attention of private capital, which is critical for growth. But, with increased mobility, private capital has become fickle. It goes where the environment is conducive to making high rates of return and leaves when the environment turns sour. Policies friendly to the private sector are the way to get the attention of private investors.

Capitalists in the MENA region continue to "vote with their feet" by holding assets abroad where returns are safer. Estimates of the stock of capital abroad from the region are about $350 billion, more than any other region in the world as a share of GDP.[5] The GCC accounts for about half the total capital flight, although investing these assets abroad is economically optimal for major oil exporters who need to diversify their investments. In the rest of the region, countries with the least hospitable environment for investors, as measured by capital flight, are Egypt, Iran, Iraq, and Syria. In contrast, capital flight is not much of an issue in the Maghreb, particularly in Morocco and Tunisia.

What policies bring in private capital? Political and macroeconomic stability are an essential precondition, but so are government policies that affect the private sector's rates of return. In fact, the productivity of investment in MENA countries has deteriorated substantially, as evidenced by the low level of output obtained from every 1% increase in investment (figure 1.7). Most MENA countries get about half the output per unit of investment that East Asian countries do, despite the more rapid growth of the labor force in MENA.

In a world of intense competition for capital, underdeveloped financial systems, burdensome tax rules, and regulatory hassles are a sure way to deter investors (box 1.3). In Morocco, despite recent liberalization, as many as 20 documents are needed to register a business, and it typically takes six months to complete the formal steps for commercial establishment. Resolving a commercial case takes 2.0–2.5 years in Egypt, Jordan, and Lebanon—compared with 1.2 years in Canada. A World Bank study estimates that up to 30% of the average entrepreneur's time in Egypt is spent resolving problems with regulatory compliance (Saba 1995). In Jordan legislation intended to encourage private investment adds three months to a year to processing an application. In Lebanon clearing customs can require as many as 18 signatures, and the lack of clear regulations in such areas as health and safety creates substantial uncertainty for business.

FIGURE 1.7

Additional output per unit of new investment is low

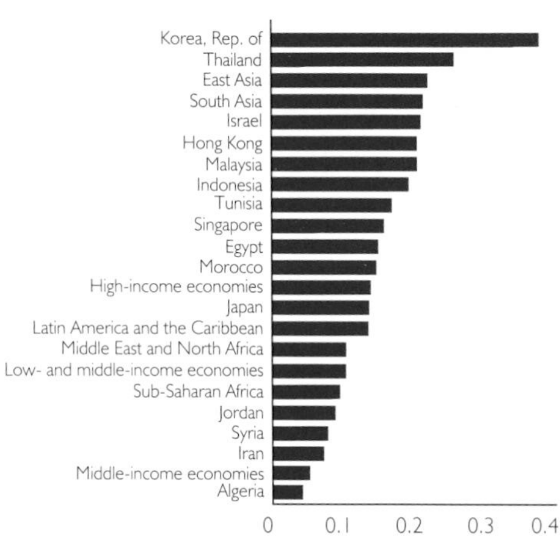

Source: World Bank staff calculations.

The litmus test of government commitment is often privatization. Is the government willing to withdraw from certain areas and allow the pri-

BOX 1.3

Investor ranking of constraints

What do investors look for in the business environment when deciding where to put their capital? Surveys of investors have identified a number of constraints to investment in MENA countries.

Despite the common practice of rolling over short-term loans as a means of financing some fixed assets, the lack of long-term finance greatly increases the risk associated with fixed investment. Moreover, the costs of borrowing tend to be high and are compounded by the costs of complying with regulations. Foreign investors tend to be more concerned with political stability, the rule of law, and policy predictability.

MENA countries need to address constraints to investment

Constraint	Rank
Finance (cost and availability)	1
Taxation (level and administration)	2
Inadequate skills	3
Poor infrastructure	3
Complex regulations	4
Legal system	4

Source: Anderson and Martinez 1995.

FIGURE 1.8

The share of public enterprises in economic activity is high . . .

(percent)

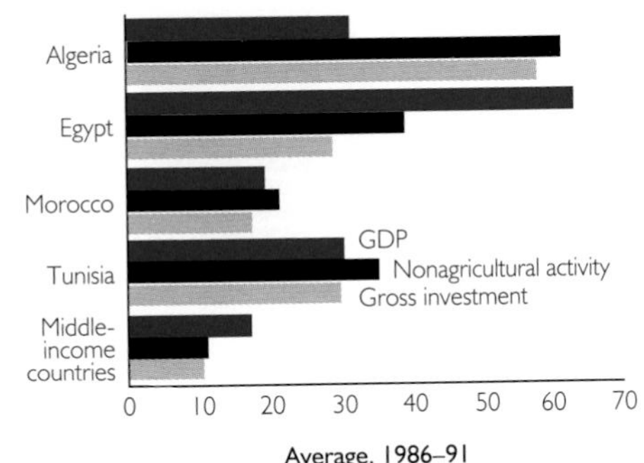

Source: World Bank 1995a.

FIGURE 1.9

. . . the privatization transactions, few . . .

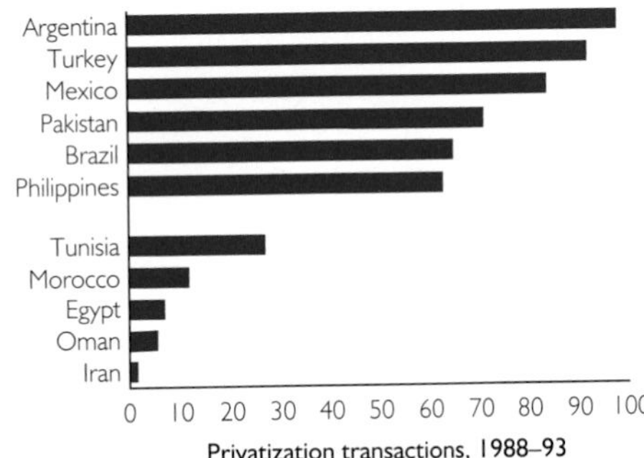

Note: Privatization transactions are defined as any sale of shares in state-owned enterprises.
Source: Anderson and Martinez 1995.

FIGURE 1.10

. . . and privatization revenue, small

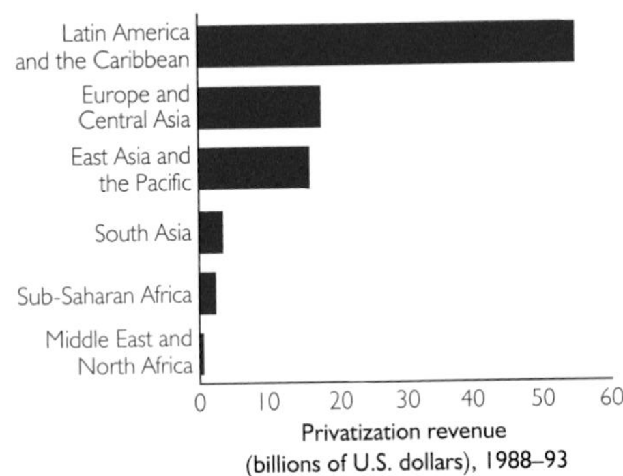

Note: Middle East and North Africa does not include Bahrain, Kuwait, Qatar, Saudi Arabia, and United Arab Emirates.
Source: Anderson and Martinez 1995.

vate sector to take the leading role? On this measure, MENA countries lag substantially behind other regions. The share of public enterprises in economic activity is higher in MENA countries than in other middle-income countries (figure 1.8). There have been very few privatization transactions (figure 1.9). And revenues from divestiture have been small (figure 1.10).

The size of the public sector in most MENA countries is bigger than is good for growth. International evidence indicates that where the public sector's share of total investment exceeds 40%, both the productivity of investment and overall growth tend to deteriorate markedly (World Bank 1991). In the MENA region many countries' public sectors exceed 40% of total investment, with such exceptions as Lebanon and selected Gulf countries. In Jordan a study of industrial companies showed that those with less than 15% government ownership had higher productivity, faster sales growth, and greater profitability than those with more than 15% government ownership (Kanaan 1995). Poor performance of public enterprises imposes large direct fiscal burdens (about 2% of GDP in Morocco and Yemen). It also results in the accumulation of bad debts by the banking system. And it crowds out private firms that could have been productive and contributing tax revenue. In Algeria, despite massive investment in the past (about 50% of GDP), public enterprise losses reached $5 billion in 1990. There is also evidence that state-owned enterprises create less than half the number of jobs per dollar invested as private firms—in part because public enterprises are often in more capital-intensive sectors (Anderson and Martinez 1995).

Financial systems in the region are relatively large. Financial depth in MENA, as measured by the ratio of M2 to GDP, is higher than in Latin America, South Asia, and, until recently, East Asia. But their lack of competitiveness has raised costs for the private sector.

State-owned banks dominate financial systems. In Egypt four public sector commercial banks control 70% of the system's assets. In Tunisia the state has majority shares in five of the six largest commercial banks. And in Algeria the financial system essentially consists of five state banks, traditionally specializing in a particular sector.

Such state-dominated systems have meant above-average financing costs for the private sector. Intermediation margins (the difference between lending and deposit rates) for non-GCC MENA countries averaged about 9% in 1991–93, compared with about 4% in OECD countries and South Asia and about 3% in the high-performing East Asian economies. The differences across countries are significant. In Algeria the relatively high spreads of 8.5% to 13% for short-term loans are due to the lack of competition. Morocco, with significant private ownership and foreign participation, has relatively low spreads (4%). Securities markets in most MENA countries (except Israel, Jordan, and, to a lesser extent, Egypt) are underdeveloped.

The poor quality of services increases production costs and lowers competitiveness

The importance of infrastructure to any integration strategy also requires a major improvement in the quality of services. Quantity is less of a problem. Most countries in MENA supply infrastructure services to households in quantities analogous to countries with similar incomes. Jordan again is the major exception, providing a level of infrastructure services to households in excess of most other countries with similar income levels (World Bank 1994d). The GCC countries too have made massive investments in infrastructure and the quality of services is high by international standards.

But the poor quality of services in many countries hits production costs and competitiveness. For example, waiting time to obtain a telephone connection in 1992 was 4.4 years in Tunisia, 5.8 years in Jordan, 6.1 years in Egypt, and 10.0 years in Algeria. The share of unsuccessful calls was 34% in Tunisia, 46% in Yemen, 50% in Lebanon, 57% in Morocco, and 60% in Jordan. Less than half the paved roads in most of the region are considered to be in good condition (compared with 85% in most high-income countries).

Labor is losing competitiveness

More than half a billion workers in developing countries will enter the labor force over the next 15 years, most at wages well below the MENA average. Nearly all will have attended primary school and acquired basic numeracy and literacy skills. More than 150 million of the new workers will have completed secondary school. And the growing numbers of workers qualified to perform basic manufacturing tasks in such countries as China and Indonesia will make the markets for mass-produced goods intensely competitive. To maintain living standards, MENA countries will have to improve labor productivity and increase female participation in the labor force.

Productivity in MENA countries has fallen dramatically (figure 1.11). The creation of new jobs has stagnated, and unemployment rates are the highest in the world (figure 1.12). Labor has borne the brunt of the adjustment—with real wages falling more than in any other region. The average worker in MENA today is earning no more in real terms than in the early 1970s. Only Sub-Saharan Africa has such a poor track record.

This deterioration in wages occurred even as massive investments in human capital continued. MENA countries devote a greater share of their national income to education than any other region. But these investments in human capital appear to have generated poor returns, as evidenced by low completion rates, high unemployment among graduates, and low labor productivity. Extensive distortions create incentives for the wrong kinds of education and training services, reduce the social returns to investments in human capital, and lower the external benefits associated with the accumulation of skills. Quality also has deteriorated, especially where student numbers have increased rapidly under publicly dominated systems.

FIGURE 1.11
MENA is losing competitiveness

Average change in total factor productivity (percent), 1960–90

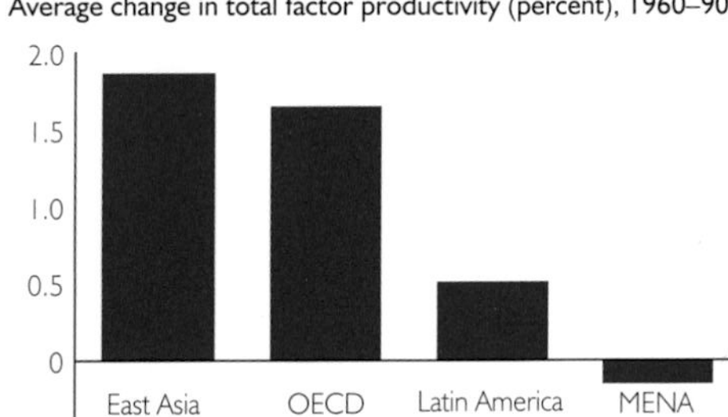

Source: World Bank 1993.

FIGURE 1.12
Unemployment rates are the highest in the world

(percent)

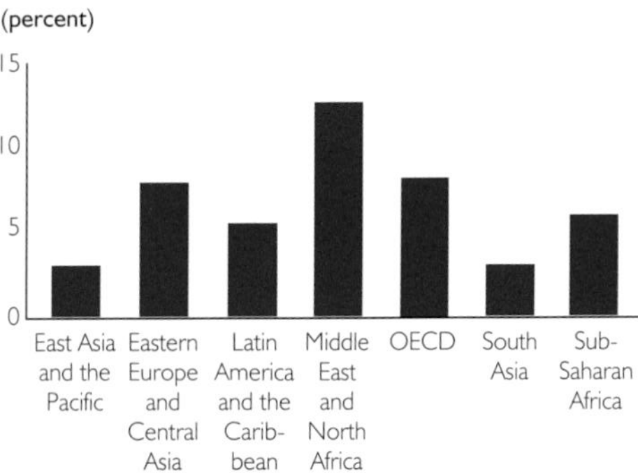

Note: Unemployment rates for most countries represent the most recent estimates available between 1990 and 1995. MENA does not include GCC countries.
Source: Filmer 1995.

Poverty, especially of opportunities, has worsened

The failure to generate growth has increased the number of poor people in the region. Based on household surveys, the number of people surviving on less than $1 a day reached 11 million—an increase of 700,000 between 1985 and 1990 (table 1.3). Which groups were most affected? The poor are largely rural, especially farmers with little or no land, and have large households and little education. The poor in urban areas tend to be unskilled or self-employed. Even countries that have fairly good social indicators and extensive social assistance programs, such as Iran and Jordan, witnessed a sharp increase in poverty as growth stalled and population increased rapidly.

Despite the recent deterioration in poverty associated with slow growth, the region has been moderately successful

TABLE 1.3

The number of poor has increased with rising populations, 1985, 1990, and 1994

Country	1985		1990		1994[a]	
	Thousands	Percentage of population	Thousands	Percentage of population	Thousands	Percentage of population
Algeria	400	1.83	290	1.16	439	1.60
Egypt	3,465	7.45	2,936	5.60	3,438	6.05
Iran	3,005	6.48	4,987	8.94	4,394	6.94
Jordan	110	4.16	413	12.60	589	13.83
Morocco	1,569	7.11	625	2.49	432	1.58
Tunisia	336	4.63	233	2.89	148	1.60
Total	8,885	6.06	9,484	5.59	9,440	5.01
MENA region[b]	10,291	..	10,995	..	11,028	..

.. Not available.
Note: Poor is defined as average spending of less than $1 a day at 1985 purchasing power parity.
a. Preliminary estimate based on GDP growth rates.
b. The six countries above plus estimates for Lebanon, Syria, and Yemen using the regional average poverty rate.
Source: van Eeghen 1995.

at reducing the poverty of incomes. But opportunities—in access to effective education and health care—remain severely inadequate for many. Consider Morocco. It translated growth (helped by bountiful rainfall) into one of the sharpest reductions in income poverty in the world by 1991. Yet primary school enrollment ratios fell from 79% in 1985 to 66% in 1990—the lowest in the region and rivaled only by Sub-Saharan Africa. The majority of Moroccan women (62%) are illiterate. All this is problematic for the skills development central to competitiveness.

Natural resources are being mined unsustainably

Most MENA countries have relied excessively on mining natural resources as a development strategy, but many are also beginning to face serious resource constraints. More than half the MENA countries derive about half their GDP from natural resource–based sectors—defined as oil and gas, mining, and agriculture (table 1.4). But reserves of nonrenewable resources are falling rapidly in Algeria, Egypt, Oman, and Syria. And such renewable resources as water are being tapped unsustainably, with use rates that exceed 100% of renewable supplies in Bahrain, Gaza, Israel, Jordan, Kuwait, Libya, Oman, Qatar, Saudi Arabia, United Arab Emirates, and Yemen (table 1.5). Meanwhile, lost productivity from land degradation is estimated to cost $11.5 billion a year (World Bank 1995c).

TABLE 1.4

Economies are dependent on natural resources, 1992
(percent)

Country	Share of GDP	Share of exports
Syria	53	62
Algeria	52	97
Kuwait	52	..
Oman	52	95
Saudi Arabia	52	99
United Arab Emirates	49	96
Iran	37	96
Egypt	36	65
Yemen	35	..
Tunisia	32	27
Morocco	29	45
Jordan	20	50

.. Not available
Source: World Bank 1994d.

TABLE 1.5
Water quantity and quality are problems

Water quality	High water quantity[a]	Low water quantity[b]
High	Algeria, Egypt, Iran, Iraq, Lebanon, Morocco, Syria, Tunisia	Gaza, Jordan
Low		Bahrain, Israel, Kuwait, Libya, Oman, Qatar, Saudi Arabia, United Arab Emirates, Yemen

a. Use is less than 100% of renewable supplies.
b. Use is more than 100% of renewable supplies.
Source: World Bank 1995c.

Increasing urbanization, industrialization, and vehicle use also mean that air and water pollution levels have become a serious threat to health and to tourism. Lack of access to safe drinking water and safe sanitation translates into about 10 million lost years of productive life each year in MENA countries. Almost 60 million people breathe dangerously polluted air from highly polluting industries, inefficient vehicles, leaded gasoline, and high-sulfur fuels. The combined cost of such unsustainable resource use is estimated at $12–14 billion a year, roughly 3% of the region's GDP (World Bank 1995c). Moreover, air pollution takes a severe toll on the region's antiquities, as does coastal pollution on tourist beaches.

Given the disengagement from the world economy and the ill-suited domestic policies, the need for reform seems obvious. So, what prevents reform? Why has the old economic structure failed to generate growth, jobs, and improved living standards over the past decade? And how insurmountable are the constraints to reform? Chapter 2 looks at these more complex issues of political economy to reconcile economic efficiency with political viability.

Notes

1. MENA is defined to include Algeria, Bahrain, Egypt, Iran, Iraq, Israel, Jordan, Kuwait, Lebanon, Libya, Morocco, Oman, Qatar, Saudi Arabia, Syria, Tunisia, United Arab Emirates, West Bank and Gaza, and Yemen. The oil-exporting countries are included in regional aggregates (depending on data availability) unless otherwise stated. Data for Lebanon, Libya, Qatar, and the West Bank and Gaza are scarce but are included wherever possible.

2. Maghreb includes Algeria, Libya, Morocco, and Tunisia; the Gulf Cooperation Council (GCC) includes Bahrain, Kuwait, Oman, Qatar, Saudi Arabia, and United Arab Emirates; and Mashreq includes Egypt, Jordan, Lebanon, Syria, and Yemen.

3. Although intraregional trade activity may appear low, the region only absorbs 3–4% of global exports. As such, MENA countries have a higher than average propensity to trade with one another, given their low propensity to trade at all (Yeats 1995).

4. Preliminary estimates for 1994 indicate that foreign direct investment in Morocco may exceed $700 million.

5. Capital flight from MENA is about $85 billion based on the World Bank's residual method, where capital flight is defined as (external borrowing + foreign direct investment) – (current account deficit + increase in reserves).

However, compounding of hypothetical earnings at LIBOR results in an estimate of $600 billion. To the extent that such earnings are repatriated through recorded flows, estimates of the base for such calculations would be commensurably lower. On balance, for MENA as well as other developing regions, the "true" levels of capital flight lie somewhere in between, hence the $350 billion estimate reported here.

CHAPTER 2

Yesterday's Achievements, Today's Predicament

History matters. Proximity to Europe meant that countries in the Middle East and North Africa had one of the most intense encounters with colonialism in the world. The legacy of that period of exploitation has permanently colored attitudes toward economic policy, political legitimacy, and the appropriate role of the state. Colonial states tended to be politically authoritarian and discriminatory, but economically laissez-faire. Such policies were intended to integrate the economies of the region into world trade, but on unequal terms and with minimal benefits to local people.

In response to that experience, almost all the states in the region (except Lebanon) adopted statist development strategies in the post-colonial period. The state was to play a modernizing role, taking control of investment and production, providing mass access to education and social services, and redressing the huge inequalities that had emerged in society. The instruments of such policy were nationalization, protection for domestic industries, large public investment programs, and extensive systems of subsidies for basic goods and services.

FIGURE 2.1

Past growth was rapid . . .

Growth of GDP per capita, 1960–85 (percent)

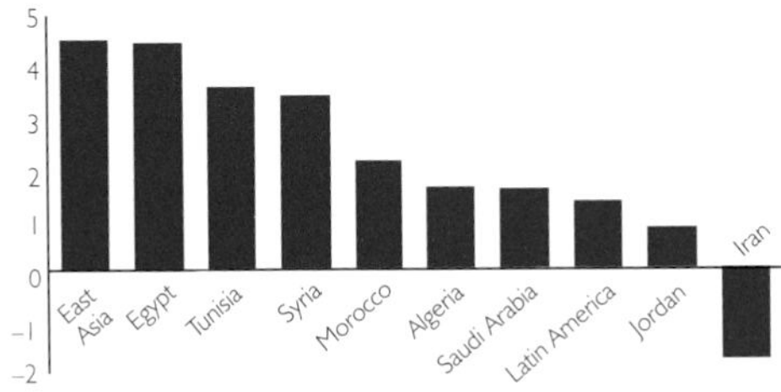

Note: East Asia includes China, Hong Kong, Indonesia, Republic of Korea, Malaysia, the Philippines, Singapore, and Thailand. Latin America includes Argentina, Bolivia, Brazil, Chile, Colombia, Ecuador, Peru, Paraguay, Uruguay, and Venezuela.
Source: World Bank data.

FIGURE 2.2

. . . and equitable

Growth of GDP per capita (percent), 1965–89

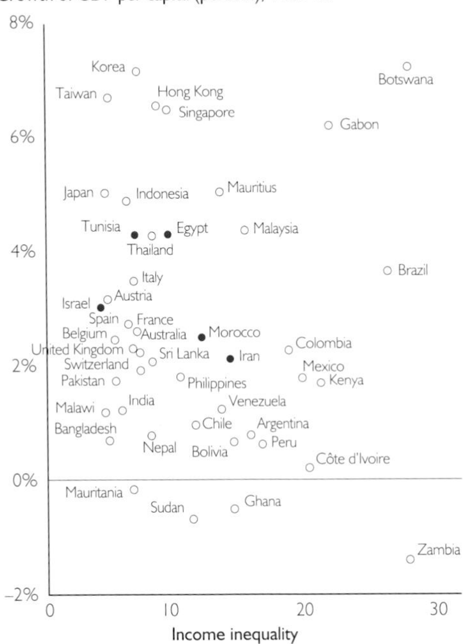

Note: Income inequality is measured as the ratio of the income shares of the richest 20% and the poorest 20% of the entire population.
Source: Page 1995.

Achievements of the statist era were considerable

During 1960–85 the MENA region outperformed all other regions of the world except East Asia, not only in income growth per capita, but also in the equality of income distribution. Growth rates in MENA were among the highest for countries at their level of per capita income (figure 2.1). Income inequality was low for countries growing so rapidly (figure 2.2). Improvements in social indicators were dramatic. A Middle Eastern child born in 1990 could expect to live 13 years longer than his or her parents. Infant mortality

FIGURE 2.3

Poverty in MENA has been low . . .

Poor (percentage of total population)

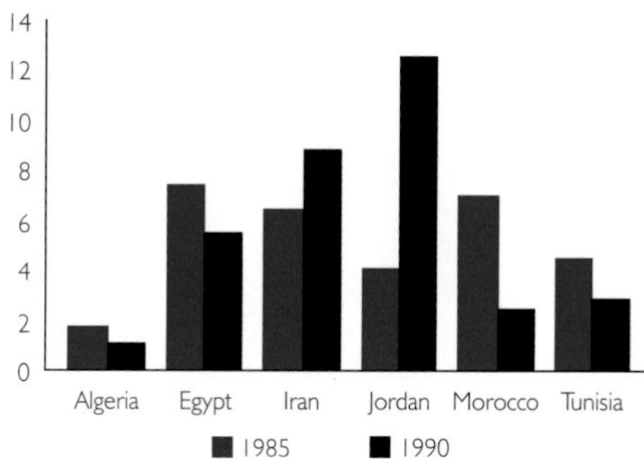

Note: Poor is defined as average spending of less than $1 a day at 1985 purchasing power parity.
Source: van Eeghen 1995.

FIGURE 2.4

. . . compared with the rest of the world

Poor (percentage of total population)

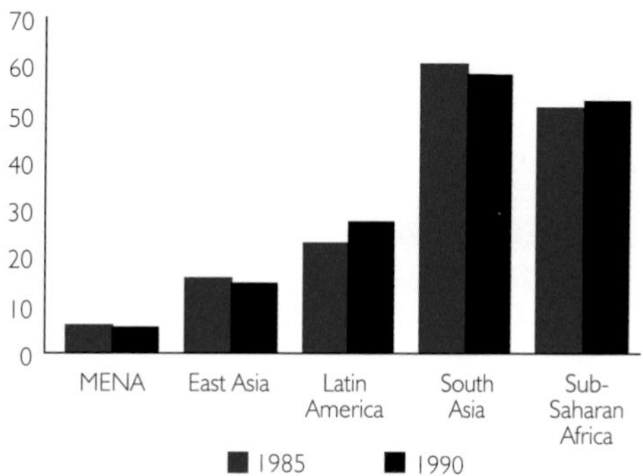

Note: Poor is defined as average spending of less than $1 a day at 1985 purchasing power parity. MENA includes Algeria, Egypt, Iran, Jordan, Morocco, and Tunisia.
Source: Chen, Datt, and Ravallion 1993; van Eeghen 1995.

more than halved over 25 years—from 151 deaths per 1,000 live births in 1965 to 61 per 1,000 in 1991. Primary school enrollment improved markedly, from 61% in 1965 to 98% in 1991. And literacy among adults improved from 34% in 1970 to 53% in 1990, with particular progress in the oil-exporting countries.

Middle East and North African governments were also effective at reducing poverty (figure 2.3). By 1990 only 5.6% of the population in MENA lived on less than $1 a day, compared with 14.7% in East Asia and 28.8% in Latin America (figure 2.4). For any given per capita income, poverty was lower in MENA countries than elsewhere (figure 2.5). And the share of income that goes to the richest 20% of the population relative to the poorest 20% of the population tends to be lower in MENA countries than in many countries in East Asia and Latin America. These achievements were the result of rapid growth in the 1970s and early 1980s and the introduction of generous transfers to large portions of the population (table 2.1).

Making MENA's achievements particularly remarkable is the prevalence of armed conflict in the region. No region has been characterized by so many persistent conflicts—the Arab-Israeli conflict, the Iran-Iraq war, the Gulf war, the conflict in former Spanish Sahara, the civil wars in Algeria, Lebanon, and Yemen—to name a few. The losses in human life and in physical capital from these conflicts can only have hurt economic welfare and slowed progress in development.

Past successes were the outcome of easier times, not statist policies

The era of statism coincided with a far more accommodating international context for MENA countries. Oil prices were high, the world economy was buoyant, industrialization was still in the "easy" stages, and the world was a less competitive place. Times have changed, and many of the policies and institutions that seemed to serve MENA countries well in the past have become stumbling blocks to the future.

FIGURE 2.5

Given income levels, the number of poor is below average, 1990

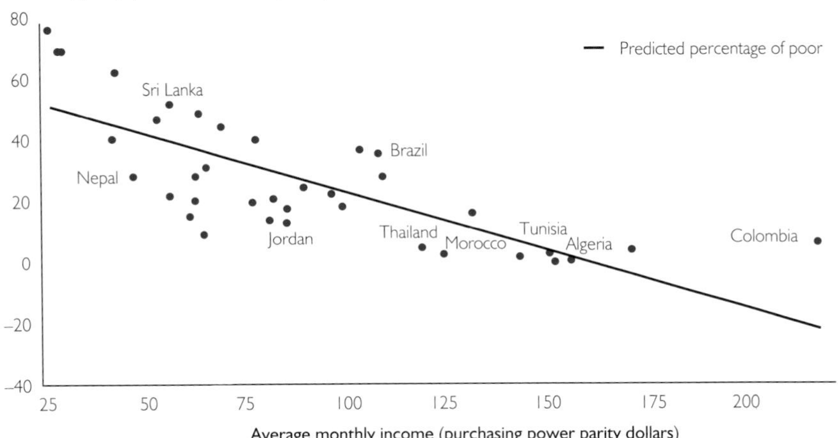

Note: Sample includes all low- and middle-income countries for which data were available.
Source: Chen, Datt, and Ravallion 1993.

Past success was driven by oil and investment

The oil boom was an unprecedented time. During 1973–85 one of the largest transfers of income in world history occurred from oil importers to oil exporters—so large as to contribute to one of the most prolonged recessions in the industrial countries. At its peak, the effect of the windfall on oil producers was equivalent to a 50% increase in their national incomes. (figure 2.6). The spillovers for the rest of the region (through aid flows, remittances of migrant workers, and exports) were substantial and equivalent to a 35–40% increase in GDP for the Middle East and North Africa as a whole.

The windfall enabled a massive buildup of public investment, in excess of the already high levels prevailing since the 1960s (figure 2.7). The state invested heavily in both human and physical capital. Because of the windfall and government policies, firms adopted capital-intensive technologies, despite the need to create jobs for a growing population. State-owned enterprises were effective at generating growth in an era of mass production and relatively little competition, while large oil and other rents meant that non-oil exports and international competitiveness were not a priority. The

FIGURE 2.6

The oil windfall was massive

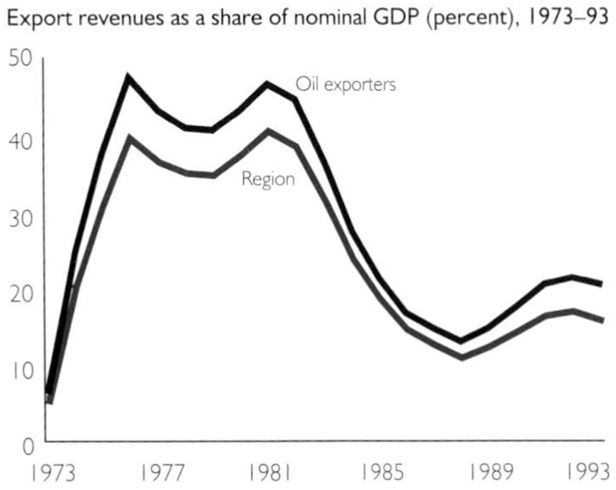

Export revenues as a share of nominal GDP (percent), 1973–93

50
40
30
20
10
0
Oil exporters
Region
1973
1977
1981
1985
1989
1993

Note: Three-year moving average of differences between actual and "counterfactual." Oil exporters include Algeria, Egypt, Iran, Iraq, Yemen, and the GCC countries.
Source: Riordan and others 1995.

TABLE 2.1
Social safety nets are large and leaky

Measure	Number of people affected	Impact	Budgetary cost	Leakage
Algeria				
Family allowance[a]	6 million	Little because of its small size	1.25% of GDP	Large. No link between family income and eligibility
School allowance	All families with children aged 6–21	Small because it only goes to families contributing to social security	0.2% of GDP	Large. No link between family income and eligibility
Health care	Available to social insurance contributors and noncontributors without distinction	Large	2.6% of GDP	Large. No link between income and eligibility
Consumer subsidies[a]	Available to all. Cover basic foodstuffs, some energy products and public services	Large.	2.0% of GDP	Households in the top income decile receive more than twice the subsidy of those in the lowest decile, and top five deciles of households receive 60% of food subsidy expenditures
Public works and cash transfers	Public works provide compensation to those able to work and cash transfers provide financial support to those unable to work	Cover 7% of the population	Less than 0.5% of GDP in 1994	Large. Some people receive multiple benefits
Unemployment insurance	Was introduced in July 1994 to facilitate industrial restructuring	Targeted to the retrenched workers	Not available	Not available
Egypt				
Food subsidies	87% of the population	Large, although some of the poorest segments are not reached because providing the necessary documentation is costly for them	4.8% of GDP	Large because most of the population benefits
Social assistance	2.7 million beneficiaries	Small—the payment is only 5% of the absolute poverty line	0.15% of GDP	None
Casual workers scheme	771,000	Total number of beneficiaries represents only 30% of the total poor	0.16% of GDP	None
Electricity subsidy	Available to all	Regressive (ranges from 86.4% of cost for the lowest to 19.2% for the highest consumption groups)	1.71% of GDP	Large because the entire population benefits
Water subsidy	All users, but price discrimination is applied in favor of low-volume users.	Large	4.9% of GDP	Large because higher-income people benefit by more than their share in the population
Education subsidy	Entire population, to varying degrees	Poorest do not benefit proportionally	4.9% of GDP	Large because higher-income people benefit by more than their share in the population
Jordan				
Education	Entire population	Poor benefit proportionately less	5.4% of GDP	Large. Benefits are regressive
Health care	5.5 million visits	Military personnel are main users	3.7% of GDP	Moderate. Those with low incomes pay lower fees
Cash transfers to the unemployed poor	22,400 households	The program relies on individual assessment and self-selection of the chronically poor	0.25% of GDP	Limited because extensive documentation is required and monitoring activities ensure that all beneficiaries deserve the transfer

TABLE 2.1 (CONTINUED)

Measure	Number of people affected	Impact	Budgetary cost	Leakage
Jordan, continued				
Food coupons	All households	Self-selection	0.48% of GDP	Large. Of every Jordanian dinar, only one-third accrues to the bottom 20% of the population
Morocco				
Health care	Available to all	Moderate. There are vast regional imbalances in health expenditures	3.5% of total public expenditure	Large. The richest 20% of the population appropriates 40% of public spending in health, while the bottom 40% receive less than 20%
Certificates for health care	Aimed, in principle, at giving free access to basic services to the poor	Local authorities have insufficient information to target effectively	Not available	Large
Activities of national mutual aid	Not available	Targets needy populations through nutrition assistance, preschool education, vocational training, and aid	0.7% of total central government budget expenditures.	Not available
Food support and nutrition programs	2.5 million. 875,000 children are getting food at school	Poor children are less likely to benefit since they are more likely to reside in rural areas and not to attend school	0.5% of GDP	Large
Public works program	Was initiated in 1961 and employs on average 50,000 persons annually	Public workers undertaken are in the areas of agricultural development, basic infrastructure, and social equipment. Workers are remunerated at the minimum wage and in some cases partly in food	Not available	None. Although there are no established targeting mechanisms, the public works program appears to reach the poor
Women's programs	56,000 poor and illiterate women	The programs consist of vocational training and technical and financial assistance to women's workshops and cooperatives	Not available	Not available
Tunisia				
General compensation fund	Until 1990 subsidies on food, animal food, and fertilizers were available to all	Food subsidies are regressive as a percentage of income	2% of GDP	Self-targeting mechanisms reduced the leakage, but further steps should be taken to sharpen the effectiveness of the reform
Direct transfers	Targeted through indicators and include: food aid in school cafeterias and food rations for preschoolers; financial aid to the handicapped and the elderly poor; cash transfers to poor families who need income support	Services 300,000 preschoolers, 5,000 handicapped people, 4,700 elderly poor, and 101,000 needy families	0.43% of GDP in 1994	Large. Eligibility lists are rarely updated, and eligibility criteria are very general. Some people receive multiple benefits
Health care	Basic health care services are available to almost the entire population, regardless of income	Provides essentially uniform subsidies to the entire population	5.2% of GDP	Large. More than half the population enjoys free or heavily subsidized health care
Public works program	Aimed to provide employment for the poor in urban and rural areas	The largest and the most effective programs for unskilled workers	About 0.12% of GDP in 1994	None. Has been effective in targeting the poor through self-targeting mechanisms

a. Recent reforms to Algeria's program of family allowances and consumer subsidies have resulted in improvements. However, estimates of the impact of these reforms are not yet available.
Source: van Eeghen 1995.

FIGURE 2.7

Public investment far outpaced private investment

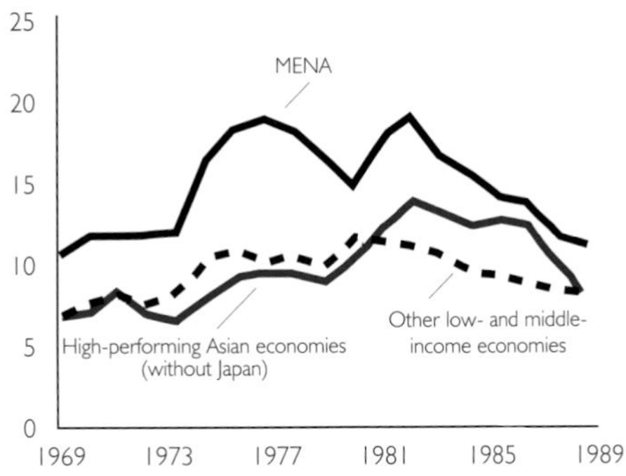

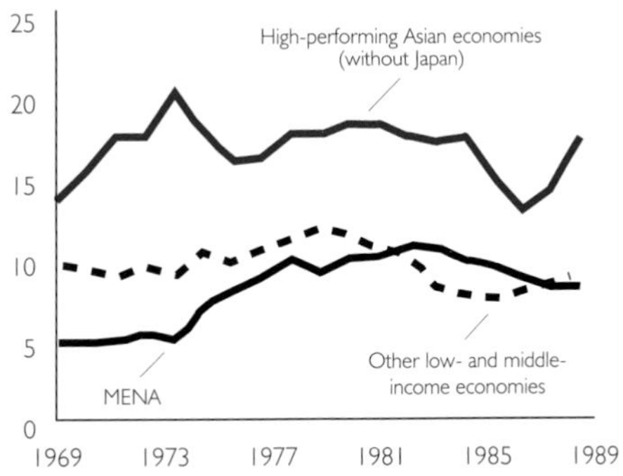

Note: MENA includes Algeria, Egypt, Iran, Iraq, Jordan, Morocco, Syria, and Tunisia.
Source: Umari 1993.

fact that many governments were not "picking winners" but "picking favorites" did not seem to matter where indigenous private sectors were small and did not constitute a major engine of growth.

Most MENA countries could afford relatively generous social expenditures during this period. Enrollments increased rapidly and expenditures per pupil as a share of national income rose to some of the highest levels in the world (figure 2.8). There tended to be a spectrum of educational traditions in the MENA region—the more exclusive or elitist tradition typical of Morocco (with low coverage and higher repetition rates associated with higher quality standards) and the more inclusive or populist tradition typical of Egypt (with high access but poor quality). Excess demand for skilled labor in an expansionary public sector obscured the fact that many graduates lacked skills relevant to the private market (box 2.1). Extensive safety nets, substantial consumer subsidies, and free health care and education were introduced with little targeting (see table 2.1).

But what matters today is productivity, flexibility, and speed

The economic crisis affecting the region since 1986 was the product of two fundamental factors—the collapse in world oil prices and the decline of productivity. For the oil exporters, the fall in output closely paralleled developments in oil prices (figure 2.9). Investment in MENA countries declined in the 1980s, but the fall in output was more extreme than the collapse of investment—implying that not only did the quantity of investment fall, but so did its productivity (figure 2.10). Economic policies have been slow to adjust to these changed circumstances.

The importance of productivity improvements for sustaining growth can be illustrated by contrasting MENA countries with those of East Asia (figure 2.11). What would have happened to growth if MENA countries (whose per capita incomes differed from East Asia's by only $80 in 1960) had achieved the same rates of investment and educational attainment as the East Asian "superstars" during 1960–91? Raising the average rate of investment in MENA to East Asian levels—increasing it by 7.6% on average for the period—would have increased 1991 per capita income from

FIGURE 2.8

Education spending is high, even accounting for young populations

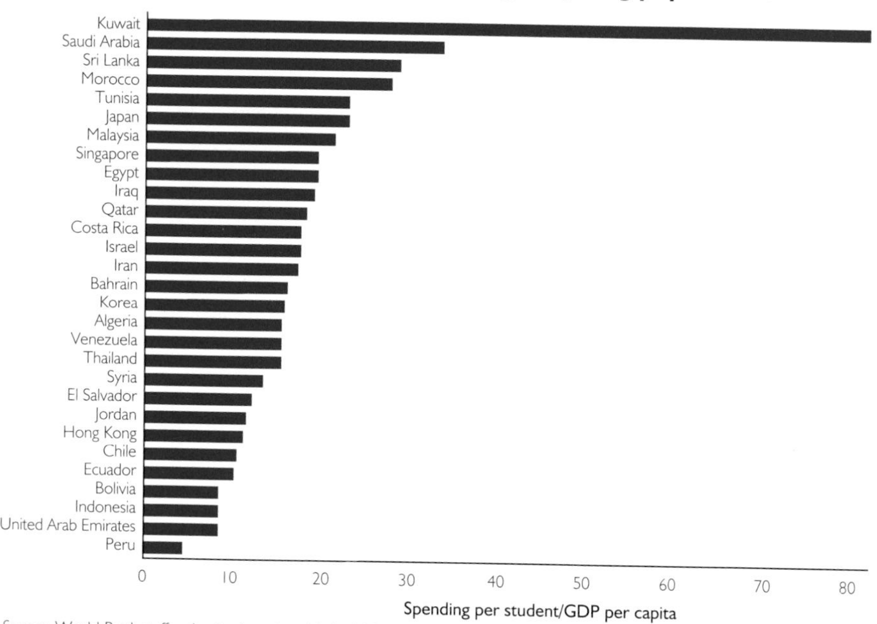

Source: World Bank staff estimates based on United Nations Educational, Scientific, and Cultural Organization and World Bank data.

$3,342 to $3,863. Adding East Asia's levels of human capital to the higher investment levels results in a further increase to $5,179. Yet East Asian incomes grew over the same period from $1,603 per capita to $8,000. More than half the difference in growth rates (55%) cannot be explained by East Asia's superior performance in accumulating human and physical capital. Instead, it was due to differences in the productivity of using capital.

The fierce competition in world markets at the close of the 20th century requires producers to be fast, to have low costs, and to innovate continuously, as have the successful economies in East Asia. In the past it often took up to a year between the placing of an order for wearing apparel and the arrival of the goods at the retailer. Today, it might take days—as successful companies have learned to be very responsive to shifts in consumer demand. Intense price competition has forced firms worldwide to reduce middle management jobs by shifting supervision and management functions to workers with improved qualifications. Competition also drives up quality and consistency standards because customers can easily find alternative suppliers whose products have lower defect rates and lower maintenance requirements.

FIGURE 2.9

Oil and output go together for oil exporters

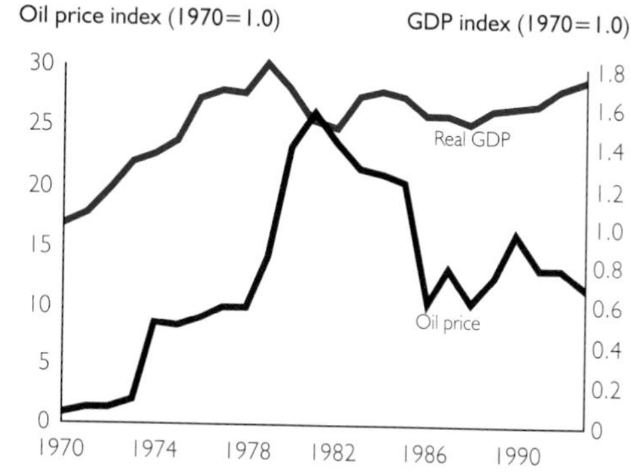

Source: Riordan and others 1995.

BOX 2.1

Educational quality for a changing world

Jordan has one of the best-educated labor forces in the MENA region, but recent measures of quality indicate weaknesses in precisely those skills needed for international competitiveness. Jordan is the only country in the MENA region to have participated in international comparative assessments of student achievement. The results show that of all the countries assessed, Jordanian students scored the lowest in terms of average correct answers on both math and science achievement tests. Jordan is in good company—its results are just below those of much wealthier countries, such as Spain and the United States.

Most interesting are Jordan's results for different cognitive processes. Students performed better on "conceptual understanding" for mathematics and "knows" for science (referring to grasp of facts and concepts) than on "problem solving" in mathematics and "integrates" in science. These latter skills are central to the changing requirements of work in internationally competitive economies, where workers are expected to solve nonroutine problems, adapt to change by learning, and make decisions based on an understanding of the broader context of their companies' priorities.

To address these issues, Jordan is developing a system to assess and evaluate its educational programs. Under the auspices of the National Center for Education Research and Development, its monitoring and policy research capacity will enable ongoing evaluation of whether the educational system is teaching the skills essential for the future.

Source: Golladay, Beryman, and Avins 1995.

International assessment of educational progress of students, age 13, 1990–91

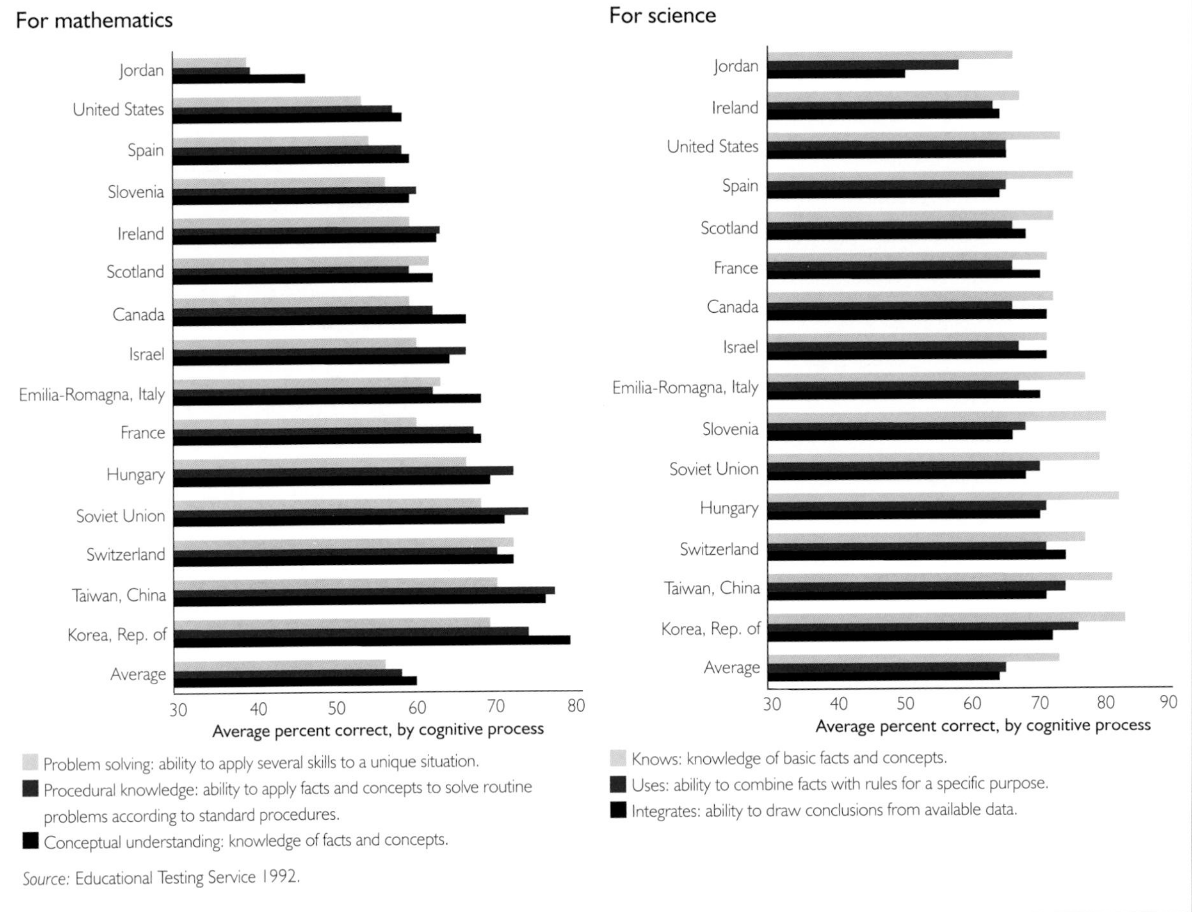

Source: Educational Testing Service 1992.

Successful firms must monitor the preferences of customers closely, constantly looking for ways of reducing costs and improving goods and services.

Past successes sowed the seeds of today's reform predicament

But the achievements of the past also sowed the seeds of today's economic predicament. The huge investments in state-owned enterprise assets—and in human skills no longer relevant to the market place—are the nub of the adjustment problem facing most MENA economies. As in the post–centrally planned economies of Eastern Europe, the productivity of capital has deteriorated steadily under statist strategies in Algeria, Egypt, and Jordan (figure 2.12). Despite relatively high investment rates, returns to investment declined under policies that thwarted competition.

Inflexibility of enterprises and workers. Trade liberalization, public sector retrenchment, and privatization imply considerable losses for a small but powerful minority of the labor force in the short run. This is especially the case for skilled labor in the Mashreq, where secondary school graduates constitute 80% of the labor force in the state-owned enterprises and only 20% of that in the private sector. Similarly, in the Maghreb a two-tier labor market has emerged with high levels of pay, benefits, and job security for a small number of educated workers alongside temporary contracts and minimal protection for the vast majority of workers. Exposing such protected workers and firms to international competition is politically complex. Governments in some MENA countries are already feeling the effects as labor unrest has increased. In Egypt there were 8 strikes in 1990, 63 in 1993 (Ibrahim 1994).

Weak incentives to be productive. The old social contract—linking years spent in school to guaranteed high-wage jobs—needs to be renegotiated. Governments are already unable to fulfill their part of the bargain. The vast majority of the unemployed in the region are first-time job seekers. In Algeria, Egypt, Jordan, and Syria educated young workers account for 60–80% of the unemployed. Graduates in

FIGURE 2.10

Output fell more than investment—so productivity fell

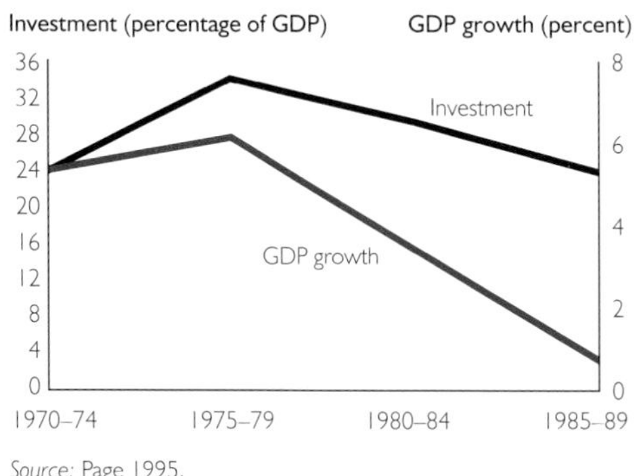

Source: Page 1995.

FIGURE 2.11

Low productivity accounts for differences between MENA and East Asia

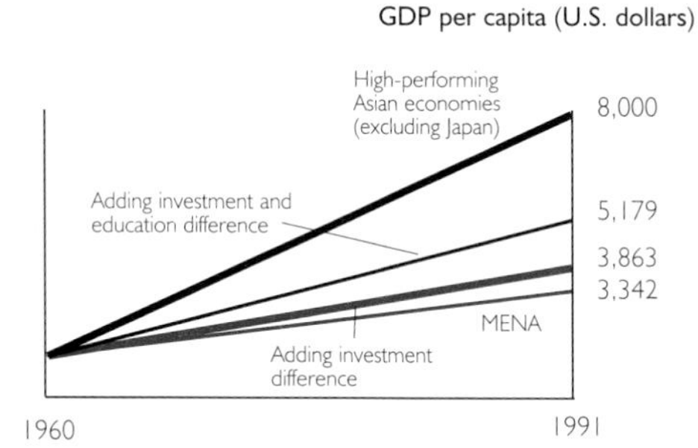

GDP per capita (U.S. dollars)

Source: Page 1995

FIGURE 2.12

Marginal productivity of capital

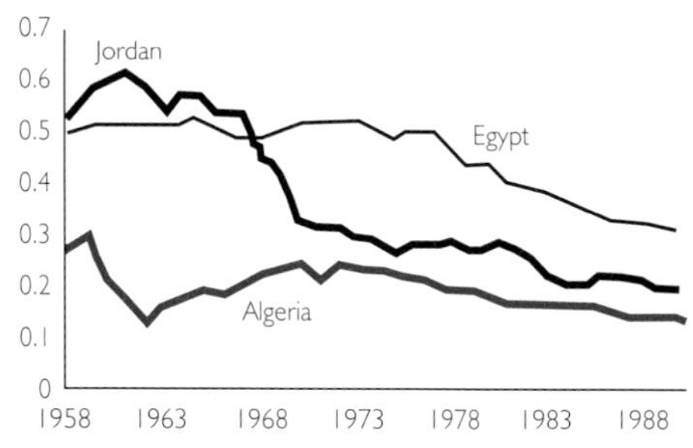

Note: Marginal productivity of capital = alpha * (Y/K), where capital's share alpha is estimated from a constant returns to scale Cobb-Douglas production function with three subperiods (1958–72, 1973–86, and 1987–90). Alpha = 0.66 (Algeria), 0.603 (Egypt), and 0.49 (Jordan).
Source: World Bank staff estimates; Nehru and Dhareshwar 1993.

Egypt now have to wait seven to eight years for their public sector jobs, resulting in a deteriorating quality of civil servants since the most talented workers find alternative employment before their turn comes. In Kuwait undemanding government employment has become the mechanism for transferring oil wealth to citizens, deterring the vast majority of Kuwaitis from taking on productive private sector jobs.

Expensive subsidies and transfers. Fiscal retrenchment in an era of diminishing rents will also involve asking producers and consumers to pay for services that they have always received for free. The situation is perhaps most extreme in some of the Gulf countries, where even token user fees for electricity, education, or health care have met with strong protest. The subsidies involved were often massive—estimates for Saudi Arabia in 1985 showed a total subsidy bill equivalent to about 18% of GDP (Askari 1990). In Kuwait operating subsidies for electricity and water alone amounted to 8% of GDP in 1992. In Bahrain electricity subsidies amounted to 6.5% of GDP and water subsidies were 8% of GDP in 1992. The 1995 budget in Saudi Arabia reveals a considerable effort to move toward more realistic pricing. Gasoline prices were doubled. Electricity and water prices were raised for commercial users, although they remain below the real costs of provision. And telephone charges were increased.

Oil and strategic rents have enabled many countries to postpone reform

Why change has been slow

Why have countries in other parts of the world been able to overcome the political obstacles to reform while most states in the MENA region still struggle with change? In many cases it is because countries in other regions started to adjust earlier because the shocks hit them sooner. For example, the debt crisis in Latin America was the catalyst for a major rethinking of development strategy and the emergence of the "Latin American consensus" on market-oriented reform. Moreover, the availability of oil and strategic rents enabled many countries in MENA to postpone reform. It is no accident that the countries farthest along in integrating with the world economy—Jordan, Morocco, and Tunisia—lacked substantial natural resource rents.

Postponing reforms has meant that interest groups that profit from the old regime are deeply entrenched. Firms that have benefited from protection and cheap credit—and a middle class accustomed to subsidized commodities and such benefits as education and well-paying public sector jobs—are reluctant to see their privileges erode. And many governments have been slow to respond with better policies, improved service delivery, and more transparent procedures.

Competitive pressures from the world economy combined with domestic pressures for new and better job opportunities are the most likely forces for triggering change in MENA countries. In many of them, there are the additional domestic challenges of fundamentalism and disaffected poor and middle classes. Incumbent regimes are sometimes poorly placed to initiate change because that would assume blame for past failures and undercut important support coalitions. But in other parts of the world, reforms have been possible where leaders have successfully marshalled domestic political support, technical expertise, and external financing to provide the basis for effective reforms.

Reforms have been successful where leaders have marshalled political support, technical expertise, and external financing

What is the region's economic potential, and what direction would these reforms have to take? These are the subjects of chapter 3.

CHAPTER 3

The Promise of Prosperity

The global economy presents vast opportunities

Despite the bleak prognosis in previous chapters, there are many rays of hope. The world economy is tough, but it handsomely rewards those that can compete. The peace process and Europe's Mediterranean Initiative offer new possibilities for the MENA region. And some countries—such as Jordan, Morocco, and Tunisia—are taking advantage of their potential and reaping considerable rewards.

Some aspects of the international environment are favorable

The global economic environment, invigorated by buoyant world trade that promises to grow by more than 6% a year over the next ten years, is better than it has been since the 1960s. The speed of integration—the growth of world trade minus the growth rate of output—has risen steadily as trade liberalization has progressed and countries have benefited from greater globalization. The economic recovery in the industrial countries combined with the continuing decline in inflation will mean favorable markets for MENA exports.

The tightening of world capital markets has resulted in higher long-term interest rates, and private capital flows to developing countries have decelerated somewhat. Nevertheless, net private capital flows to developing countries are expected to grow on the order of 7–10% a year over the next decade as savers in industrial countries seek higher returns.

If policies remain supportive, growth in developing countries could approach 5% a year over the next decade. For countries positioned to take advantage of the opportunities that globalization brings, the external environment in the future will be very favorable. But for the ill-equipped, the trends will be adverse as growing competitiveness results in some countries being "left behind."

Globalization brings opportunities

Taking advantage of globalization begins at home. The best example is the array of new trading opportunities offered by the Uruguay Round. There are two key issues for MENA governments: adopting a trade policy regime that fosters integration into the world economy and establishing a set of institutions that make this trade policy stance credible. The World Trade Organization (WTO) can help on both fronts. First, members of the WTO must fulfill obligations that ensure that trade policies are largely nondiscriminatory, avoid the use of most quantitative restrictions on goods or the prohibition of market access by service providers, restrict the use of export subsidies, eliminate some trade-related investment measures (such as local content requirements or export performance rules), encourage reliance on international product standards, protect intellectual property, and ensure that rules and enforcement procedures are transparent. Second, the WTO provides a legal mechanism—bindings—for countries to signal the seriousness of their commitments (box 3.1). And lastly, improved dispute settlement procedures provide a mechanism for resolving conflicts.

Taking advantage of globalization begins at home

The European Union's Mediterranean Initiative is a strategic opportunity

Guided by the fear that poor economic development in MENA countries would cause instability on Europe's southern flank, the European Union (EU) has proposed to negotiate a free trade area with the countries of the Mediterranean. The basic objective is to incorporate the Mediterranean countries into the European Economic Area through a series of agreements, with the ultimate goal of creating a free trade zone in the region by 2010. These objectives are to be achieved gradually, and the European Union has committed to assist in financing the adjustment costs associated with free trade. The budget for such assistance amounts to about ECU 9.4 billion ($12 billion) for 1995–99, divided evenly between funds from the European Union and loans from the European Investment Bank. About half the funds are earmarked to prepare for free trade (private sector development, trading infrastructure) while the remainder will be devoted to poverty alleviation, rural development, and the environment. By the end of the century the Mediterranean Initiative could increase official resource flows to the region by more than half.

BOX 3.1

Committing to stay put or to move forward? Liberalization and the World Trade Organization

Credibility is the key to reform, especially in countries that take a gradual approach. A major advantage under the WTO is the requirement that a schedule of bound tariffs be presented for all industrial products. This enables governments to commit themselves to maximum tariff rates that can be applied in the future. But evidence from a number of MENA countries indicates that bindings have been used to "lock in" the status quo, not to signal further progress on trade liberalization (box table 3.1).

Similarly, MENA's WTO members did little to open their services markets despite the potential benefits in fostering more efficient domestic services and in enhancing the competitiveness of both goods and services in export markets. Commitments were made by Algeria, Bahrain, Egypt, Kuwait, Morocco, and Tunisia—while commitments are expected from Jordan, Qatar, Saudi Arabia, Sudan, and United Arab Emirates. But the only substantial commitments have been in hotel and restaurant services. Otherwise, no liberalization occurred, and little use was made of the option to bind policies under the General Agreement for Trade in Services (GATS).

Even Egypt, the Arab country with the fewest restrictions on market access and national treatment in the service sector, essentially did not liberalize under the GATS. The share of foreign personnel in foreign-owned enterprises is restricted. A maximum of 49% of shares is set for foreign capital in such industries as construction and related engineering services, tourism projects in the Sinai region, and insurance. Foreign banks and insurance companies are restricted from opening branches that will cause "harmful" competition to existing companies.

What are the costs of such half-hearted liberalization? The lack of bindings or "policy anchors" means that investors continue to face an uncertain environment as governments send mixed signals about their commitment to trade liberalization. The lack of liberalization in service markets means that MENA producers will be disadvantaged in a context where access to efficient global networks in communication, transportation, and other services is necessary for international competitiveness. There is thus a real opportunity for using WTO bindings (as well as EU association agreements) to signal serious policy commitments to the private sector.

BOX TABLE 3.1

Bound and applied tariff rates
(percent)

	Industry	Agriculture
Post–Uruguay Round bound average tariff rates (unweighted)		
Egypt	31	61
Tunisia	27	41
Current applied average tariff rates (unweighted)		
Egypt	23	52
Tunisia	33	40

Source: Hoekman 1995.

The Mediterranean Initiative is strategically important for both the European Union and the MENA countries. In the European Union, the southern countries of France, Italy, Spain, and Portugal are seeking to counterbalance the eastward expansion of the EU led by Germany. Just as U.S. firms have used NAFTA to subcontract lower-cost Mexican producers, and Germany has used association agreements with Central European countries for outsourcing to gain competitiveness, the southern European nations seek to build similar mutually beneficial relations with their Mediterranean neighbors.

For MENA countries the Mediterranean Initiative implies a major shift in the development paradigm—and a commitment to realign policies, institutions, and companies in the direction of Europe. It is the same strategic choice that such countries as the Czech Republic, Greece, Poland, and Portugal have made. Joining the EU block gives MENA countries preferences relative to Asia and levels the playing field relative to Eastern Europe and Turkey. Moreover, deeper links with the European Union imply financial support for adjustment costs, greater credibility of policy commitments, and the possibility of attracting greater investment as part of a larger market. Wages in most MENA countries are a fraction of those in most European countries, implying substantial potential for competitiveness. Consider the Central and Eastern European countries, which have penetrated the European market (from a very low base) and are reaping the benefits (table 3.1).

The export payoff from harmonization can be surprisingly large

Not much can be expected from the European Union in market access for sensitive products (like some agricultural goods), although such improved access could provide immediate benefits to many MENA exporters. Nevertheless, improved market access is not the main benefit of the EU agreement over the long run. The key is that the agreements provide MENA countries the opportunity to "lock in" policy commitments and begin to harmonize domestic laws and standards with international norms—making it easier for domestic producers to penetrate foreign markets. The "export payoff" of such harmonization can be surprisingly large (box 3.2).

Using the next decade (as the Multi-Fibre Agreement is phased out) to improve productivity and move to higher value-added activities in the European market is a way to ensure that MENA countries get to participate in the prosperity brought by the growth in world trade. Moreover, because the EU agreements will create strong incentives for Mediterranean economies to open up to each other, greater intra-

TABLE 3.1
Eastern European economies have exploited outsourcing from the EU
(net exports as a share of total exports to EU)

Export	Central and Eastern Europe 1989	Central and Eastern Europe 1993	MENA 1989	MENA 1993
Leather	38.9	34.5	8.0	8.5
Garments	60.8	74.5	15.6	11.1
Machinery	8.1	14.4	5.4	2.6
Transport	12.3	4.7	4.5	2.3
Instruments	6.4	11.9	6.5	2.5
Furniture	26.5	13.9	1.2	1.5
Total	10.4	17.9	1.6	1.7

Note: Net exports includes an adjustment for outsourcing. MENA does not include Bahrain, Iran, Oman, Qatar, and Yemen.
Source: Hoekman 1995.

BOX 3.2

The benefits of free trade agreements? Not necessarily what you would expect

Recent studies of the impact of free trade agreements with the European Union on the economies of Morocco and Tunisia produced some surprising results (Rutherford, Rustrom, and Tarr 1993 and 1995). Despite the fact that Morocco and Tunisia already have preferential access to European markets (without having to reciprocate by giving European producers access to their own markets), the welfare gains from a free trade agreement are large. The reason is that the bulk of the welfare gains stem not from the reduction of tariff and nontariff barriers but from the gains in competitiveness that result from the harmonization of standards and the reduction in trading costs from improved infrastructure financed by the EU. In Tunisia, for example, three-quarters of the welfare gains in the short run and more than half in the long run come from harmonization and improved trading infrastructure. Further export gains can be attributed to the real exchange rate depreciations that are induced by trade liberalization.

Although the estimates of welfare gains appear small—1.5% of GDP in Morocco and 4.7% of GDP in Tunisia—these gains persist every year. To give a sense of the magnitudes, if Morocco per capita income without the free trade agreement were $1,400 in 2004, it would be $1,600 with the agreement, reflecting the compounding of welfare gains over the years. More dramatically in Tunisia, per capita incomes would increase by about 60%—to $2,800 in 2004—as a result of the free trade agreement.

Perhaps the most striking finding is that the benefits increase even more when free trade agreements are combined with unilateral trade liberalization. If Tunisia were to undertake full trade liberalization with the rest of the world, the welfare gains would increase to 5.3% of GDP in the long run. In Morocco the combination of an EU agreement and liberalization of tariffs with the rest of the world increases welfare by 2.5% of GDP. The cumulative impact is reflected in per capita incomes rising to almost $1,800 in Morocco and $3,000 in Tunisia (box figure 3.1). These welfare gains are achieved with very low additional adjustment costs for labor and capital because less trade is diverted to higher-cost suppliers in the EU when liberalization is comprehensive.

BOX FIGURE 3.1

Free trade agreements and unilateral trade liberalization produce significant benefits

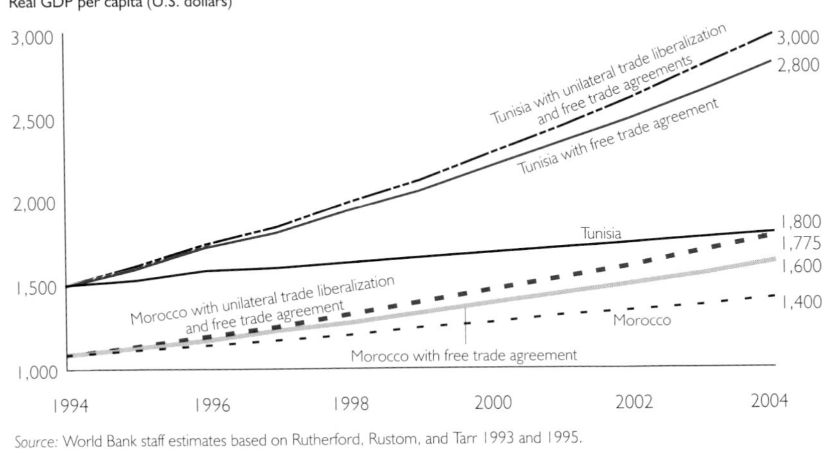

Source: World Bank staff estimates based on Rutherford, Rustom, and Tarr 1993 and 1995.

regional trade among MENA countries is a likely by-product of the process.[1]

The peace process will reduce perceptions of risk in the long run

Much of the talk of "peace dividends" is exaggerated. MENA's military spending as a share of GDP is the highest in the world, but it is fueled by more than the Arab-Israeli conflict—conflicts in the Gulf region have been an important source of higher military expenditures in recent years (table 3.2). It is thus unlikely that there will be sharp reductions in arms spending, even in the medium term, although over the long run the gradual decline in military expenditures is likely to continue. Substantial rewards for peace in the form of aid, like that for Egypt after the Camp David accords, are also unlikely to materialize in an era of donor fatigue.

Peace will reduce the region's perceived risks

The biggest potential dividend from peace is a reduction in perceived risk for the region. Private investors' subjective assessments tend to rank MENA countries as risky because of the persistence of conflict and civil strife, rather than because of commercial risks. For some countries, being in a region perceived as being in a "risky neighborhood" has adverse effects on country risk. These risks translate into lower investment and higher interest rates for international borrowing. Political risks also affect expectations about the stability of policy and the revenue from such key growth sectors as tourism.

Many of the conditions in MENA are favorable

Many of the basic elements of competitiveness are there

Most countries in MENA are advanced in stabilizing their economies and are at various stages of implementing structural reforms. Unlike many Latin American countries prone to high inflation, MENA countries have been characterized by macroeconomic stability in recent years (table 3.3). Much of the windfall of the past was invested in infra-

TABLE 3.2
MENA countries excel at spending on the military, 1992

Country	Millions of US dollars (1985 prices)	Per capita (US dollars)	Share of GNP (percent)
Kuwait	10,185	5,000	62.4
Oman	1,498	943	17.5
United Arab Emirates	4,249	2,418	14.6
Saudi Arabia	14,535	1,371	11.8
Jordan	586	133	11.2
Israel	3,984	783	11.1
Yemen	682	59	9.3
Egypt	3,427	60	6.0
Lebanon	18	7	5.0
Morocco	692	27	4.0
Tunisia	355	42	3.3
Algeria	1,592	59	2.7
All developing countries	119,350	31	3.5

Note: Kuwait's level of military spending was exceptionally high in the wake of the Gulf War in 1990. From the mid-1980s to 1990, Kuwait's military spending as a share of GDP ranged from 5 percent to 7 percent.
Source: International Institute for Strategic Studies 1993.

structure—so MENA households have adequate access to telephones, electricity, paved roads, and safe water, although quality is still an issue. Risks of contract repudiation or expropriation are limited in MENA, though measures of the quality of bureaucracy indicate problems in some countries. Nevertheless, the region as a whole ranks higher than Latin America, South Asia, and Sub-Saharan Africa in several institutional investor ratings. Sometimes this reflects the existence of well-established mechanisms (such as commercial agents or legal advisors) to steer investors clear of what would otherwise be a difficult business environment.

TABLE 3.3
Macroeconomies are stable in relative terms
(percent)

Region	Average annual inflation,[a] 1988–93	Average annual depreciation or devaluation, 1988–94
Maghreb	10	13
Mashreq	16	84
GCC	3	0
MENA	10	34
LAC	319	255
South Asia	12	8
East Asia	7	2

a. Calculated from the consumer price index.
Source: World Bank data.

Some of the legacy of past policies has also been positive—with a large human resource base in most countries. MENA countries have invested heavily in human capital—public spending on education is higher than that in any region in the world. Large portions of GDP have been devoted to education in countries like Saudi Arabia (10.6%), Jordan (6.5%), Egypt (5.5%), Tunisia (5.4%), and Kuwait (5.1%). Those investments are beginning to pay off, with the mean years of schooling in many MENA countries approaching that in other countries at similar incomes (figure 3.1). But as with infrastructure services, the varying quality of education has emerged as a key issue for future competitiveness.

Many countries have a strong entrepreneurial tradition that has been channeled into unproductive rent-seeking and trading activities as a result of the structure of economic incentives. This could be redirected. And nascent clusters of competitiveness exist in some areas (box 3.3).

Financing is available for those committed to reform

The flip side to the substantial capital flight from the region is that large foreign savings held abroad could finance new investment if the domestic conditions for investors improve. Investors in several countries have already brought money home. In Egypt private capital inflows amounted to $31.5 billion between 1987 and 1993 (including remittances) after a successful stabilization program was initiated in 1987 (IMF 1994a). In Lebanon private capital amounting to about $16 billion flowed in between 1989 and 1994 after the civil war ended. But in both cases private capital flows are largely financing needed reserve accumulation and

FIGURE 3.1

Average education levels are approaching those of comparators

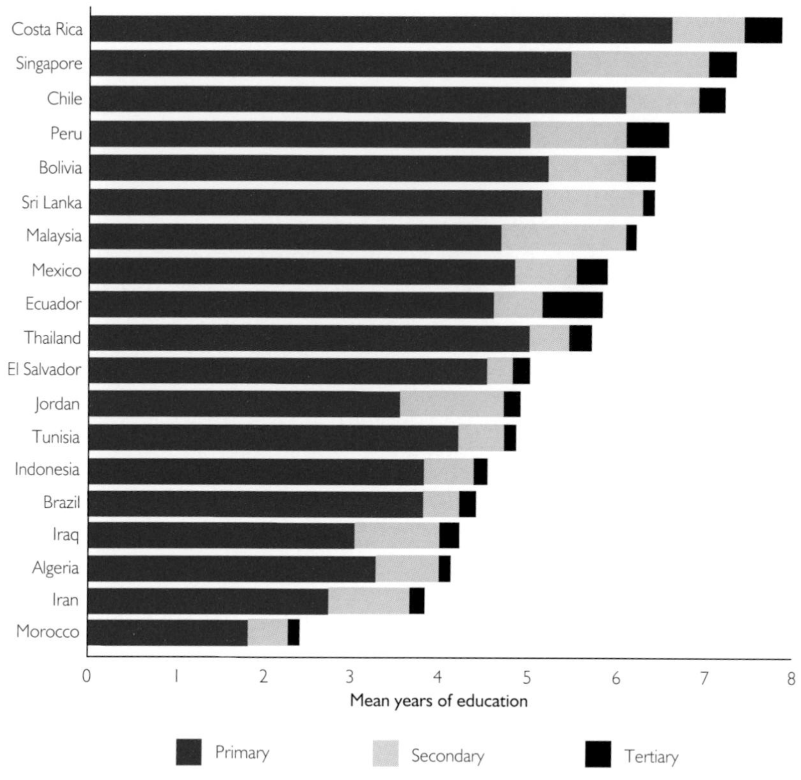

Source: Nehru, Swanson, and Dubey 1993.

International capital and official financing are available

short-term government debt at high interest rates to finance sizable deficits. Only a small portion has gone to direct investment—$4.3 billion in Egypt and $2.0 billion in Lebanon—evidence that the investment climate is not yet sufficiently attractive for private capital to make major, long-term commitments.

In addition to financing from nationals' savings abroad, international capital is available to finance new investment and adjustment costs, but only to serious reformers. Private capital flows to developing countries amounted to a staggering $158 billion in 1993. But it was concentrated in a handful of countries in East Asia and Latin America that had made substantial and sustained progress on reform—55% of the aggregate flow went to China (23%), Argentina (14%), Mexico (10%), and Brazil (8%). Official financing is also possible, particularly from the European Union, but that too will increasingly be tied to economic performance.

BOX 3.3

Building on existing clusters of firms to gain competitiveness

In many parts of the world groups of firms or "clusters" have been an important source of competitiveness. Northern Italy, Southern Germany, and Catalonia in Spain have industrial districts in which small firms specialize in different stages of the production process, both competing and cooperating in markets. Although many of these clusters produce goods such as shoes and textiles (usually associated with low wages), they manage to generate high value added and high wages by concentrating on high quality. The success of these industrial districts has been based on small scale and flexible production, continuous innovation, vertical (supplier to purchaser) and horizontal (rivalrous) relationships, and mutual trust and strong interfirm relations often led by a local authority or professional association. Similar clusters have emerged in some developing countries: the footwear clusters of Sinos Valley in Brazil, Trujillo in Peru, and Agra in India; the textiles clusters in Deagu in Korea and Ludhiana and Tirupper in India; and the diamond polishing cluster of Surat in India.

Italian shoe cluster

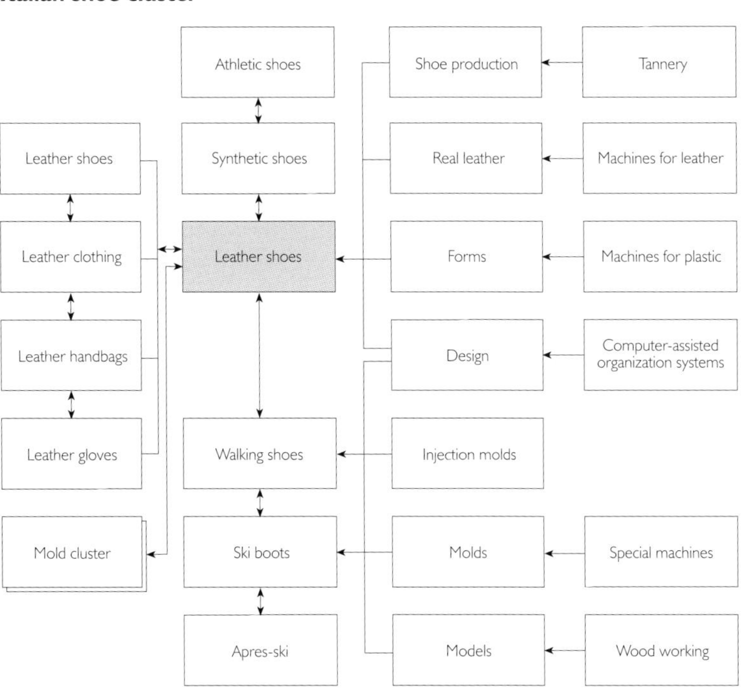

In Morocco a geographically concentrated leather and textile industry in Fez and Casablanca has a tradition of high-quality handicraft production and a bazaar culture of business relationships based on mutual trust. But it has not yet emerged as a competitive cluster because of a lack of technological innovation, institutional infrastructure, and cooperative solutions. The most striking difference between Morocco's embryonic leather and shoe cluster and that of the world-famous Italian leather and shoe industry is the absence in the Moroccan industry of the more sophisticated functions—such as design, dies, and specialized equipment—necessary to innovate and produce higher value-added exports. To develop this potential in Morocco, a tripartite committee (private sector, government, and the World Bank) has been established with support from the European Union to identify the missing components of export-oriented clusters and to find private sector solutions to improving the export potential of these firms.

Moroccan shoe cluster

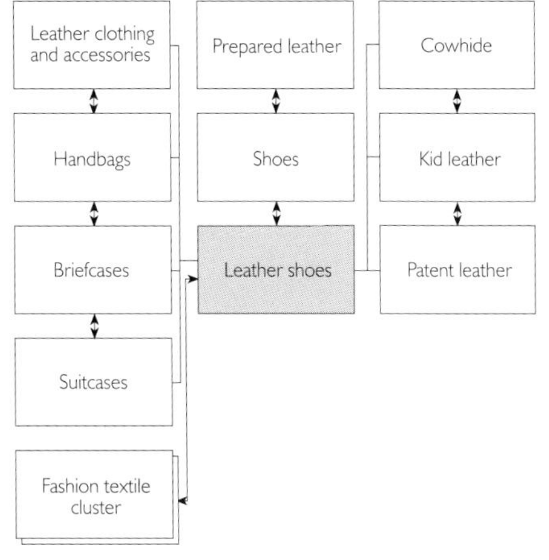

Source: Pyke, Becattini, and Sengenberger 1990; Nadvi and Schmitz 1994; and Ettori 1995.

Jordan, Morocco, and Tunisia are beginning to reap the rewards of reform

The diversity of economic strategies in MENA countries is probably greater today than at any time in their recent history. While almost all the region's countries adopted statist strategies in the 1960s and 1970s, a few have adopted a different strategy—Jordan, Morocco, and Tunisia are notable examples. Lebanon is the major exception: throughout its history it has had a private sector–dominated economy, held back by political instability. How have these early reformers in the MENA region fared?

Jordan, Morocco, and Tunisia have been consistent, building credibility over time

Jordan, Morocco, and Tunisia all instituted reforms gradually. But unlike many of their neighbors, they have been fairly consistent in the direction of reform, building credibility over time. None of the three was a major oil exporter and, with the exception of phosphates in Jordan and Morocco, none could draw on sizable rents to finance the public sector. Remittances from workers abroad were important to all three, but because there were profitable opportunities for the private sector at home, capital flight was low by regional standards. All three began their adjustment programs in the 1980s with macroeconomic stabilization, deficit reduction, trade liberalization, and structural reforms in pricing, regulation, and financial market development.

The payoffs to these policies are obvious (table 3.4). All three countries—Jordan, Morocco, and Tunisia—have experienced faster growth in incomes, exports, and jobs than have other countries in the region. And foreign investors have shown confidence in the business environment. Education levels in Jordan and Tunisia are relatively high (Morocco still lags), and poverty is at fairly low levels.

Jordan and Tunisia, unlike Morocco, relied heavily on human resource development as the basis of their strategies, evidenced by the data on mean years of schooling. On virtually every indicator of human resources—life expectancy, enrollment rates, infant mortality—Jordan and Tunisia are exceptional performers, by both regional and international standards. Even when controlling for per capita income, they have above-average social indicators (figures 3.2–3.4).

Adjustment costs are significant, but often lower than expected

How severe have the adjustment costs been for these countries? Unemployment rates have been high in the 1990s—13% in Jordan, 12%

in Morocco, and 16% in Tunisia—but no higher than those in other countries in the region.[2] Real wages have been flat in all three, but employment has grown substantially. In Morocco and Tunisia many low-wage jobs were created in export-oriented industries that were crucial for reducing poverty. Capital-labor ratios have remained low in Morocco and Tunisia as labor markets have given investors incentives to create jobs, unlike the situation in other countries in the region, where labor market regulations have encouraged investors to substitute for labor (figure 3.5).

Economic strategies in MENA countries vary widely

TABLE 3.4

Jordan, Morocco, and Tunisia have had better economic results

(percent, unless otherwise indicated)

Country	Per capita GDP growth rate, 1990–94	Non-oil exports growth rate, 1980–93	Average annual inflation rate,[a] 1984–94	FDI inflows/ GDP, 1993	Mean years of schooling, 1987	Population spending less than $1 a day, 1990
Jordan	0.39	4.3	5.33	–0.65	5	12.60[b]
Morocco	0.70	3.8	5.73	2.00	2	2.49
Tunisia	2.10	10.5	6.00	1.63	5	2.89
Algeria	–2.33	4.5	18.00	0.03	4	1.16
Egypt	–0.72	0.5	14.80	1.20	5	5.60
Iran	–1.04	–1.0	20.50	–0.05	4	8.94

a. Using GDP deflator.
b. This estimate was done at the time of the Gulf war. Higher growth rates since then have probably reduced poverty in Jordan.
Source: World Bank data; van Eeghen 1995.

FIGURE 3.2

Jordan and Tunisia do better on life expectancy

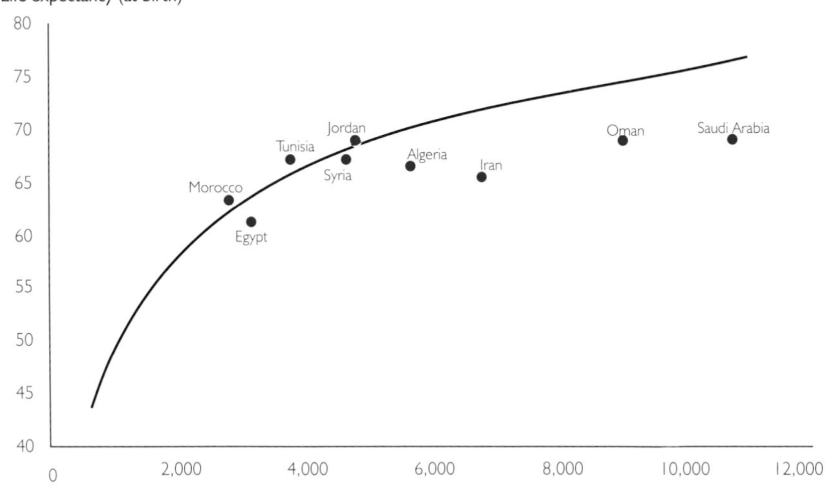

Note: Line represents regression estimate for all low- and middle-income countries.
Source: Shafik 1994.

Who gains and who loses from further integration into the world economy? In general, sectors that are tradable gain, while those that are nontradable lose, but the effects are quite country-specific (table 3.5). In Tunisia the textiles sector is a major gainer, doubling over the long run. In Morocco textiles suffer (but only in relative terms) compared with

FIGURE 3.3

Tunisia's primary enrollment exceeds the average for its income

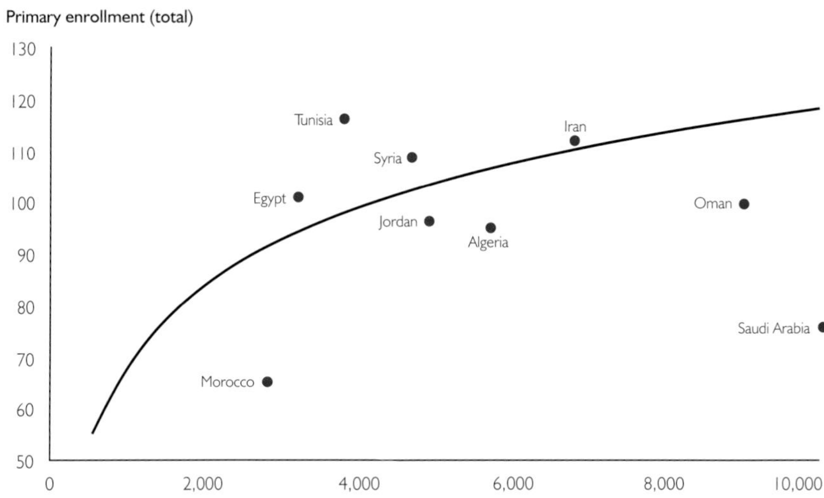

Note: Line represents regression estimate for all low- and middle-income countries.
Source: Shafik 1994.

FIGURE 3.4

Tunisian and Jordanian infants are less likely to die

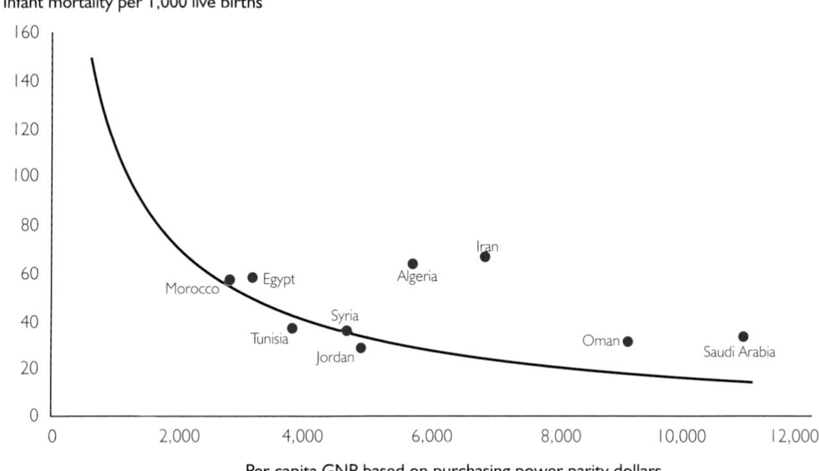

Note: Line represents regression estimate for all low- and middle-income countries.
Source: Shafik 1994.

phosphates, which are the biggest beneficiary. In the short run, 2.1% of the labor force will have to change jobs in Tunisia, but in the long run as many as 8.8% will change jobs. These adjustment costs are significant, but unlike the cumulative welfare gains from trade liberalization (see box 3.2), the adjustment costs are one-off.

And what have been the dislocations caused by privatization? The few instances of privatization in the MENA region have had negligible effects on unemployment—often because the firms chosen for early sale were better ones not plagued by overstaffing, as in Morocco. In Tunisia, too, the effect on employment has been fairly small. Only 4% of the 6,483 workers in the privatized state-owned enterprises were laid off, 46% were transferred to the new purchaser of the privatized enterprise, 16% departed voluntarily with severance packages, 29% retired, and 5% were transferred to other areas (Saghir 1993).

TABLE 3.5

Impact of free trade agreements on employment in Morocco and Tunisia

(percent change in labor use)

Sector	Morocco
Textiles	–3.7
Cereals	–9.4
Meat and dairy	–52.0
Phosphates	68.5
Electrical equipment	–6.1
Leather and shoes	10.9
Trade	–1.9
Transport	2.2

Sector	Tunisia
Textiles	26.0
Chemicals	9.2
Agriculture	–6.5
Private services	–8.1
Electrical industries	–5.5
Manufactures	–6.9
Trade	6.8
Transport	–5.9

Source: Rutherford, Rustrom, and Tarr 1993 and 1995.

Reform often has been good for the poor

The success of Morocco and Tunisia in reducing both the percentage and the number of poor reveals the gains from good policies. In both countries poverty was cut nearly in half—exceptional performance by international standards. In Morocco reductions in the poverty rate were particularly sharp—decreasing from 22% in 1985 to 11% in 1991 in rural

FIGURE 3.5

Morocco and Tunisia have created more jobs with lower capital-labor ratios

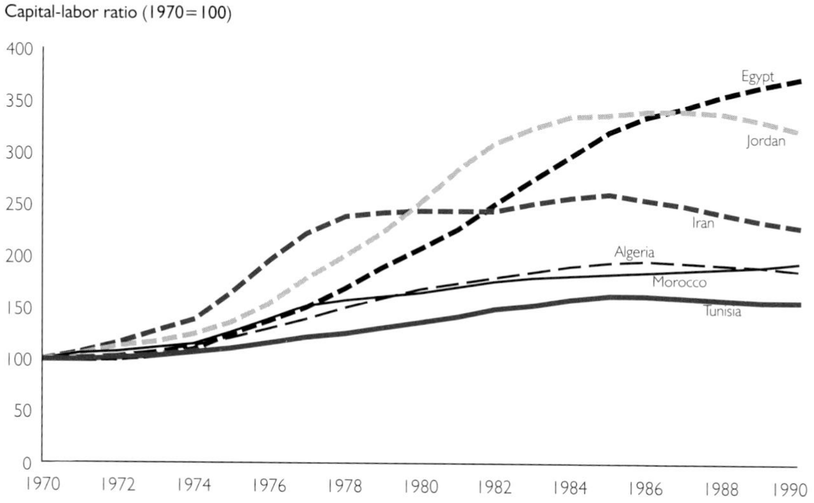

Source: World Bank staff estimates based on data from Nehru and Dhareshwar 1993.

areas and from 9% to 3% in urban areas (table 3.6). Some of this reduction in poverty can be attributed to the fact that 1990 was a year with good rainfall, hence the especially sharp reduction in rural poverty. The creation of many low-wage jobs and the rise in female participation rates in the labor force made important contributions to the incomes of poor households in both countries. More recently, a series of droughts may have worsened Morocco's poverty performance, particularly in rural areas.

Adjustment costs are manageable

The outcome in Jordan is more complex since the adjustment period was accompanied by a major external shock—the Gulf war—which caused a massive drop in output as well as an influx of unemployed labor. Both had severely negative consequences for the poor. The percentage of poor in the Jordanian population increased from 2% in 1987 to almost 16% in 1992. This deterioration occurred despite Jordan's impressive achievements in the social sectors—school enrollments and health indicators in Jordan are among the highest in the region. Nearly all the increase in poverty in Jordan was due to the 8.8% contraction of GDP between 1986 and 1991. But output growth of 16% in 1992 and 6% in 1993, combined with falling unemployment, is likely to have improved conditions for Jordan's poor.

Poverty reduction in MENA tends to be responsive to growth, and when combined with effective social policies, as in Tunisia, the effect on human welfare is dramatic. In addition to having one of the lowest rates of income poverty in the world, Tunisia has provided its citizens with social services that have generated some of the best social indicators in the region. The average Tunisian citizen lives longer, has fewer children die, and is more likely to have basic education and be literate than any country in MENA at an equivalent per capita income. A large part of these achievements stem from a long-standing commitment to female education and the provision of services and opportunities to women.

TABLE 3.6
Morocco and Tunisia have reduced poverty substantially

	Morocco		Tunisia	
	1984/85	1991	1985	1990
Head-count index	6.06	1.64	4.63	2.89
Poverty-gap index[a]	1.62	0.23	0.89	0.64
Squared poverty gap index[b]	0.82	0.06	0.31	0.28

Note: Poverty is defined as average spending of less than $1 a day at 1985 purchasing power parity.
a. The shortfall in expenditure (from the poverty line) of the average poor person, expressed as a percentage of the poverty line.
b. A measure of the distribution of income of those below the poverty line.
Source: van Eeghen 1995; Chen, Datt, and Ravallion 1993.

Better resource management can have high payoffs

Protecting the environment has been an important avenue for achieving efficiency and productivity gains. For example, energy intensity in Morocco and Tunisia is about half the MENA average, implying less energy-related pollution per unit of output. A major reason for the higher energy efficiency in these two countries is higher energy prices that reflect economic costs. Gasoline prices in 1992 were about $0.83 a liter in Morocco and $0.58 a liter in Tunisia—compared with $0.25 in Lebanon, $0.14 in Saudi Arabia, and less than $0.05 in Iran.[3] Fuel consumption per vehicle in Morocco and Tunisia is less than half the average in the non-Gulf MENA countries and less than a third of that in Iran. Prices of industrial fuel oils are also substantially higher in Morocco and Tunisia than in most MENA countries, providing incentives to conserve energy in the industrial sector.

Jordan, Morocco, and Tunisia still have important reforms ahead, but are moving in the right direction

Jordan, Morocco, and Tunisia still have important reform agendas ahead. All three countries need to improve productivity to meet greater competition from Europe as they enter association agreements. Morocco needs to achieve much more on its social agenda, especially education of girls in rural areas. Jordan and Tunisia must learn to better manage environmental fragility. But all three countries are moving in the right direction and provide examples of the way forward for the rest of the region.

Notes

1. If the European Union only negotiates bilateral free trade agreements with countries of the Mediterranean, a "hub and spoke" pattern will emerge, providing strong incentives for investors to locate in the "hub" in order to have access to the markets in the "spokes." To avoid such a diversion of investment, countries in the Mediterranean will have strong incentives to open up to each other (Hoekman 1995).

2. Unemployment data for Morocco are from 1991 and for Jordan and Tunisia are from 1993. In Jordan unemployment fell from a high of 19% in the immediate aftermath of the Gulf war in 1991 to 13% in 1993 as returnees from the Gulf were gradually absorbed into the labor force.

3. Gasoline prices in Saudi Arabia were raised to $0.16 a liter in 1995, which is close to the world wholesale price.

CHAPTER 4

From Politics to Economics

"The strength of a country is no longer measured by its military might, size of population, geographical situation, or material resources. The strength of a country is measured by the wealth of its scholars and its scientists, by its innovative capabilities and ability to discover, achieve, and apply."

Naguib Mahfouz, 1994

Now is the time for action

Reforms must be credible and consistent

Most countries in MENA have relied on gradualist strategies—sometimes sacrificing growth for lower adjustment costs. But in the new, fast-paced world economy, gradual reform may mean no growth (given the mobility of capital) if countries lack credible policies. And half-hearted or stop-go approaches to reform are a sure way to lose credibility. Attracting investors usually requires up-front commitments, and promises about the future direction of economic policy are adequate only if they are made by credible public institutions with a clear long-term reform strategy. Catching up in the future will become more difficult because trade and investment linkages are increasingly self-reinforcing. Emerging as competitors are some of the world's lowest-income countries—India and China—whose real wages are a third to half the average in MENA countries. Only a few countries in MENA (like Egypt and Yemen) have low wages that can compete at these levels.

Competing will be more difficult because serious demographic pressures will coincide with an increasing scarcity of public resources. During 1970–93 MENA's population growth rate was the highest in the world—and at current trends the region's population will reach 400 million before 2010. The age structure is very young, with half the population under the age of 15 (World Bank 1994a). Greater demand for education and social services from a young population will result in severe financing pressures. Reducing educational quality or access is not an option for relieving the pressures since enhanced skills are the key to higher incomes in the future. The impetus for reforms that create good jobs and improve welfare can only increase (box 4.1).

Potential winners from reform far outnumber the potential losers

The "pressure points" in box 4.1 spotlight the losers from the lack of reform and growth—and their numbers are growing. The costs of inaction are growing with them. In many countries in the MENA region, those interested in new job creation (the unemployed and those entering the labor force) now outnumber those interested in the preservation of old jobs (those employed in the state sector). In several MENA countries the number of potential winners from structural reform are far greater than those who stand to lose in the public enterprise sector. Even under conservative assumptions about surplus workers in the public sector as a whole (including the civil service), the winners always outnumber the losers by at least three times. In Egypt, for example, the poor number 3.2 million and the unemployed another 1.7 million, while those

BOX 4.1

Pressures for reform are mounting

Most MENA countries are at a critical juncture where simultaneous pressures are emerging:

- While the region's population is growing at 2.7%, the labor force is growing at a much faster 3.3%. Jobs for 47 million new entrants into the labor force will have to be found by 2010.
- The number of unemployed in the region stands at 9 million. By 2010 they will number 15 million if the current high rates of unemployment persist.
- Rising productivity in agriculture is likely to free up even more labor from rural areas to join the ranks of the unemployed or the urban informal sector.
- Real wages remain stagnant at 1970 levels.
- Current projections for GDP growth indicate that the number of poor (those living on less than $1 a day) will rise to about 15 million by 2010 if reforms are not introduced.

Unemployment usually exceeds 10%

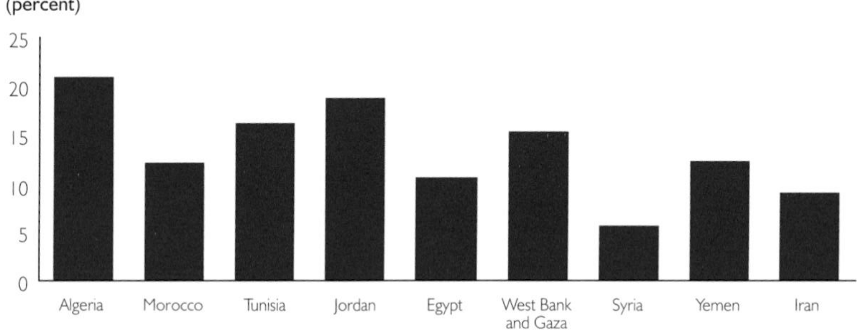

Note: Some sources report higher unemployment rates based on different definitions of unemployment. Unemployment numbers are for 1991, except for Tunisia (1993), West Bank and Gaza (1993), and Yemen (1992).
Source: World Bank data.

with protected jobs in the state-owned enterprises number only about 1 million. Obviously not all the "potential winners" would be winners—the chronic poor are always difficult to reach, and some of the unemployed lack marketable skills. And not all "potential losers" will lose since some employees in the public sector will keep their jobs or find good alternative jobs in the private sector. Experience elsewhere indicates that structural reforms necessarily involve some job destruction, but that it would be more than made up for in new jobs created as a result of more efficient investment and higher growth.

Choosing to be prosperous

Perhaps the greatest change in today's world is that no country is destined to be poor because of a bad endowment of natural resources, an isolated location, or a concentration on certain products. Production, finance, and trade have changed such that human talent is more important than natural endowment, agility more than location, and quality and innovation more than mass production. The implication is that countries can choose, through their policies, whether to be rich or poor (box 4.2).

No country is destined to be poor

BOX 4.2

Portugal and the European Union: A model for MENA?

Portugal's per capita income in 1970 was $790—well below the MENA average and only slightly exceeding that of the poorest states, Egypt and Yemen, today. Throughout the 1970s Portugal's policies closely paralleled the statism in the MENA region—a leftist coalition government nationalized private holding companies, expropriated land, and restricted foreign direct investment. Persistent balance of payments crises forced the government to turn to the International Monetary Fund in 1977 and 1983. But the economy continued to flounder with current account deficits of 14% of GDP, unemployment at 12%, real wages falling by 17% in 1983–85, and stagnant private investment.

After eight years of negotiations, Portugal acceded to the European Union in 1986, and a serious effort at structural reform was launched in 1987. Economic policy focused on fiscal consolidation and tax reform, privatization, easing regulations against dismissal, and promoting growth.

What was the impact of joining the EU? The trade balance worsened as barriers were removed and imports from the EU flooded in. Trade diversion was small (less than 1% of total trade) and concentrated in the agricultural sector. The benefits of trade creation were concentrated in Portuguese manufacturing and services, both of which grew rapidly. The economic response was significant—during 1986–90 output grew by 4.4%, investment increased by 43%, and unemployment fell to 6.4%.

The negative effects on Portugal's trade balance were offset by two benefits—transfers from the EU and foreign direct investment. Transfers from the EU amounting to almost 4% of Portugal's GDP helped to cushion the adjustment to a more competitive environment. Every fourth escudo spent by the Portuguese state in 1988 came from the EU cohesion policy coffers—such as the European Social Fund, European Investment Bank, European Regional Development Fund, and the short- and medium-term funds for balance of payments support. More important, foreign investment boomed, increasing threefold in the second half of the 1980s as Portugal's business climate improved. The Portuguese experience contrasts sharply with Greece's, where there has been little structural adjustment, stagnant foreign direct investment, and continuing heavy dependence on transfers from the European Union.

Source: Axt 1992.

For too long the MENA region has squandered its potential

For too long the MENA region has squandered its potential. Political energy was spent on regional conflicts and rivalries rather than on economic development. Oil wealth was sometimes misspent on activities with low social returns but high payoffs for a few. Large investments in human capital were underused because of misguided labor market distortions intended to help the disadvantaged—who eventually became the privileged. And the region's endowment of natural resources was mined to fuel this process.

That era is waning. The peace process, with all its vicissitudes, is bound to reduce the political risks in the region and make space for more determined efforts at economic reform in the long run. The domestic voices for change are growing more numerous. To attract private investment, all countries will have strong incentives to liberalize trade and offer access to the vast EU market through association agreements and to the numerous regional markets by forging cross-regional association agreements.

An ambitious vision

What could the region look like for the next generation? Achievable social and economic goals for the MENA region are shown in table 4.1. The social goals imply longer and healthier lives and a better-educated population. These improvements, desirable in their own right, also contribute to higher levels of output and reduced population growth. The targets are feasible because they are consistent with improvements achieved in the past. Egypt, for example, already has managed to reduce its infant mortality from 145 per 1,000 live births to 66 in a 25-year period. Tunisia did even better, with a reduction from 145 to 41 between 1965 and 1990. Similarly, the gains in life expectancy are not unusual—in both Jordan and Tunisia people can expect to live 67 years. The educational goals also have precedents—Tunisia reduced the illiteracy from 80% in 1965 to 35% in 1990

TABLE 4.1
Major economic and social improvements are possible

Region	Infant mortality (per 1,000 live births)		Life expectancy at birth (years)		Illiteracy (percentage of total population)		Gross secondary school enrollment (percent)	
	1990	2010	1990	2010	1990	2010	1990	2010
Mashreq	70	32	60	71	48	25	76	85
Maghreb	64	36	64	72	45	20	48	70
GCC	23	10	71	75	29	15	68	80

Source: Diwan and Squire 1992; World Bank data.

and Algeria increased secondary school enrollment from 6% to 61% between 1965 and 1990.

Economic projections indicate that, despite having to accommodate 120 million more inhabitants by 2010, per capita incomes in the region could double in the long run. This ambitious target assumes that per capita growth rises from 3.5% in the 1990s (as reforms are undertaken) to about 5.0% in the later years. A more probable "base case" scenario is per capita growth of about 2.5% (which translates into a still sizable 5% growth in GDP), resulting in a 50% gain in per capita incomes by 2010. These levels of economic performance are achievable—almost every country in the region experienced per capita growth rates of 3–4% or more between 1965 and 1980 and many East Asian economies have sustained even higher rates of growth. But achieving such growth rates now will mean that the economies of the region will have to look quite different from today.

Promoting non-oil exports

Today, MENA's non-oil exports (with 260 million people) are less than Finland's (with 5 million people). Meeting future import requirements (such as food) means that exports will have to grow, and non-oil merchandise exports are the biggest opportunity for the future if there is sufficient progress on trade liberalization and competition policies.

How fast must non-oil exports grow to achieve the 2.5% base-case target growth rate for per capita incomes (figure 4.1)? Riordan and others (1995) show that:

- For one group of countries, "required" growth in exports for the 1995–2010 period is either below the performance achieved over the past decade (Tunisia) or should be readily attainable in a favorable external environment (Jordan, Morocco). Although the targeted growth in per capita GDP lies above the historic average for these countries, it is likely that actual outturns will well exceed annual gains of 2.5% (figure 4.2). It is no accident that this group includes the early reformers—Jordan, Morocco, and Tunisia.
- For a second group of countries, including those of the Mashreq, as well as Bahrain and United Arab Emirates,

FIGURE 4.1

MENA's GDP and per capita income growth

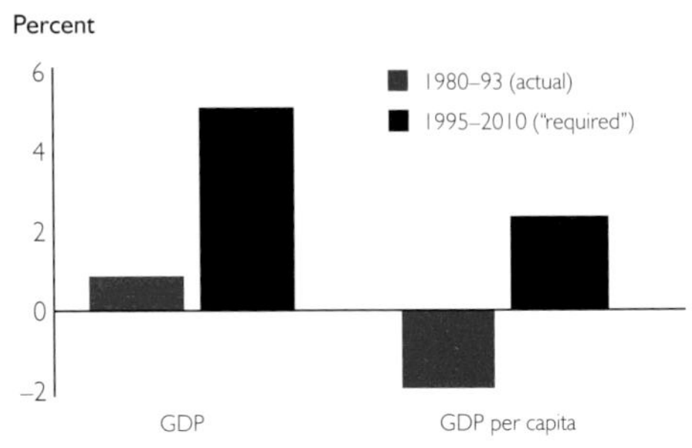

Source: Riordan and others 1995.

FIGURE 4.2

Readily achievable non-oil export growth

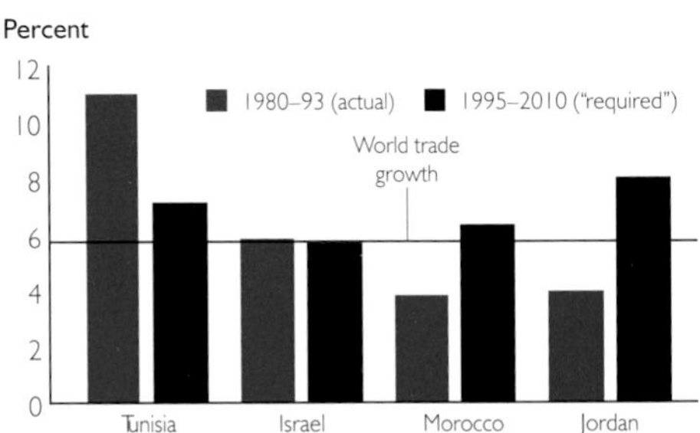

Source: Riordan and others 1995.

FIGURE 4.3

Policy-supported non-oil export growth

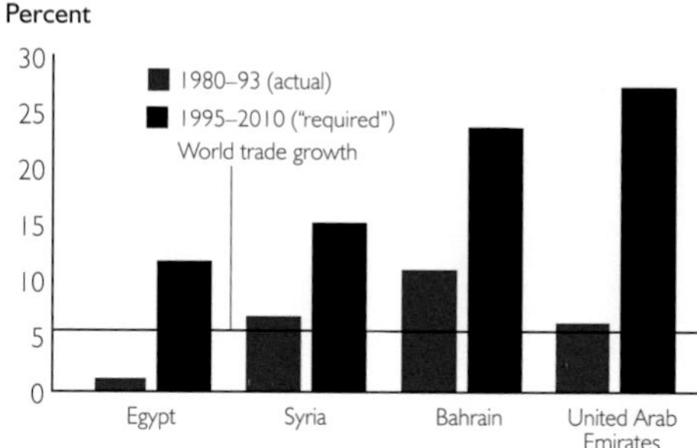

Source: Riordan and others 1995.

FIGURE 4.4

Paradigm change non-oil export growth

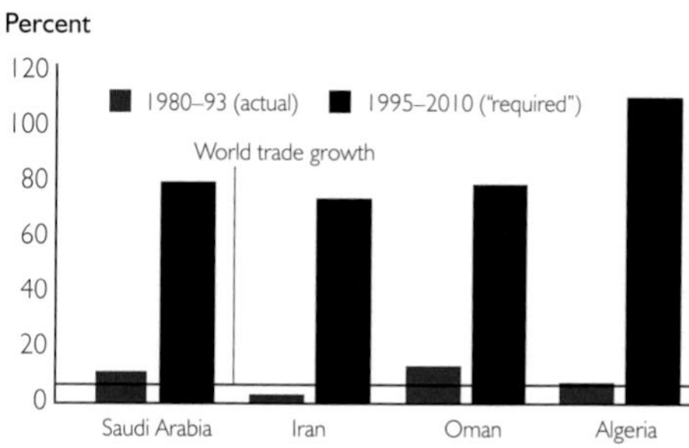

Source: Riordan and others 1995.

targeted exports will require a doubling of historic growth, but are within reach if significant efforts are made to improve competitiveness and to diversify the product and market mix (figure 4.3).

• The third group comprises those economies in which fuels account for more than 90% of exports. Although the growth in petrochemical exports has been favorable for these countries in recent years, the group will require a tenfold improvement in performance (figure 4.4). Export growth will have to rise from 5% a year to more than 50% for incomes to outpace rapid population growth. Relying on non-oil exports to maintain living standards in the future is not an option for these countries. The problem is clearly more acute for those countries with large population densities and import requirements, including Algeria, Iran, and Iraq. As targets for non-oil exports are unlikely to be achieved over the next decade, this group of countries will need to find alternative means of generating foreign exchange, such as commercial services, higher savings, and earning higher returns on foreign asset holdings. This will require a shift in the prevailing development paradigm and social contract.

In the early stages building competitive advantage on the basis of this existing export capacity is more promising than starting from scratch in new areas. Revealed comparative advantage indices are an indication of where opportunities for expanded trade exist (table 4.2). For MENA countries the opportunities are in refined fuels, chemicals, foods and feeds, and manufactures. The most rapid growth in non-oil exports has been in chemicals, machinery, and manufactures (particularly clothing and textiles, but also carpets and jewelry; figure 4.5). The countries that have achieved the greatest gains in non-oil exports have been Bahrain, Jordan, Oman, Qatar, Saudi Arabia, Syria, Tunisia, and United Arab Emirates.

In textiles the biggest export gains have been in Tunisia, Morocco, Egypt, and Syria. Much of the growth in Tunisia has been based on outsourcing of European multinationals, which import textiles for final assembly and ship clothing for sale in Europe. So, while Tunisian exports of clothing rose from $0.3 billion in the early 1980s to $1.1 billion in the early 1990s, net exports of textiles and clothing increased fivefold, from

TABLE 4.2

Competitiveness already exists in many sectors

(revealed comparative advantage indices for processed products classified by major SITC groups, 1992)

Exporter	Foods and feeds	Beverages and tobacco	Crude minerals	Refined fuels	Animal and vegetable oils	Chemicals	Manufactures by material[a]	Machinery and transport	Other manu-factures
Bahrain	0.01	0.02	0.08	**18.43**	0.07	0.54	**1.21**	0.17	0.53
Cyprus	**2.41**	**7.22**	0.26	**1.70**	**1.25**	0.68	0.65	0.30	**2.68**
Egypt	**1.07**	0.10	0.00	**9.06**	0.00	0.62	**1.75**	0.34	0.87
Iran	**6.62**	0.02	0.08	**110.40**	0.00	0.11	**2.58**	0.09	0.15
Israel	**2.62**	0.11	0.25	0.44	0.01	**1.32**	**2.10**	0.49	0.88
Jordan	0.15	0.39	0.00	0.00	0.00	**4.95**	0.85	0.37	0.47
Lebanon	**2.90**	**3.73**	0.02	0.08	0.03	0.32	**1.38**	0.30	**2.54**
Libya	0.01	0.00	0.01	**26.94**	0.00	**1.34**	0.25	0.06	0.01
Oman	0.25	0.00	0.00	**13.59**	0.00	0.18	0.37	0.64	**1.29**
Qatar	0.01	0.00	0.05	**15.89**	0.20	**3.02**	0.25	0.07	0.63
Saudi Arabia	0.15	0.00	0.16	**19.59**	0.01	**2.26**	0.23	0.23	0.17
Syria	**2.32**	0.01	0.03	**22.10**	0.00	0.06	0.45	0.06	**1.17**
Turkey	**5.10**	0.10	0.38	0.70	0.24	0.31	**1.44**	0.24	**2.57**
United Arab Emirates	0.57	**3.28**	0.38	**10.27**	0.12	0.57	**1.01**	0.39	**1.20**

Note: Revealed comparative advantage is defined as a product's share in a country's exports as a proportion of its share in world trade. When the index has a value greater than 1, the country has a "revealed comparative advantage" in that product.
a. Manufactures based on raw material inputs.
Source: Yeats 1995.

$60 million to $300 million. In Morocco net exports of textiles and clothing expanded almost fivefold, from $120 million to $570 million, over the same period. Egypt's performance has been less impressive, with annual net exports of textiles and clothing rising by only 10%, from $680 million in the 1980s to $750 million in the 1990s. Syria, by contrast, has made substantial gains, with net exports increasing almost fourfold over the 1980s, from $130 million to $510 million.[1]

The region's strong comparative advantage in petrochemicals also offers some promise. Both organic petrochemicals (such as fertilizers from the GCC countries) and inorganic chemicals (such as phosphatic fertilizers from Jordan, Morocco, and Tunisia) have grown rapidly, from less than $100 million a year in the early 1970s to $4.9 billion in the early 1990s. Saudi Arabia alone accounts for almost half the region's exports of chemicals. Other important exporters are Morocco, Tunisia, United Arab Emirates, Jordan, Egypt, and Bahrain, in that order. Petrochemicals do not face particularly high tariffs in the OECD countries, and tariffs are being reduced under GATT arrangements, but trade disputes over dumping remain an issue. For exporters of phosphatic fertilizers, moreover, the reduced protection of agricultural products expected in the European Union is likely to soften demand in that market. Growing markets for fertilizers in Asia could nevertheless hold promise for MENA exporters.

FIGURE 4.5

Clothing and chemicals have been MENA's largest exports, 1992–93

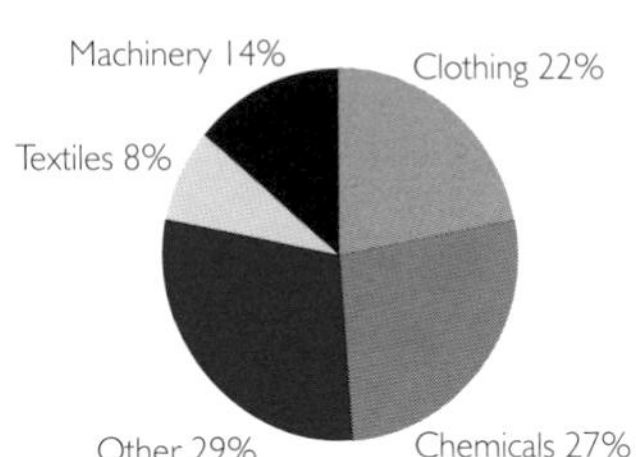

Note: Excludes Israel.
Source: Riordan and others 1995.

There also is some potential for growth in food exports—such as dried fruits (Iran, Morocco), vegetables (Morocco, Egypt), spices (Iran, Morocco), and fish (mainly from Morocco but also from Tunisia, Iran, Oman, and United Arab Emirates). Such exports have doubled in value in the past decade and more than quadrupled in the past 20 years. Although there is not much reason to be overly optimistic about extraregional food exports—since populations are growing fast and food prices are not expected to increase—several countries (such as Iran, Morocco, and Tunisia) are likely to find rapidly growing niche markets in both industrial and developing countries.

Making the private sector more competitive

Trade liberalization must be accompanied by internal liberalization to enable firms to compete

Opening up to promote exports must be accompanied by internal liberalization to enable domestic firms to compete with international ones. A strategy of dismantling many of the currently burdensome regulations, while simultaneously building a system that addresses the needs of a more global economy, is necessary in many MENA countries. Key elements of such a system would include:

- Intellectual property rights to encourage investment in information.
- Environmental protection to account for externalities.
- Consumer safety standards to encourage quality improvements.
- Regulations to promote competition in the provision of infrastructure.
- Liberalization of financial markets (including greater foreign investment in financial services) to lower borrowing costs and provide greater long-term and equity finance.

The World Trade Organization and the association agreements with the European Union provide mechanisms for achieving the first three regulatory objectives, while the introduction of new rules for infrastructure services permits a new approach to infrastructure development.

The infrastructure upgrading needs of MENA countries provide an important opportunity to mobilize new private investment and increase the competitiveness of existing firms by improving the quality of services. For example, expanding and modernizing infrastructure in Egypt will cost about $2 billion a year and in Jordan about $500 million a year for the foreseeable future. Governments are unlikely to be able to afford more than 20% of these costs, and donors may cover about 15%. The remainder, if it is to be financed, will have to come from the private sector (figure 4.6). Since the government's financing capacity can barely

FIGURE 4.6

Required investment in infrastructure is large, and private financing is necessary

Egypt

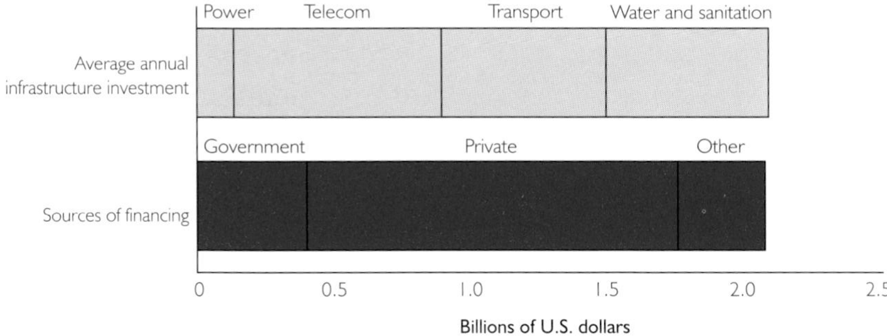

Jordan

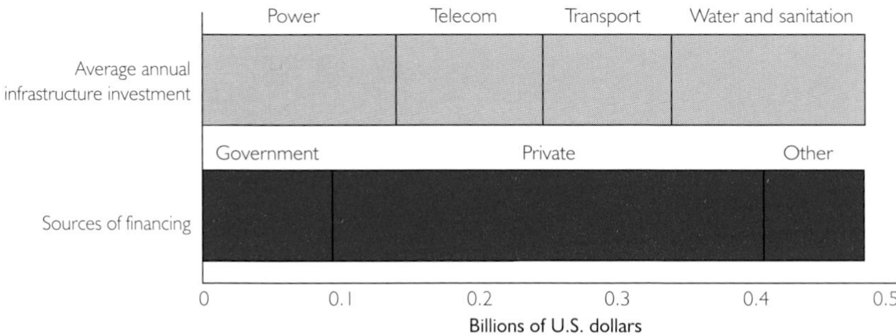

Note: The figures represent estimated average annual investment for 1995–2004.
Source: Anderson and Martinez 1995.

cover the investment requirements in water and sanitation (which the private sector is least likely to finance), virtually all new investment in power, telecommunications, and transport will require private financing.

Infrastructure needs provide an opportunity to mobilize new private investment

Improvements in quality will require greater technical efficiency and productivity. For example, system losses in electricity of 12–16% of total production will have to be eliminated. And in telecommunications the 40–48 main telephone lines maintained by each employee will have to rise to the OECD average of about 200 lines per employee.

But for private sources to make long-term investments in infrastructure and for consumers to get efficient, high-quality services, the right rules must be in place. The rules must provide clarity for the investor—by enabling reasonable rates of return. And they must provide sufficient protection for consumers—by encouraging competition and productivity gains in the delivery of services. An effective mechanism is price-cap regulation, whereby the price of infrastructure services is set under an agreed formula and producers are allowed to keep any cost savings from greater productivity.

For some countries in the MENA region, focusing on improving the business environment will have a huge payoff. But for those with large and inefficient public sectors (such as Algeria and Egypt), privatization is essential. Attempts to reform public enterprises while retaining public ownership show some initial success but no ability to sustain improved performance. So, for fiscal reasons and to signal government commitment to a private sector–based strategy, accelerated privatization will be a central element of the region's future (box 4.3). Countries with less burdensome public enterprise sectors (like Jordan, Lebanon, Morocco, Tunisia, and many Gulf countries) will be able to focus more on attracting private investment into infrastructure and other services that are crucial to long-term competitiveness.

Privatization will be essential to the region's future

Privatization of commercial firms and infrastructure services also provides an important mechanism for attracting foreign investment. The lack of viable investment opportunities available to foreign participants is one of the most tangible limitations to higher capital inflows. Equity market capitalization is minimal, and investments by foreigners are restricted in several markets (table 4.3).[2] Slow progress on privatization in the region has also meant that buying shares in former state

BOX 4.3

What it takes to privatize

Privatization programs in MENA countries are at different stages of implementation and have taken a variety of approaches. In general, privatization programs have been among the slowest of all reforms, reflecting the political difficulties of subjecting public enterprises to market forces.

International experience points to several lessons for countries that want to accelerate privatization:

- *Centralize.* Multiple agencies and reviews complicate implementation, and sectoral ministries or holding companies often have substantial vested interests in avoiding sales of their public enterprises. A single privatization agency, headed by a "champion" of privatization, has proven most effective elsewhere.
- *Simplify the process.* The most effective method is a simple, transparent auction in which price is the sole determinant of who buys the enterprise. Restrictions on potential buyers, complicated post-privatization conditions, and the use of multiple criteria for assessing competing bids have slowed the process considerably.
- *Sell privatization to the public.* Public information campaigns are needed to explain the process, show that it is fair, and persuade the public and workers of the advantages.
- *Reward managers.* Incentives should be given to boards of directors and managers to implement privatization.
- *Use consultants and investment bankers.* While responsibility for privatization should be centralized, implementation should be decentralized. Consultants or investment bankers should be paid a fee based on the sales price of the firm to ensure that they will have a strong incentive to sell enterprises quickly and at the highest price.

enterprises has not been a significant option. Although the share of infrastructure in emerging market capitalization has grown to almost $300 billion, the lack of financing opportunities for the private sector in MENA infrastructure has provided no scope for attracting foreign capital. Lack of information also has been a drawback—there was no Standard and Poor's rating for any MENA country at the end of 1994. That discourages inflows from institutional investors required to observe such ratings (see table 4.3).

Producing more skilled and flexible workers

To create competitive workers, labor markets will have to be liberalized (to ensure investments in human capital have high payoffs) and access to education will have to increase (World Bank 1995e). MENA countries will have to set a goal of nine years of basic education for all children. By 2010 minimum enrollment rates should be 100% for primary school in all

TABLE 4.3

Portfolio, bond, and equity investments remain small

	Level of capital flows		Investors' country risk perception[a]		Investment opportunities		
	Average foreign direct investment, 1990–92 (millions of US$)	Portfolio equity and bond flows, 1993 (billions of US$)	Euromoney country risk rating,[b] 1994 (0–100)	Standard & Poor's credit rating, December 1994	Eurobond issues, 1993	Market capitalization of local equity market, 1993 (millions of US$)	Planned privatizations, October 1994
Middle East and North Africa							
Algeria	8	0	96	..	0	..	1
Bahrain	–6	0	35	..	0	5,600	..
Egypt	482	0	82	..	0	2,922	23
Jordan	22	0	71	..	0	4,734	1
Morocco	303	0	59	..	0	1,876	112
Saudi Arabia	283	0	38	..	0	51,000	..
Syria	67	0	75	..	0	..	..
Tunisia	190	0	51	..	0	46	..
Eastern Europe							
Czech Republic	637	633	39	BBB+	2	10,807	..
Hungary	880	3,897	46	BB+	8	4,796	36
Poland	353	0	73	..	0	2,072	110
South Asia							
India	176	1,498	47	BB+	5	71,811	10
Pakistan	278	185	63	BB–/B	0	7,622	17
Latin America							
Argentina	2,818	5,603	49	BB–/B	37	35,419	26
Brazil	1,109	6,239	62	B	69	76,571	13
Mexico	3,929	17,397	44	BB+	43	145,154	5

.. Not available.

a. Ratings for foreign currency and long-term/short-term ratings.

b. Higher ratings indicate greater risks.

Source: World Bank 1994c; *Euromoney*, various issues; Azzam 1995; Standard & Poor's *Creditweek International*, January 2, 1995; and *International Financing Review*, January 8, 1994.

countries, 70% for lower and upper secondary education, and 25% for higher education. Given the age structures in most MENA countries, meeting these enrollment targets means increasing the number of primary enrollments by about 50%, with particularly large expansions in Jordan and Iran, where population growth rates are rapid. The numbers in secondary education would about double, with increases varying from less than 50% to 400%. The secondary school age cohort will expand by about three-quarters in Iran, more than half in Jordan, and a third in Morocco. The effects in tertiary education will be the most dramatic, with enrollments increasing by two-and-a-half to three times. Quality improvement will depend less on lowering student-teacher ratios and more on providing better educational materials, upgrading teachers, introducing early childhood development programs (such as Morocco's efforts to improve teaching in Koranic preschools), and, most important, reducing the factors impeding girls' participation, especially in rural areas.

Training programs need to be closely linked to employers

Vocational training programs, which have often been used as "warehouses" for unemployed youth, will have to be transformed to flexible systems that respond to the changing skill requirements of labor markets. In Egypt, for example, despite the higher costs relative to general secondary school, 61% of secondary students attend vocational and technical schools, often to divert the numbers seeking admission to higher education. The consequence is that the vocational training system supplies five to seven times the number of technical workers required by the economy. In Morocco a payroll tax on employers goes solely to finance publicly provided vocational training, resulting in training that is often divorced from the needs of the private market.

In most MENA countries training programs need to be closely linked to employers through joint private and public financing, management, and goal-setting, as is starting to happen in Iran, Jordan, Tunisia, and Yemen. For example, the employment and training fund in Tunisia has been effective because it provides training to workers who already have job offers and finances training within enterprises.

Increasing enrollments, demographic pressures, and the need to improve quality will put severe financing pressure on education. The total annual cost of achieving these goals for educational expansion—adjusted for population growth, higher teachers salaries, and modest quality improvements—would be about $17.5 billion (1990 dollars) in 2010 in Egypt, Iran, Jordan, Morocco, and Tunisia alone. This represents a tripling over what governments spent in 1990. The largest efforts will have to be made in Morocco, where spending will increase fourfold, and in Iran and Tunisia, where increases of almost threefold are required. The growth in expenditures in Egypt and Jordan would be less dramatic, but even in these countries expenditures would have to about double. These increases in spending can only be achieved if economies of the region are growing rapidly.

The priority use of public financing should lie in ensuring universal literacy, numeracy, and social and cultural values through high participation rates in primary, lower secondary, and eventually upper secondary education. Economic growth will bring higher incomes to enable private financing of higher levels of education, where the benefits are considerable. This is already taking place in Lebanon (where private higher education predominates), Iran (box 4.4), and Jordan (where 20% of higher education enrollments are in the private sector). The policy of assisting university students with tuition, food, housing, and other expenses consumes more than a quarter of all expenditures in higher education in Morocco and Tunisia—and must change. These subsidies benefit the well-off and are not necessary to achieve reasonable levels of university enrollment. But removing them and relying on greater private financing of higher education should be coupled with loans and scholarships for the poor.

Ensuring literacy and numeracy should be a primary objective of public financing

BOX 4.4

Iran's Islamic Azad University

Iran's Islamic Azad University, a privately financed, nonprofit institution founded in 1983, is possibly the largest private education enterprise in the world. By all measures, the institution's growth has been spectacular during the past ten years. Student enrollments are up from 2,500 to more than 300,000, degree programs from 10 to 126, and the number of campuses from 9 to 116, in 105 cities.

The university's students represent half the higher education enrollments in the country, while the remainder attend the public, tuition-free system. Remarkably, this has been achieved without state support for recurrent expenditures, most of which are covered by tuition fees. The state has helped the university's capital development by providing land and building grants during campus start-up. Private donations from local business and civic groups also have been instrumental.

This rapid expansion, coupled with the near-exclusive reliance on student tuition for recurrent spending, has nevertheless led to some qualitative deficiencies. Only 14% of faculty are full-time. Laboratories and libraries lack basic provisions. And central management tools are weak. The university's current long-term development plan, with its emphasis on educational quality enhancement, aims at redressing these deficiencies.

Source: World Bank 1992a.

Shifting away from agriculture

More sustainable resource use of scarce material resources, especially water, will require fundamental changes in the structure of many MENA economies. Nonrenewables like oil and minerals need to be replaced by alternative sources of income, possible only from higher rates of investment. More realistic pricing of water would reallocate scarce water away from low-value users in agriculture (who now consume more than 80% of total water) toward higher-value industrial or residential uses. The agricultural sectors in many countries are likely to shrink and to change in composition. Moreover, crop substitution—away from such water-intensive crops as rice and sugar cane and toward less water-demanding, more valuable crops like fruits and vegetables—is a likely trend. The social impact of such reallocation will be small in most countries since irrigated agriculture employs a small share of the labor force (except in Egypt, Oman, and Yemen).

Expand the pie to reduce poverty

Reforms could dramatically reduce abject poverty

Higher growth is a prerequisite to reducing income poverty and to providing a sustainable basis for adequate social spending and safety nets in the future. The difference between 0% and 1% average growth in the MENA region has a huge impact on poverty—no growth means 8 million more poor people in the region. Without the higher growth that reform can bring, the number of poor (living on less than $1 a day) would rise to about 15 million by 2010 (figure 4.7). And because there are many people in the MENA region who are very close to the poverty line, their vulnerability to poor economic outcomes is great. With reform, abject poverty could be dramatically reduced, although at higher incomes the definition of poverty would have to change.

The export orientation needed for growth is good for the poor because it creates lower-wage jobs that the poor can do. To ensure that growth is good for the poor, it is essential that wages are kept in check and remain flexible, especially in the early stages of reform. Morocco and Tunisia's recent success in reducing poverty stems in large part from the fact that growth created employment in the lower-wage jobs that favor the poor. Such expansion in low-wage job opportunities is the first step in lifting people out of poverty.

FIGURE 4.7

Reform will bring down poverty

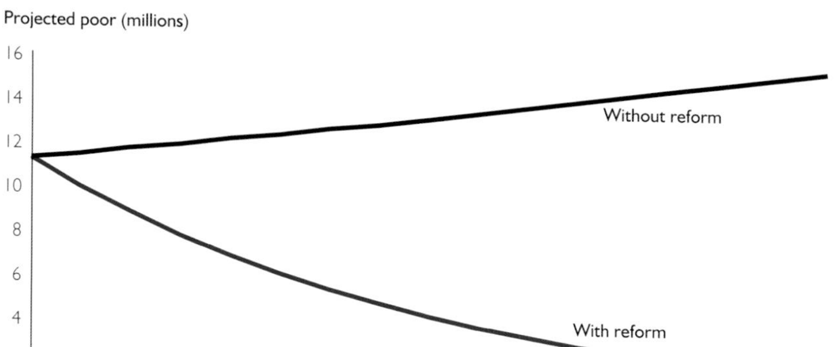

Note: Poor is defined as average spending of less than $1 a day at 1985 purchasing power parity. The growth elasticitiy of poverty used here is –4.48. Without reform, GDP per capita grows at –0.46% for MENA. With reform, GDP per capita grows at 2.5%. Includes Algeria, Egypt, Iran, Jordan, Lebanon, Morocco, Syria, Tunisia, and Yemen.
Source: van Eeghen 1995.

Antipoverty measures change at higher levels of growth because additional GDP growth has far less impact—an increase in average growth from 5% to 6% would reduce the number of poor by only 1.5 million in the next decade. So, policies need to become much more specific and targeted to address the needs of the chronic poor.

To design such targeted programs, governments will need much better information about the characteristics of the poor. Where most of the poor are rural, policies might include investments in rural infrastructure, schools, and health facilities, as well as liberalization of agricultural markets. But proper targeting of the large social transfers outlined in table 2.1 will be crucial for keeping costs under control and for maximizing the resources that get to the needy. The actual amounts needed to hypothetically eliminate poverty are quite small (table 4.4). But some leakage is inevitable and targeting itself can be costly, both politically and administratively. Tunisia's subsidy program, which includes some targeting, still costs three times what would be required to give all the poor the equivalent of the poverty-line income each year. Egypt's social assistance program provides very small payments (about 5% of the poverty line) to 2.7 million beneficiaries, but administrative costs consume 12% of total costs.

TABLE 4.4

Transfers required to eliminate poverty under perfect targeting are small

Country	Number of poor (thousands)	Transfer required (thousands of US$)	Transfer as a share of GDP
Jordan (1992)	551	7,705	0.16
Morocco (1990/91)	3,738	25,684	0.08
Tunisia (1990)	600	2,369	0.01

Source: van Eeghen 1995.

Perhaps the easiest way to expand the pie is to use resources better—and women may well represent the most important untapped economic potential in many MENA countries. With the lowest female labor force participation rates in the world, women's human capital is underused in almost all MENA economies. In Morocco and Tunisia rising female labor force participation has been important in the recent decline in poverty. Moreover, the poor social indicators in many MENA countries can be directly attributed to the neglect of female education and the inability to capture the enormous externalities from educating girls—in life expectancy, infant mortality, and nutrition. Yet the financial cost of redressing the gender gap in education in MENA countries is less than 1% of GDP, a trivial sum relative to the payoff in both incomes and social indicators. Overcoming the more binding social and cultural constraints to educating girls must be an important element of any strategy for the future.

Women may be the most important untapped potential in the region

The payoff from reform

What are the benefits to the reforms outlined above? Illustrative medium-term projections for the level and efficiency of investment and growth of per capita GDP for a sample of MENA countries are shown in table 4.5. There is a sharp contrast between the levels of per capita income growth with and without reform, as well as between the implied potential gains in health, education, and nutrition. Instead of rising unemployment and domestic tension (without reform), economies will

TABLE 4.5
Impact of reform: Investment, productivity, and growth

	Investment/GDP		Incremental capital-output ratio		Average growth of GDP per capita (medium term)	
Country	With reform	Without reform	With reform	Without reform	With reform	Without reform
Mashreq	27	17	5.9	9.0	1.8	–1.0
Egypt	25	18	6.0	9.0	2.1	0.0
Jordan	30	19	5.5	7.0	1.5	–0.5
Lebanon	30	15	5.0	10.0	4.5	0.0
Syria	30	15	6.0	9.0	0.8	–1.6
Yemen	30	15	6.0	10.0	1.4	–1.7
Maghreb	26	29	5.5	9.0	2.6	0.0
Algeria	27	33	6.0	18.0	2.1	–0.5
Morocco	25	25	5.0	7.0	3.0	1.6
Tunisia	25	23	5.0	7.0	3.3	1.6

Note: Projections are for the medium term, which refers to the period following implementation of the main reforms (assumed to require five to seven years depending on country circumstances).
Source: Diwan and Squire 1992; World Bank staff estimates.

grow fast enough to absorb their expanding labor forces while experiencing a gradual rise in real wages (with reform). With reform, all countries can realize positive growth rates in per capita incomes. Without reform, all countries experience falling per capita GDP except in countries that have already initiated reforms, like Morocco and Tunisia.

Politics in the service of economics

Identifying needed reforms is always far easier than implementing them. But with planning and fresh ideas policymakers can manage the politics of preparing for a more prosperous future (box 4.5).

The costs of reform

Economic reform costs in the short run. The costs result because a substantial share of existing capital—both human and physical—must be retrained, converted, or simply retired to allow for the accumulation of more appropriate types of capital. These costs translate into higher unemployment and lower consumption (to allow for greater investment) during the transition. Estimates of the magnitude of these short-run adjustment costs in MENA countries are about a 1–2% loss in per capita consumption and a 3% rise in the rate of unemployment relative to the no-reform scenario (Diwan and Squire 1992).

Initial conditions determine the magnitude of adjustment required

Initial conditions are an important factor in determining the magnitude of adjustment required, which varies a great deal across countries. Unusually high levels of investment (and commiserate sacrifices in consumption) of around 30% of GDP are required where population growth rates exceed 3% a year, as in Algeria, Jordan, Syria, and Yemen (see table 4.5). The problem is exacerbated where there are already high levels of unemployment. Moreover, where economies are dominated by public enterprises (such as in Algeria and Egypt), the development of a dynamic private sector will take more time than in a more advanced reformer like Tunisia. This is reflected in the greater efficiency of investment (the smaller incremental capital-output ratio) in the countries where the reform process is more advanced. In addition, these countries can afford to consume more and invest less (around 25% of GDP) and still generate sizable growth in per capita incomes.

Equipping people to cope with change is a necessary part of the transition. In general, workers with general skills and higher education are

BOX 4.5

Getting from here to there: A reformer's checklist

For now . . .	**. . . and tomorrow**
Credible and consistent trade liberalization must lead the way	
• Use international signaling mechanisms, such as the World Trade Organization and the association agreements with the EU, to lock in reforms and gain credibility. • Support non-oil exports through assistance in financing and market penetration.	• Move toward free trade or uniform tariffs not in excess of 5% by 2010.
Create a high return, nimble investment environment	
• Abolish burdensome licensing requirements, excessive customs fees, and protracted conflict resolution. • Encourage competition in the financial sector to reduce financing costs for producers and develop securities markets, payment and trading systems, and regulatory capacity.	• Reduce the costs of doing business by upgrading infrastructure services with private sector financing.
Make privatization a priority	
• Centralize the management of the program under a high-level privatization "champion." • Decentralize the implementation of privatization transactions by using consultants and managers who are paid fees based on the price at which they sell the firm. • Sell privatization to the public through information campaigns.	• Use simple, transparent rules for enterprise sales and for regulating private investment in infrastructure. • Reward managers for successfully implementing privatization.
Get on the international financial map	
• Provide clear, simple, and credible rules for foreign investors.	• Put information in the international arena by publishing economic data, issuing international paper, and obtaining internationally recognized credit ratings.
Integrate education and the economy	
• Increase student flexibility by focusing on basic skills and reducing early specialization. • Make vocational training demand-driven through joint public-private management, governance, and financing. • Liberalize labor markets to increase the productivity of educational investments.	• Raise access targets by level and increase quality through various feedback mechanisms to test the educational system's performance with national and international standards.
Use natural resources sustainably	
• Eliminate remaining subsidies to natural resources (energy and water) and environmental services (municipal water and sanitation).	• Impose environmental taxes to ensure that polluters pay.
Rely on growth and targeted interventions to reduce poverty	
• Aim for rapid growth and keep real wages in check. • Reassess regulations that discourage job creation for the poor (such as minimum wages and restrictions on firing and temporary contracts).	• Rely on self-targeted interventions where possible, such as differential qualities of goods or public works programs. • Provide cash transfers for the chronic poor, but monitor closely to ensure maximum benefits to the truly needy.

likely to find the adjustment easier. But for workers with narrow, specialized skills, retraining by the private sector holds the greatest promise—as does providing information on new jobs and assisting with job searches.

Reforms also cost in terms of requiring the allocation of additional resources to certain activities, often at the expense of others. But often the amounts involved are fairly small in relative terms. For example, providing everyone with a package of basic health care interventions that will reduce infant mortality and increase life expectancy by the end of the decade would cost about $30 per person per year—less than half of 1% of the region's GDP. The cost of paying every poor person enough to bring them to the poverty line is less than a fraction of 1% of GDP in countries like Jordan, Morocco, and Tunisia (see table 4.4). And while the increases in educational spending required to raise enrollments appear high (200% by 2010), they are small relative to the potential growth in GDP and the scope for greater private financing (especially of higher education).

Sharing costs with the private sector and donors can ease the burden

The difficulties often arise from the politics of reallocation (especially when sensitive budgets such as the military are involved) and achieving efficiency gains. Reducing transfers to politically important groups is often only feasible if it is done gradually. That is why growth makes higher spending on the key sectors for the future more politically viable. For example, with no growth, maintaining per student expenditures on education in Jordan would require a doubling of the education budget's share of total spending over the decade—an unlikely event. But with growth, higher social expenditures can easily be accommodated with existing budget shares. Achieving efficiency gains through mechanisms such as public enterprise or civil service reform or better targeting of benefits is also politically problematic, but economically profitable. Sharing costs with the private sector and donors (as described below) can ease the burden on public finances.

Use the private sector as partners

The public sector does not have to do everything. The financial and creative capacity of the private sector can be harnessed by good public policy to serve social objectives. Doubts linger, however, over whether the private sector can "carry the ball." In many MENA countries the private sector thrived during the era of rents and grew accustomed to protection, subsidies, and little competition.

Can such a private sector be the engine of future development? Yes. MENA's private sector is the product of government policies, and there is no reason to think that energies devoted to rent-seeking in the past cannot be channeled to productivity gains in the future, if the incentive regime changes. Jobs for 47 million new entrants into the work force will have to be created by 2010. The investment required to create that many jobs (based on current capital-labor ratios) is large—$31 billion in Iran, $30 billion in Morocco, $25 billion in Algeria, $14 billion in Egypt, and $12 billion in Tunisia.[3] Achieving such high rates of investment and job creation will require governments to bring the private sector in as serious partners.

Governments must be open to private initiatives

In addition to expanding production, services, and infrastructure, private initiatives can often solve other types of problems—if the public sector gives the space to find solutions. In many MENA countries private education and health care have grown rapidly as the quality of public services has deteriorated. In countries like Lebanon the private sector has a long tradition of providing education, and business associations are increasingly involved in training, setting industry standards, and promoting self-regulation. Nongovernmental organizations have been active in providing social services and promoting community development in Egypt and in the West Bank and Gaza. Governments often are suspicious of such private initiatives, and often curtail the activities of legitimate groups. But, regulations requiring transparency and public accountability (such as publication of regular financial statements) as well as adherence to standards (such as educational curriculum or health regulations) are a more effective way of harnessing these private energies for the social good and developing a vibrant civil society.

Compensate the losers

In cases where adjustment is difficult, compensating the losers from reform with cash transfers is often the most cost-effective approach. Transfer payments are used in more than 50 countries to compensate those hurt by downsizing the public sector. Countries in Eastern Europe devote as much as 1% of GDP to such compensation. There is now considerable experience on how to design voluntary compensation schemes that provide redundant workers with a choice among early retirement, cash, annual payments, retraining programs, subsidies to new employers, and transfers within the public sector. Estimates of the costs of severance payments for redundant workers in the state-owned enterprises in Egypt amount to just $1 billion to cover three years of pay, or less than 3% of GDP. If surplus labor in the public sector as a whole is given severance payments, the cost rises to about 7% of GDP (Diwan 1994).

Get financing from supporters

There is no shortage of potential financing for the MENA region. There is, however, a shortage of good policies and projects to make that financing real. The approximately $350 billion in assets held abroad is just one potential source of financing for the massive investments in new industries, infrastructure, and commercial and social services outlined in this report. The $158 billion of private capital flows to developing countries in 1993 is another potential source of financing. Donor funds are still considerable and institutions like the World Bank could double their lending to the region under the right circumstances. The European Union's Mediterranean Initiative (amounting to about $12 billion during 1995–99) could increase official resource flows to the region by more than half.

There is no shortage of potential financing

The key is that international support will reinforce rather than replace the reform process. Private financing will not materialize unless the conditions are right—and that means serious progress on structural reforms that create a competitive business environment. Public external financing has traditionally been motivated by political objectives, but that is changing. Donors, however, are willing to finance the political costs of reform—such as severance payments or targeted transfers—which can ease the short-run difficulties for reform-minded governments. Moreover, debt relief can be provided where countries are constrained by liquidity problems.

Have a long-term strategy

Taking on numerous reforms and interest groups simultaneously may be economically optimal, but politically suicidal. So, having a long-term strategy—and sequencing and setting priorities in the interim—is key. In most cases major changes get their first impetus from some external pressure. Trade liberalization plays precisely that role in any effort to improve a country's competitiveness. Once the pressures of international competition are felt at home, the reforms needed to adjust to that pressure follow—deregulation, privatization, educational reform, financial market development, and the creation of jobs that are good for the poor. Meanwhile, the institutional capacity to regulate judiciously and achieve social objectives needs to be built up in parallel.

Often, problems can be anticipated and adjustments phased. The pressure on wages in MENA textile firms from low-cost competitors in Asia will be felt gradually as the Multi-Fibre Arrangement is phased out over the next few years. But the pain of adjusting to that greater competition (by moving to higher-value products) can be gradual if the adjustment begins now. Similarly, the rising scarcity of water in many MENA countries should trigger preparations for fundamental changes in the agricultural sectors of most countries.

Having a long-term strategy and properly sequencing and setting priorities in the interim are key

Many of the reforms described in this report will challenge the short-term interests of important groups in many MENA countries—workers employed in protected industries, those growing water-intensive crops, polluters, and civil servants who are paid to deal with cumbersome regulations. But there are more gainers from these reforms than losers over the long run—the difference is that the losers are organized and the gainers are not. The beneficiaries from the policies described here include the unemployed, the vast number of new entrants into the labor force, the poor, and those working in the informal sector. Giving these groups a greater voice in public policy must be a central part of claiming a prosperous future for the Middle East and North Africa.

Notes

1. Some of Syria's textile exports gains may reflect one-off barter settlements of debts with the former Soviet Union.

2. Equity markets in the Gulf countries, for example, are restricted to GCC nationals. But this is starting to change. In Bahrain, Kuwait, and Oman foreigners have been allowed to buy shares, usually through investment funds. See Azzam (1995) for details.

3. More labor-intensive technologies would result in lower investment requirements.

Bibliography

Further details and supporting analysis for the findings in this report can be found in the following background papers, prepared as part of this study and available from the World Bank's Middle East and North Africa Regional Office.

Anderson, Robert E., and Albert Martinez. 1995. "Private Sector Development in the Middle East and North Africa."

Golladay, Fred, Sue Berryman, and Jon Avins. 1995. "A Human Capital Strategy for Competing in World Markets."

Hoekman, Bernard. 1995. "Implications of the World Trade Organization for MENA Countries."

Larsen, Bjorn. 1995. "Environmental and Natural Resource Management in the Middle East and North Africa Region: Some Selected Issues."

Page, John. 1995. "From Boom to Bust—and Back? The Crisis of Economic Growth in the Middle East, 1960–1993."

Riordan, E. Mick, Uri Dadush, Jalaleddin Jalali, Shane Streifel, Milan Brahmbhatt, and Kazue Takagaki. 1995. "The World Economy and Implications for the Middle East and North Africa Region, 1995–2010."

van Eeghen, Willem. 1995. "Poverty in MENA."

Waterbury, John. 1995. "The State and Economic Transitions in the MENA Region."

In addition to the background papers, the following provided useful input:

Abdel Jaber, Tayseer. 1995. "Key Long-Term Development Issues in Jordan." Paper presented at the Economic Research Forum and World Bank workshop on strategic visions for the Middle East and North Africa, Tunis, June.

Abdullah, Samir. 1995. "The Middle East Peace Dilemma: Multilateral Conflict Resolution through Bilateral Negotiations." Paper presented at the Economic Research Forum and World Bank workshop on strategic visions for the Middle East and North Africa, Tunis, June.

Abed, George. 1995. "Economic Prospects for Palestine." Paper presented at the Economic Research Forum and World Bank workshop on strategic visions for the Middle East and North Africa, Tunis, June.

Askari, Hossein. 1990. *Saudi Arabia's Economy: Oil and the Search for Economic Development.* Greenwich, Conn.: JAI Press.

Axt, Heinz-Jurgen. 1992. "Liberalization and Cohesion: Southern Europe's Development and Prospects within the European Community." *International Journal of Political Economy* 22 (1).

Azzam, Henry. 1995. "Gulf Capital Markets: Development Prospects and Constraints." In *Development of Financial Markets in the Arab Countries, Iran, and Turkey*. Cairo: Economic Research Forum for the Arab Countries, Iran, and Turkey and AUC Press.

Boughazala, Mongi. 1995. "Key Long-Term Development Issues in Tunisia." Paper presented at the Economic Research Forum and World Bank workshop on strategic visions for the Middle East and North Africa, Tunis, June.

Chen, Shaohua, Guarav Datt, and Martin Ravallion. 1993. "Is Poverty Increasing in the Developing World?" Policy Research Working Paper 1146. World Bank, Washington, D.C.

Corm, George. 1995. "Reconstruction and Development Issues in Lebanon." Paper presented at the Economic Research Forum and World Bank workshop on strategic visions for the Middle East and North Africa, Tunis, June.

Diwan, Ishac. 1994. "Public Sector Retrenchment and Severance Pay: Nine Propositions." Middle East and North Africa Region. World Bank, Washington, D.C.

Diwan, Ishac, and Lyn Squire. 1992. "Economic and Social Development in the Middle East and North Africa." Middle East and North Africa Discussion Paper 3. World Bank, Washington, D.C.

Diwan, Ishac, Chang-Po Yang, and Zhi Wang. 1995. "The Arab Economy, the Uruguay Round Predicament, and the European Union Wildcard." Paper presented at the Economic Research Forum and World Bank workshop on strategic visions for the Middle East and North Africa, Tunis, June.

Economic Research Forum. 1995. *Development of Financial Markets in the Arab Countries, Iran, and Turkey.* Cairo: Economic Research Forum for the Arab Countries, Iran, and Turkey and AUC Press.

Educational Testing Service. 1992. *International Assessment of Educational Progress.* Princeton, New Jersey.

El-Badawi, Ibrahim. 1995. "The Challenges of Peace and Development in the Sudan: Towards a Strategic Vision in a Changing World Environment." Paper presented at the Economic Research Forum and World Bank workshop on strategic visions for the Middle East and North Africa, Tunis, June.

El-Erian, Mohamed A., and Manmohan Kumar. 1995. "Equity Markets in Middle Eastern Countries." *IMF Staff Papers* 42 (2). Washington, D.C.

Ettori, François. 1995. "Competitiveness Clusters in Morocco." Middle East and North Africa Country Department 1. World Bank, Washington, D.C.

Fergany, Nader. 1995. "Egypt 2012: Education and Employment." Paper presented at the Economic Research Forum and World Bank workshop on strategic visions for the Middle East and North Africa, Tunis, June.

Filmer, Deon. 1995. "Estimating the World at Work." Background paper for *World Development Report 1995*. World Bank, Washington, D.C.

Hamdouch, Bachir. 1995. "Strategic Issues for Morocco." Paper presented at the Economic Research Forum and World Bank workshop on strategic visions for the Middle East and North Africa, Tunis, June.

Handoussa, Heba, and Hanna Khiereldin. 1995. "Egypt in the Year 2012: A Strategy for Development." Paper presented at the Economic Research Forum and World Bank workshop on strategic visions for the Middle East and North Africa, Tunis, June.

Ibrahim, Saad Eddin. 1994. "Governance and Structural Adjustment: The Egyptian Case." Paper presented at a conference on governance and structural adjustment, World Bank, Washington, D.C., November.

ILO (International Labour Organization). 1986. *Economically Active Population: 1965–2025*. Geneva: International Labour Office.

IMF (International Monetary Fund). 1994a. *Balance of Payments Yearbook*. Washington, D.C.

———. 1994b. *Government Finance Statistics Yearbook*. Washington, D.C.

———. 1994c. *International Financial Statistics*. Washington, D.C.

International Institute for Strategic Studies. 1993. *The Military Balance, 1993–94.* Washington, D.C.

Kanaan, Taher. 1995. "The State and the Private Sector in Jordan." Paper presented at the Economic Research Forum and World Bank workshop on strategic visions for the Middle East and North Africa, Tunis, June.

Karshenas, Massoud. 1995. "Economic Reform and Reconstruction of the Iranian Economy." Paper presented at the Economic Research Forum and World Bank workshop on strategic visions for the Middle East and North Africa, Tunis, June.

Mohtadi, Hamid. 1995. "Environment and Sustainable Development: Problems, Policies and Institutions." Paper presented at the Economic Research Forum and World Bank workshop on strategic visions for the Middle East and North Africa, Tunis, June.

Nadvi, Khalid, and Hubert Schmitz. 1994. "Industrial Clusters in Less Developed Countries: Review of Experience and Research Agenda." Institute of Development Studies Discussion Paper 33a. University of Sussex, United Kingdom.

Nehru, Vikram, and Ashok Dhareshwar. 1993. "A New Database on Physical Capital Stock: Sources, Methodology, and Results." *Revista de Análisis Económics* 8 (1).

Nehru, Vikram, Eric Swanson, and Ashutosh Dubey. 1993. "A New Database on Human Capital Stock." Policy Research Working Paper 1124. World Bank, Washington, D.C.

Pyke, Frank, Giacomo Becattini, and Werner Sengenberger, eds. 1990. *Industrial Districts and Inter-Firm Cooperation in Italy.* Geneva: International Labour Organization.

Rutherford, Thomas, E.E. Rustrom, and David Tarr. 1993. "Morocco's Free Trade Agreement with the European Community: A Quantitative Assessment." Policy Research Working Paper 1173. World Bank, Washington, D.C.

———. 1995. "The Free Trade Agreement Between Tunisia and the European Union." Policy Research Department. World Bank, Washington, D.C.

Saba, Joe. 1995. "Foreign Direct Investment in the Middle East: A Comparative Assessment of Investment Regimes." Private Sector Development Department. World Bank, Washington, D.C.

Saghir, Jamal. 1993. "Privatization in Tunisia." Cofinancing and Advisory Services Discussion Paper. World Bank, Washington, D.C.

Sayan, Serdar, and Suleyman Durgun. 1995. "Incorporating Energy-Related Environmental Concerns into a Sustainable Development Strategy for Turkey." Paper presented at the Economic Research Forum and World Bank workshop on strategic visions for the Middle East and North Africa, Tunis, June.

Shafik, Nemat. 1994. "Big Spending, Low Returns: The Paradox of Human Resource Development in the Middle East and North Africa." Middle East and North Africa Region. World Bank, Washington, D.C.

Sukkar, Nabil. 1995. "Strategic Economic Issues in Syria." Paper presented at the Economic Research Forum and World Bank workshop on strategic visions for the Middle East and North Africa, Tunis, June.

Togan, Subidey. 1995. "Determinants of Economic Development in Turkey." Paper presented at the Economic Research Forum and World Bank workshop on strategic visions for the Middle East and North Africa, Tunis, June.

Umari, Nawfal. 1993. "The Public Sector in the Middle East and North Africa." Paper presented at the initiative to encourage economic research in the Middle East, Cairo, June.

World Bank. 1991. *World Development Report 1991: The Challenge of Development*. New York: Oxford University Press.

———. 1992a. "Higher Education Policy Paper." Washington, D.C.

———. 1992b. *World Debt Tables, 1992–93*. Washington, D.C.

———. 1993. *The East Asian Miracle: Economic Growth and Public Policy*. A World Bank Policy Research Report. New York: Oxford University Press.

———. 1994a. "A Population Perspective on Development: The Middle East and North Africa." Middle East and North Africa Region. Washington, D.C.

———. 1994b. "Private Sector Development in Egypt—The Status and the Challenges." Middle East and North Africa Country Department 2. Washington, D.C.

———. 1994c. *World Debt Tables, 1994–95*. Washington, D.C.

———. 1994d. *World Development Report 1994: Infrastructure for Development*. New York: Oxford University Press.

———. 1995a. *Bureaucrats in Business: The Economics and Politics of Government Ownership*. A World Bank Policy Research Report. New York: Oxford University Press.

———. 1995b. *Global Economic Prospects and the Developing Countries*. Washington, D.C.

———. 1995c. *Middle East and North Africa Environment Strategy: Toward Sustainable Development.* Washington, D.C.

———. 1995d. *Social Impact of Adjustment Operations*. Washington, D.C.

———. 1995e. *Will Arab Workers Prosper or Be Left Out in the Twenty-First Century?* Regional Perspectives on *World Development Report 1995.* Washington, D.C.

———. 1995f. *From Scarcity to Security: Averting a Water Crisis in the Middle East and North Africa.* Washington, D.C.

Yeats, Alexander. 1995. "Export Prospects of Middle Eastern Countries: A Post–Uruguay Round Analysis." International Economics Department, International Trade Division. World Bank, Washington, D.C.

Statistical Appendix

Algeria

POVERTY and SOCIAL	Algeria	M. East & North Africa	Lower-middle-income
Population mid-1994 *(millions)*	27.3	268	1,112
GNP per capita 1994 *(US$)*	1,690	..	1,510
Average annual growth, 1990-94			
Population *(%)*	2.3	2.6	1.5
Labor force *(%)*	3.7	3.1	1.7
Most recent estimate *(latest year available since 1988)*			
Poverty: headcount index *(% of population, 1990) /1*	1	..	..
Urban population *(% of total population)*	55	55	55
Life expectancy at birth *(years)*	67	66	67
Infant mortality *(per 1,000 live births)*	53	52	39
Child malnutrition *(% of children under 5)*	9	..	..
Access to safe water *(% of population)*	..	84	78
Illiteracy *(% of population age 15+)*	43	45	19
Gross primary enrollment *(% of school-age population)*	99	97	104
Male	105	103	103
Female	92	90	96

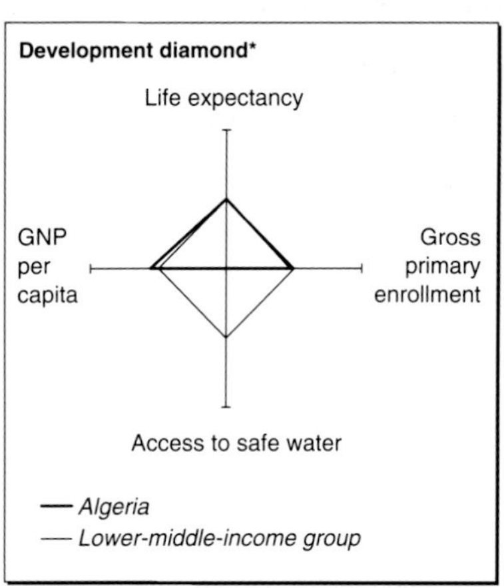

KEY ECONOMIC RATIOS and LONG-TERM TRENDS

	1975	1985	1993	1994
Gross domestic investment/GDP	45.2	33.2	29.2	32.7
Exports of goods and non-factor services/GDP	33.6	23.5	21.9	22.7
Gross domestic savings/GDP	36.0	36.4	27.8	27.3
Gross national savings/GDP	36.4	36.0	26.6	26.4
Current account balance/GDP	-10.7	1.2	1.6	-4.3
Interest payments/GDP	1.4	2.4	3.4	3.4
Total debt/GDP	29.7	31.5	51.8	64.4
Total debt service/exports	9.0	36.2	82.0	84.8
Present value of debt/GDP	..	..	49.3	..
Present value of debt/exports	..	..	219.8	..

	1975-84	1985-94	1993	1994	1995-04
(average annual growth)					
GDP	5.4	0.2	-2.4	-0.2	3.7
GNP per capita	2.0	-2.4	-3.7	-2.9	1.5
Exports of goods and nfs	2.0	2.2	-1.9	-4.0	4.4

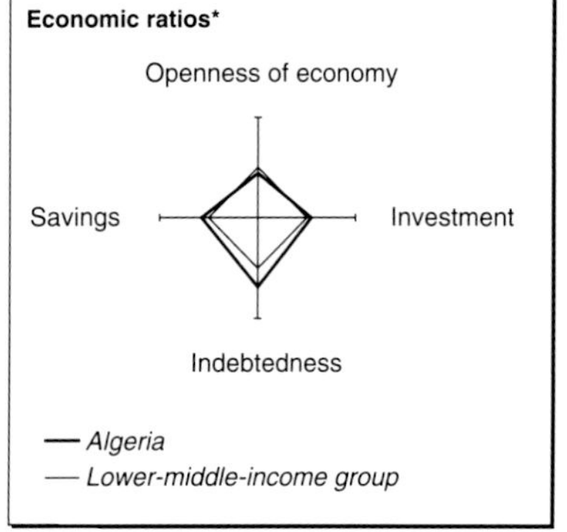

STRUCTURE of the ECONOMY

	1975	1985	1993	1994
(% of GDP)				
Agriculture	12.1	10.0	13.5	12.0
Industry	46.0	50.7	43.3	44.2
Manufacturing	8.6	12.2	11.4	10.9
Services	41.9	39.3	43.2	43.8
Private consumption	51.1	47.9	54.8	56.2
General government consumption	12.9	15.7	17.4	16.5
Gross domestic investment	45.2	33.2	29.2	32.7
Exports of goods and non-factor services	33.6	23.5	21.9	22.7
Imports of goods and non-factor services	42.9	20.4	23.2	28.1

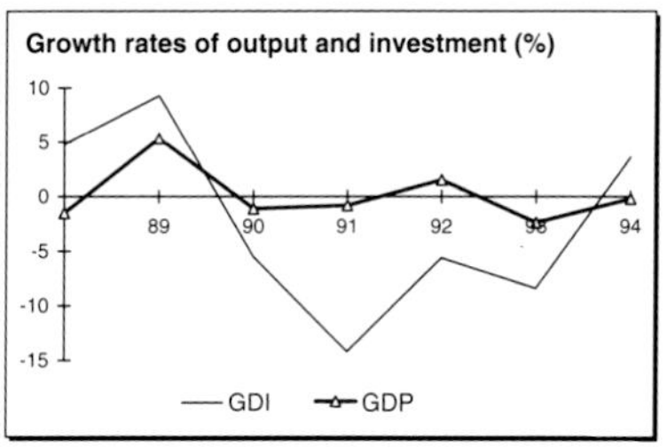

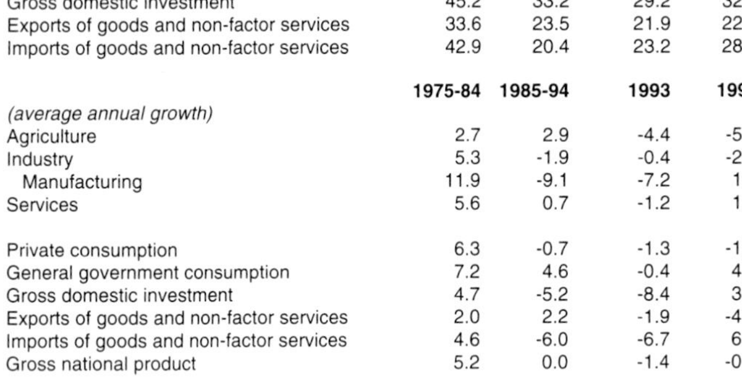

	1975-84	1985-94	1993	1994
(average annual growth)				
Agriculture	2.7	2.9	-4.4	-5.0
Industry	5.3	-1.9	-0.4	-2.4
Manufacturing	11.9	-9.1	-7.2	1.7
Services	5.6	0.7	-1.2	1.8
Private consumption	6.3	-0.7	-1.3	-1.5
General government consumption	7.2	4.6	-0.4	4.0
Gross domestic investment	4.7	-5.2	-8.4	3.7
Exports of goods and non-factor services	2.0	2.2	-1.9	-4.0
Imports of goods and non-factor services	4.6	-6.0	-6.7	6.2
Gross national product	5.2	0.0	-1.4	-0.7

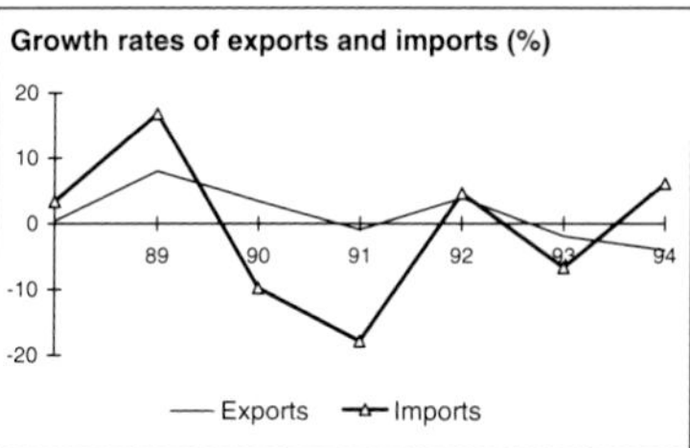

Note: 1994 data are preliminary estimates. /1 Poverty is defined as spending less than one dollar per person per day (1985$ PPP).

* The diamonds show four key indicators in the country (in bold) compared with its income-group average. If data are missing, the diamond will be incomplete.

PRICES and GOVERNMENT FINANCE

	1975	1985	1993	1994
Domestic prices				
(% change)				
Consumer prices *(1995 to March:* 8.0*)*	9.0	10.5	20.5	29.0
Implicit GDP deflator	5.4	4.4	13.9	27.9
Government finance				
(% of GDP)				
Current revenue	..	37.9	27.6	27.7
Current budget balance	..	19.3	2.7	4.5
Overall surplus/deficit	..	-8.3	-8.7	-4.4

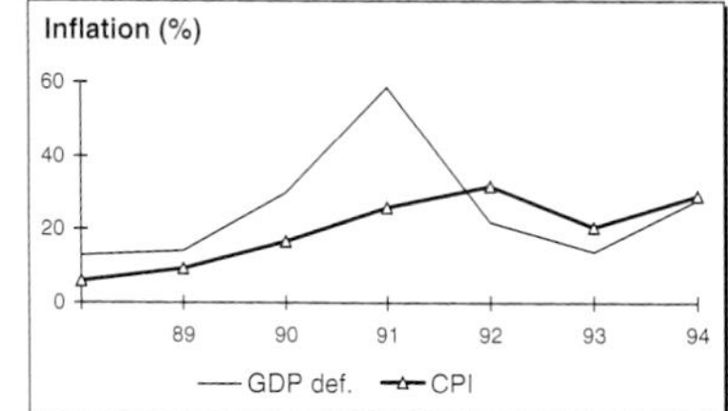

TRADE

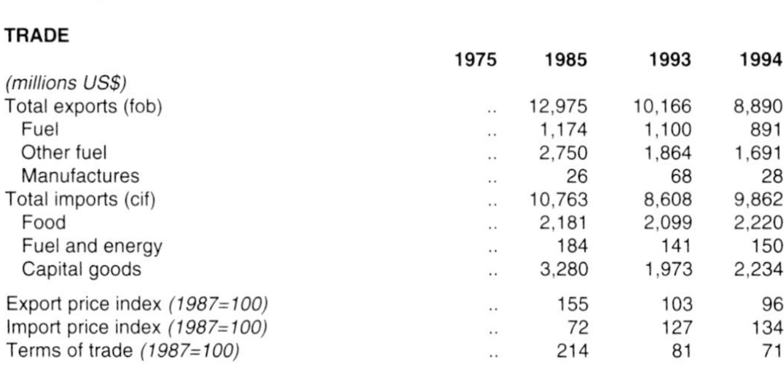

	1975	1985	1993	1994
(millions US$)				
Total exports (fob)	..	12,975	10,166	8,890
Fuel	..	1,174	1,100	891
Other fuel	..	2,750	1,864	1,691
Manufactures	..	26	68	28
Total imports (cif)	..	10,763	8,608	9,862
Food	..	2,181	2,099	2,220
Fuel and energy	..	184	141	150
Capital goods	..	3,280	1,973	2,234
Export price index *(1987=100)*	..	155	103	96
Import price index *(1987=100)*	..	72	127	134
Terms of trade *(1987=100)*	..	214	81	71

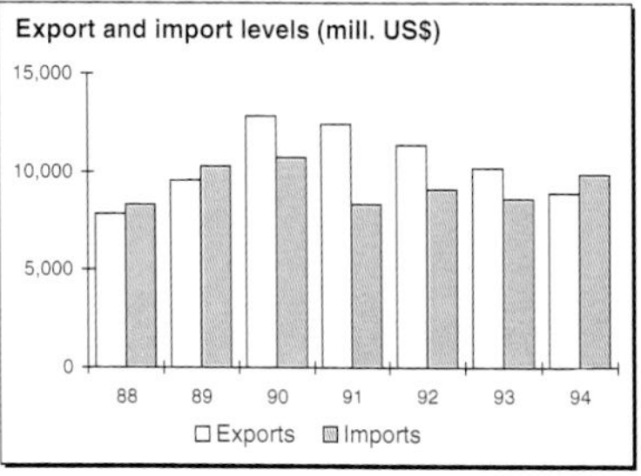

BALANCE of PAYMENTS

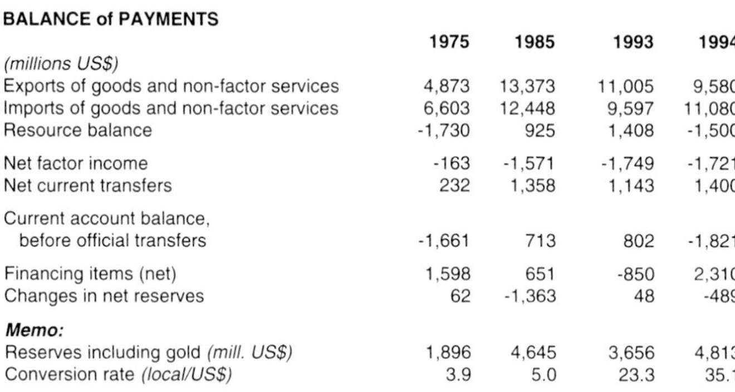

	1975	1985	1993	1994
(millions US$)				
Exports of goods and non-factor services	4,873	13,373	11,005	9,580
Imports of goods and non-factor services	6,603	12,448	9,597	11,080
Resource balance	-1,730	925	1,408	-1,500
Net factor income	-163	-1,571	-1,749	-1,721
Net current transfers	232	1,358	1,143	1,400
Current account balance, before official transfers	-1,661	713	802	-1,821
Financing items (net)	1,598	651	-850	2,310
Changes in net reserves	62	-1,363	48	-489
Memo:				
Reserves including gold *(mill. US$)*	1,896	4,645	3,656	4,813
Conversion rate *(local/US$)*	3.9	5.0	23.3	35.1

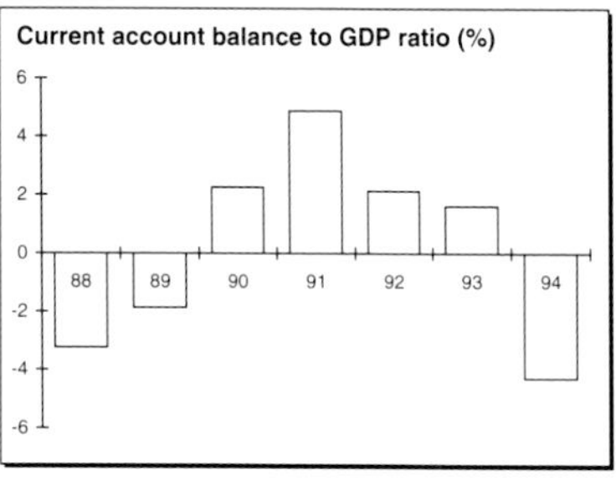

EXTERNAL DEBT and RESOURCE FLOWS

	1975	1985	1993	1994
(millions US$)				
Total debt outstanding and disbursed	4,633	18,260	25,757	27,225
IBRD	36	480	1,512	1,709
IDA	0	0	0	0
Total debt service	469	5,002	9,146	8,228
IBRD	6	72	282	327
IDA	0	0	0	0
Composition of net resource flows				
Official grants	30	41	82	80
Official creditors	115	-112	102	1,229
Private creditors	1,193	540	-581	-1,153
Foreign direct investment	119	0	15	18
Portfolio equity	0	0	0	66
World Bank program				
Commitments	48	0	240	191
Disbursements	33	148	176	300
Principal repayments	3	42	170	208
Net flows	30	106	6	92
Interest payments	3	30	113	119
Net transfers	27	76	-106	-27

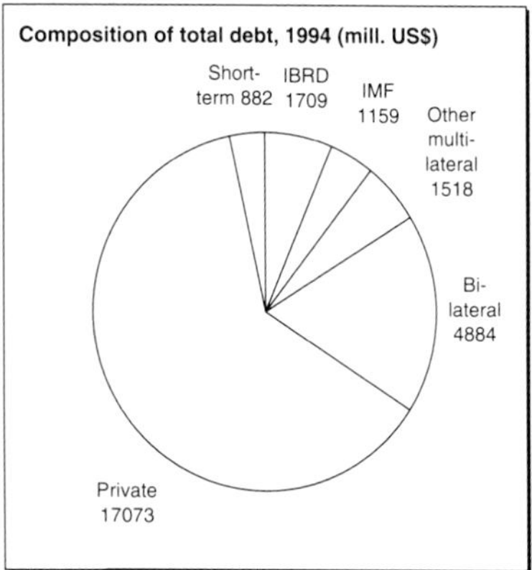

International Economics Department

Debt data are from *World Debt Tables 1994-95*.

Arab Republic of Egypt

POVERTY and SOCIAL	Egypt	M. East & North Africa	Low-income
Population mid-1994 *(millions)*	57.6	268	3,092
GNP per capita 1994 *(US$)*	710	..	390
Average annual growth, 1990-94			
Population *(%)*	2.0	2.6	1.9
Labor force *(%)*	2.7	3.1	1.8
Most recent estimate *(latest year available since 1988)*			
Poverty: headcount index *(% of population)*	..	..	19
Urban population *(% of total population)*	45	55	28
Life expectancy at birth *(years)*	64	66	62
Infant mortality *(per 1,000 live births)*	64	52	63
Child malnutrition *(% of children under 5)*	9	..	40
Access to safe water *(% of population)*	86	84	67
Illiteracy *(% of population age 15+)*	52	45	41
Gross primary enrollment *(% of school-age population)*	101	97	108
Male	110	103	116
Female	93	90	101

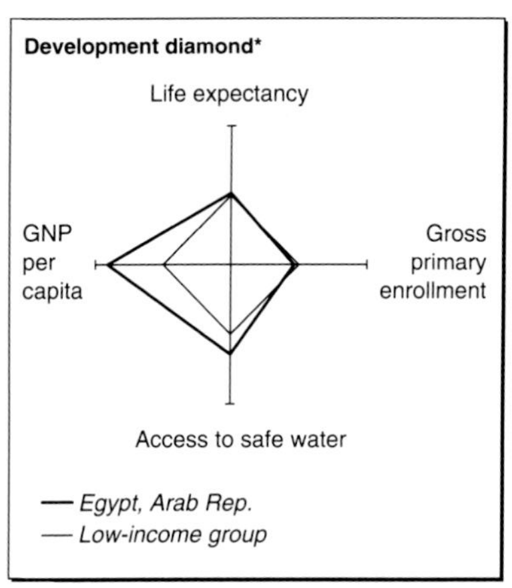

KEY ECONOMIC RATIOS and LONG-TERM TRENDS

	1975	1985	1993	1994
Gross domestic investment/GDP	33.4	26.7	17.0	17.5
Exports of goods and non-factor services/GDP	20.2	19.9	25.3	21.7
Gross domestic savings/GDP	12.3	14.5	5.4	5.9
Gross national savings/GDP	13.6	12.5	17.6	16.3
Current account balance/GDP	-21.2	-9.3	0.5	-1.2
Interest payments/GDP	0.9	2.9	2.9	3.2
Total debt/GDP	47.9	121.5	103.2	102.3
Total debt service/exports	12.4	28.4	14.9	16.2
Present value of debt/GDP	..	..	70.2	..
Present value of debt/exports	..	..	170.8	..

(average annual growth)	1975-84	1985-94	1993	1994	1995-04
GDP	8.8	2.2	0.5	2.0	2.4
GNP per capita	5.9	1.6	-1.3	0.5	0.4
Exports of goods and nfs	3.9	6.7	-11.4	-7.6	3.7

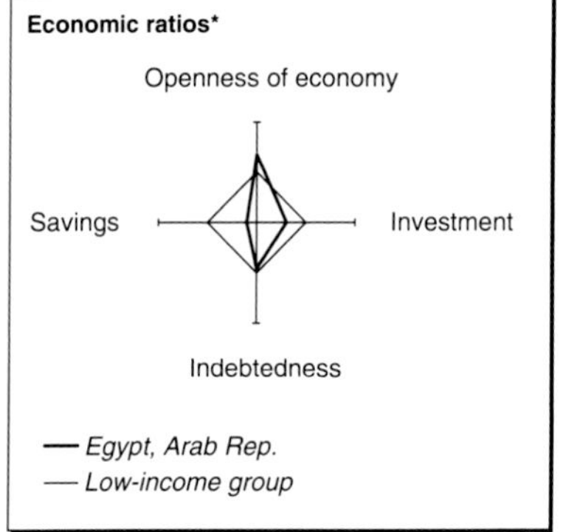

STRUCTURE of the ECONOMY *(% of GDP)*	1975	1985	1993	1994
Agriculture	29.0	20.0	17.9	19.8
Industry	26.9	28.6	22.4	21.1
Manufacturing	17.4	13.5	15.7	14.7
Services	44.1	51.5	59.7	59.1
Private consumption	62.9	68.2	81.1	80.5
General government consumption	24.9	17.2	13.5	13.5
Gross domestic investment	33.4	26.7	17.0	17.5
Exports of goods and non-factor services	20.2	19.9	25.3	21.7
Imports of goods and non-factor services	41.3	32.0	36.9	33.3

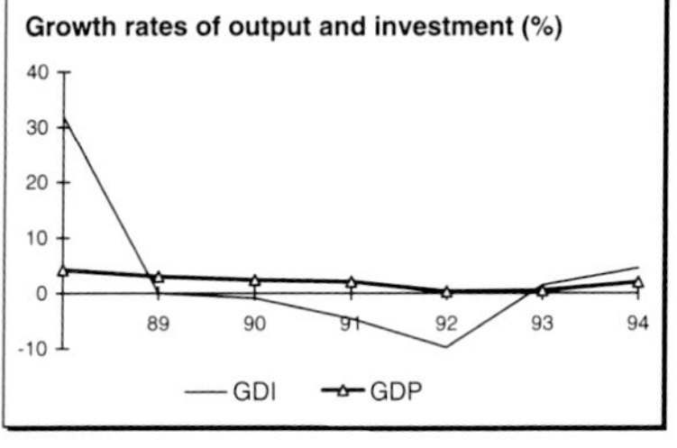

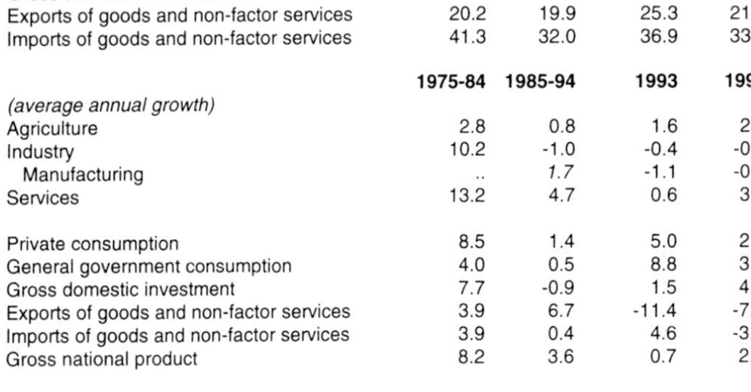

(average annual growth)	1975-84	1985-94	1993	1994
Agriculture	2.8	0.8	1.6	2.9
Industry	10.2	-1.0	-0.4	-0.3
Manufacturing	..	*1.7*	-1.1	-0.6
Services	13.2	4.7	0.6	3.1
Private consumption	8.5	1.4	5.0	2.0
General government consumption	4.0	0.5	8.8	3.3
Gross domestic investment	7.7	-0.9	1.5	4.5
Exports of goods and non-factor services	3.9	6.7	-11.4	-7.6
Imports of goods and non-factor services	3.9	0.4	4.6	-3.2
Gross national product	8.2	3.6	0.7	2.5

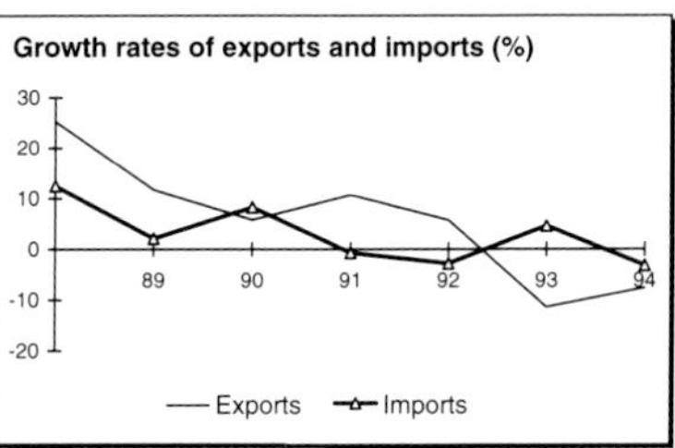

Note: 1994 data are preliminary estimates. Figures in italics are for years other than those specified.

* The diamonds show four key indicators in the country (in bold) compared with its income-group average. If data are missing, the diamond will be incomplete.

PRICES and GOVERNMENT FINANCE

	1975	1985	1993	1994
Domestic prices				
(% change)				
Consumer prices *(1995 to April:* 0.4*)*	9.7	12.1	12.1	8.2
Implicit GDP deflator	9.2	9.0	10.4	8.2
Government finance				
(% of GDP)				
Current revenue	..	22.2	33.2	33.8
Current budget balance	..	-13.7	2.0	2.6
Overall surplus/deficit	..	-21.6	-4.1	-2.5

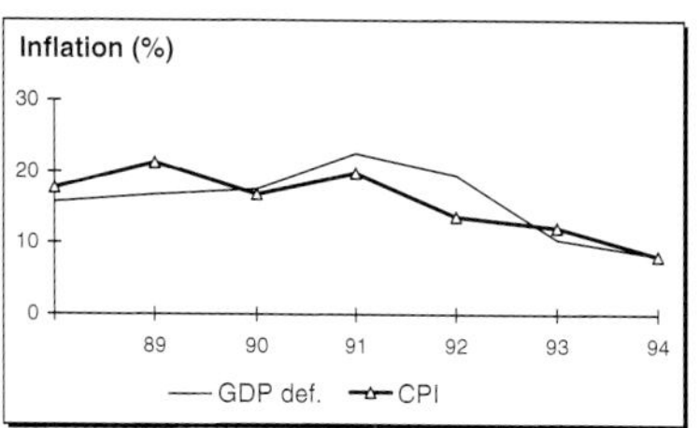

TRADE

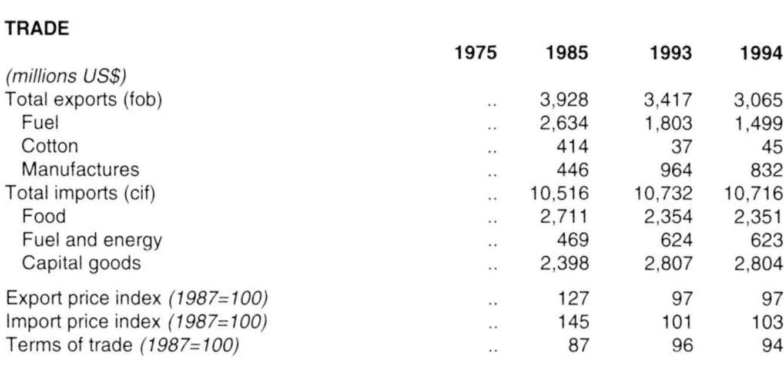

	1975	1985	1993	1994
(millions US$)				
Total exports (fob)	..	3,928	3,417	3,065
Fuel	..	2,634	1,803	1,499
Cotton	..	414	37	45
Manufactures	..	446	964	832
Total imports (cif)	..	10,516	10,732	10,716
Food	..	2,711	2,354	2,351
Fuel and energy	..	469	624	623
Capital goods	..	2,398	2,807	2,804
Export price index *(1987=100)*	..	127	97	97
Import price index *(1987=100)*	..	145	101	103
Terms of trade *(1987=100)*	..	87	96	94

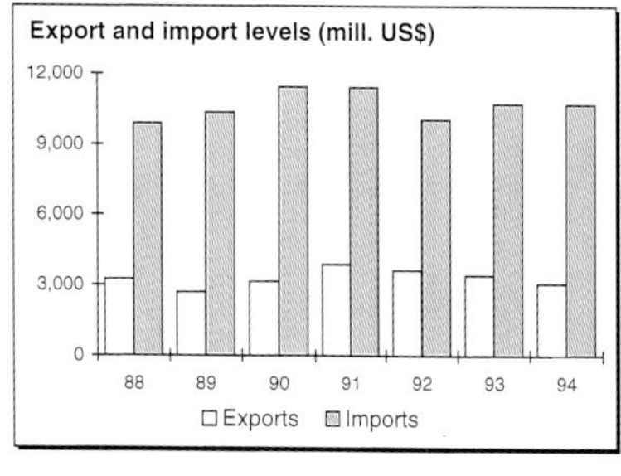

BALANCE of PAYMENTS

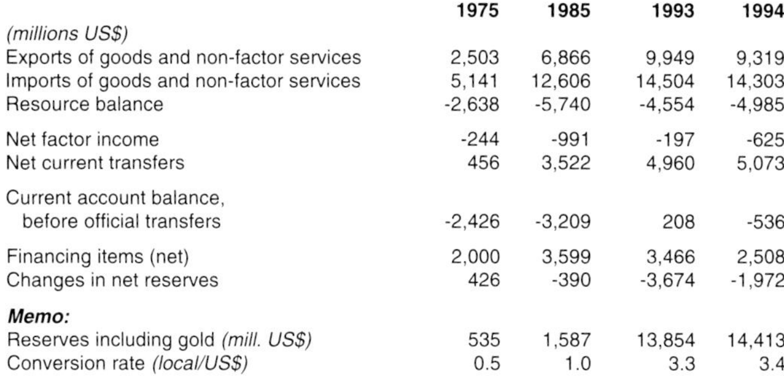

	1975	1985	1993	1994
(millions US$)				
Exports of goods and non-factor services	2,503	6,866	9,949	9,319
Imports of goods and non-factor services	5,141	12,606	14,504	14,303
Resource balance	-2,638	-5,740	-4,554	-4,985
Net factor income	-244	-991	-197	-625
Net current transfers	456	3,522	4,960	5,073
Current account balance, before official transfers	-2,426	-3,209	208	-536
Financing items (net)	2,000	3,599	3,466	2,508
Changes in net reserves	426	-390	-3,674	-1,972
Memo:				
Reserves including gold *(mill. US$)*	535	1,587	13,854	14,413
Conversion rate *(local/US$)*	0.5	1.0	3.3	3.4

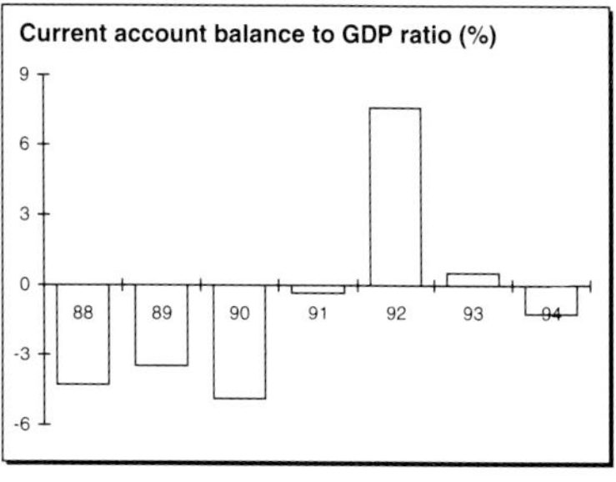

EXTERNAL DEBT and RESOURCE FLOWS

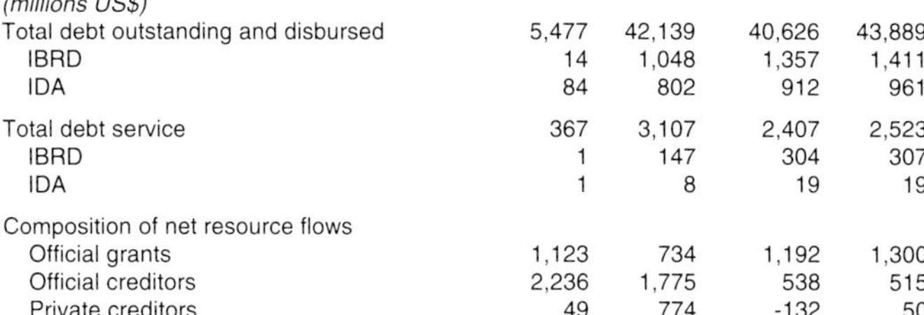

	1975	1985	1993	1994
(millions US$)				
Total debt outstanding and disbursed	5,477	42,139	40,626	43,889
IBRD	14	1,048	1,357	1,411
IDA	84	802	912	961
Total debt service	367	3,107	2,407	2,523
IBRD	1	147	304	307
IDA	1	8	19	19
Composition of net resource flows				
Official grants	1,123	734	1,192	1,300
Official creditors	2,236	1,775	538	515
Private creditors	49	774	-132	50
Foreign direct investment	8	1,178	493	530
Portfolio equity	0	0	0	0
World Bank program				
Commitments	132	59	208	121
Disbursements	62	269	163	199
Principal repayments	0	70	200	204
Net flows	62	198	-37	-5
Interest payments	1	84	122	123
Net transfers	61	114	-159	-127

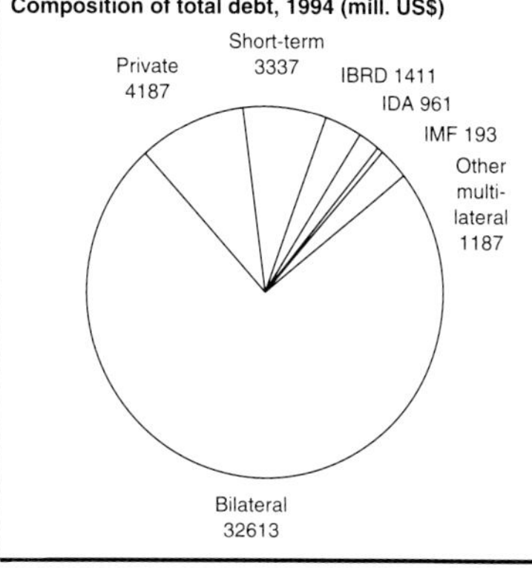

International Economics Department

Debt data are from *World Debt Tables 1994-95*.

Bahrain

POVERTY and SOCIAL	Bahrain	M. East & North Africa	Upper-middle-income
Population mid-1994 *(millions)*	0.5	268	510
GNP per capita 1994 *(US$)*	*8,030*	..	4,760
Average annual growth, 1990-94			
Population *(%)*	2.8	2.6	1.7
Labor force *(%)*	3.3	3.1	2.2
Most recent estimate *(latest year available since 1988)*			
Poverty: headcount index *(% of population)*	..	..	..
Urban population *(% of total population)*	90	55	71
Life expectancy at birth *(years)*	72	66	69
Infant mortality *(per 1,000 live births)*	18	52	36
Child malnutrition *(% of children under 5)*	..	..	..
Access to safe water *(% of population)*	100	84	87
Illiteracy *(% of population age 15+)*	23	45	14
Gross primary enrollment *(% of school-age population)*	93	97	105
Male	94	103	105
Female	93	90	105

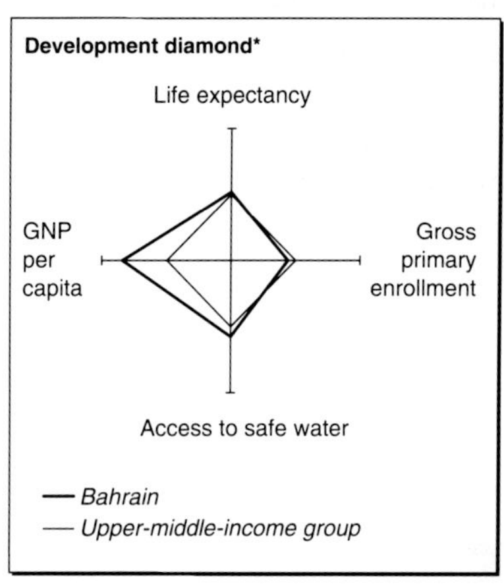

KEY ECONOMIC RATIOS and LONG-TERM TRENDS

	1975	1985	1993	1994
Gross domestic investment/GDP	..	33.8	27.8	..
Exports of goods and non-factor services/GDP	..	100.0	107.0	..
Gross domestic savings/GDP	..	45.2	37.4	..
Gross national savings/GDP	..	31.0	..	..
Current account balance/GDP	..	-2.2	..	..
Interest payments/GDP	..	..	..	..
Total debt/GDP	..	..	..	..
Total debt service/exports	..	..	..	..
Present value of debt/GDP	..	..	..	..
Present value of debt/exports	..	..	..	..

(average annual growth)	1975-84	1985-94	1993	1994	1995-04
GDP	..	*4.1*	5.6	..	..
GNP per capita	..	*-1.2*	2.6	..	..
Exports of goods and nfs	..	..	..	..	..

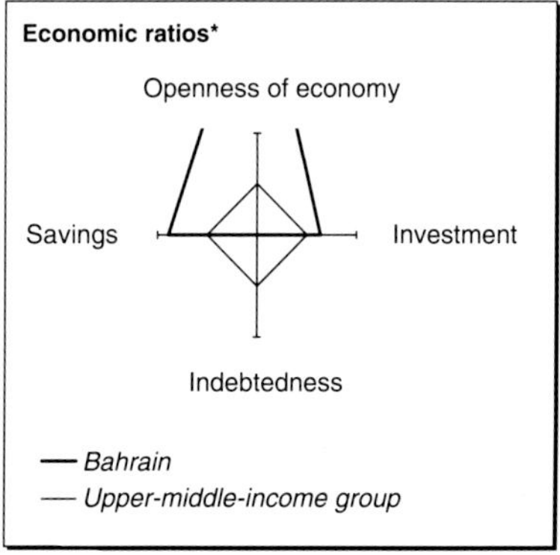

STRUCTURE of the ECONOMY

(% of GDP)	1975	1985	1993	1994
Agriculture	..	1.2	0.9	..
Industry	..	50.0	41.7	..
Manufacturing	..	10.0	16.9	..
Services	..	48.8	57.4	..
Private consumption	..	32.3	37.1	..
General government consumption	..	22.5	25.5	..
Gross domestic investment	..	33.8	27.8	..
Exports of goods and non-factor services	..	100.0	107.0	..
Imports of goods and non-factor services	..	88.5	97.4	..

(average annual growth)	1975-84	1985-94	1993	1994
Agriculture	..	*0.6*	..	..
Industry	..	*0.2*	..	..
Manufacturing	..	*4.6*	..	..
Services	..	*6.6*	..	..
Private consumption	..	..	..	..
General government consumption	..	..	..	..
Gross domestic investment	..	..	..	..
Exports of goods and non-factor services	..	..	..	..
Imports of goods and non-factor services	..	..	..	..
Gross national product	..	*2.0*	5.5	..

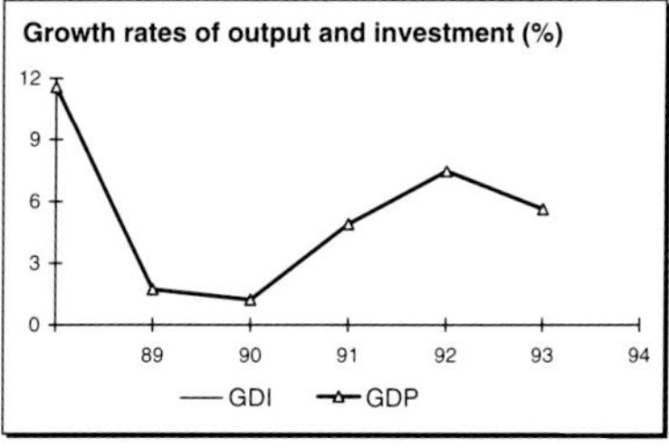

Note: 1994 data are preliminary estimates. Figures in italics are for years other than those specified.

* The diamonds show four key indicators in the country (in bold) compared with its income-group average. If data are missing, the diamond will be incomplete.

PRICES and GOVERNMENT FINANCE

	1975	1985	1993	1994
Domestic prices				
(% change)				
Consumer prices	16.2	-2.6	2.5	0.8
Implicit GDP deflator	..	-1.7	-1.1	..
Government finance				
(% of GDP)				
Current revenue	..	..	..	..
Current budget balance	..	..	..	..
Overall surplus/deficit	..	..	..	..

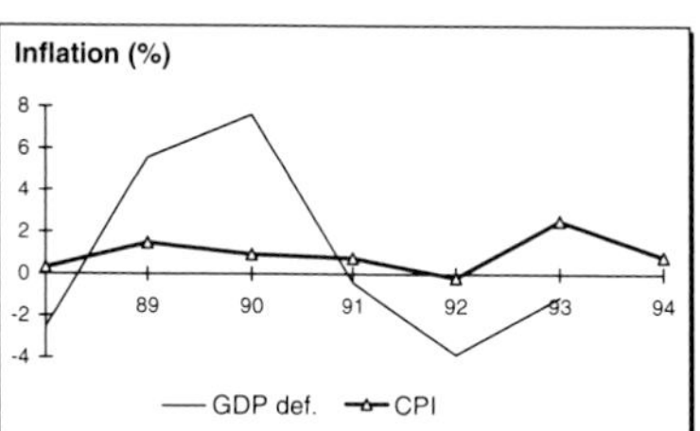

TRADE

	1975	1985	1993	1994
(millions US$)				
Total exports (fob)	..	..	..	..
n.a.	..	..	..	..
n.a.	..	..	..	..
Manufactures	..	..	..	..
Total imports (cif)	..	..	..	..
Food	..	..	..	..
Fuel and energy	..	..	..	..
Capital goods	..	..	..	..
Export price index *(1987=100)*	..	..	..	..
Import price index *(1987=100)*	..	..	..	..
Terms of trade *(1987=100)*	..	..	..	..

BALANCE of PAYMENTS

	1975	1985	1993	1994
(millions US$)				
Exports of goods and non-factor services	1,359	3,808	..	..
Imports of goods and non-factor services	1,269	3,285	..	..
Resource balance	90	524	..	..
Net factor income	-217	-370	..	..
Net current transfers	-76	-235	..	..
Current account balance, before official transfers	-203	-81	..	..
Financing items (net)	372	439	..	..
Changes in net reserves	-169	-357	96	-2
Memo:				
Reserves including gold *(mill. US$)*	311	1,709	1,361	1,227
Conversion rate *(local/US$)*	0.4	0.4	0.4	..

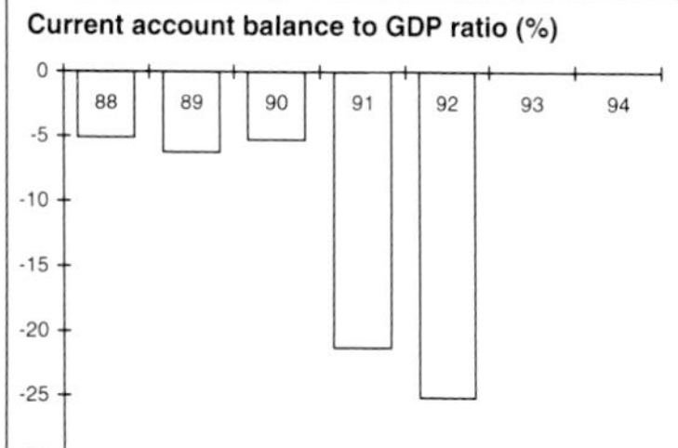

EXTERNAL DEBT and RESOURCE FLOWS

	1975	1985	1993	1994
(millions US$)				
Total debt outstanding and disbursed	..	..	..	..
IBRD	..	..	..	..
IDA	..	..	..	..
Total debt service	..	..	..	..
IBRD	..	..	..	..
IDA	..	..	..	..
Composition of net resource flows				
Official grants	18	78	104	50
Official creditors	..	..	..	..
Private creditors	..	..	..	..
Foreign direct investment	..	101	-5	..
Portfolio equity	..	..	..	..
World Bank program				
Commitments	..	..	..	..
Disbursements	..	..	..	..
Principal repayments	..	..	..	..
Net flows	..	..	..	..
Interest payments	..	..	..	..
Net transfers	..	..	..	..

International Economics Department

Islamic Republic of Iran

POVERTY and SOCIAL	Iran	M. East & North Africa	Lower-middle-income
Population mid-1994 *(millions)*	65.8	268	1,112
GNP per capita 1994 *(US$)*	*2,120*	..	1,510
Average annual growth, 1990-94			
Population *(%)*	2.7	2.6	1.5
Labor force *(%)*	3.3	3.1	1.7
Most recent estimate *(latest year available since 1988)*			
Poverty: headcount index *(% of population, 1990) /1*	9	..	..
Urban population *(% of total population)*	57	55	55
Life expectancy at birth *(years)*	68	66	67
Infant mortality *(per 1,000 live births)*	35	52	39
Child malnutrition *(% of children under 5)*	..	..	..
Access to safe water *(% of population)*	89	84	78
Illiteracy *(% of population age 15+)*	46	45	19
Gross primary enrollment *(% of school-age population)*	109	97	104
Male	114	103	103
Female	104	90	96

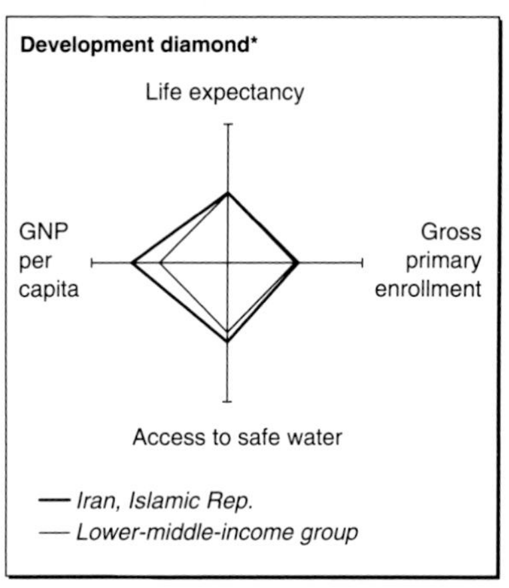

KEY ECONOMIC RATIOS and LONG-TERM TRENDS

	1975	1985	1993	1994
Gross domestic investment/GDP	24.5	21.0	29.2	23.2
Exports of goods and non-factor services/GDP	42.6	7.9	23.7	30.1
Gross domestic savings/GDP	33.7	20.9	23.8	31.2
Gross national savings/GDP	33.7	23.3	23.3	30.4
Current account balance/GDP	9.5	-0.3	-5.9	7.2
Interest payments/GDP	..	0.0	..	..
Total debt/GDP	..	3.4	30.1	30.6
Total debt service/exports	..	4.1	17.6	14.0
Present value of debt/GDP	..	..	..	..
Present value of debt/exports	..	..	106.0	..

	1975-84	1985-94	1993	1994	1995-04
(average annual growth)					
GDP	-1.8	2.5	2.3	1.8	4.5
GNP per capita	-5.3	-1.0	-0.7	..	2.2
Exports of goods and nfs	-15.6	11.6	16.1	-1.7	3.5

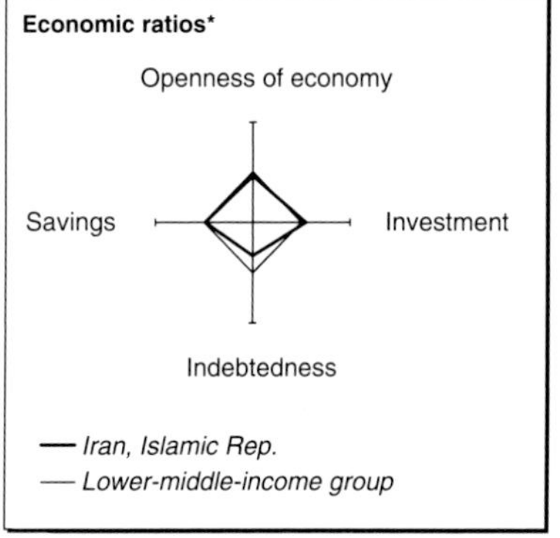

STRUCTURE of the ECONOMY

	1975	1985	1993	1994
(% of GDP)				
Agriculture	11.4	20.5	20.7	21.4
Industry	54.3	27.7	35.4	35.6
Manufacturing	9.0	8.5	13.7	11.5
Services	34.3	51.8	43.9	43.0
Private consumption	42.1	63.6	61.7	53.6
General government consumption	24.2	15.5	14.5	15.2
Gross domestic investment	24.5	21.0	29.2	23.2
Exports of goods and non-factor services	42.6	7.9	23.7	30.1
Imports of goods and non-factor services	33.4	8.0	29.1	22.1

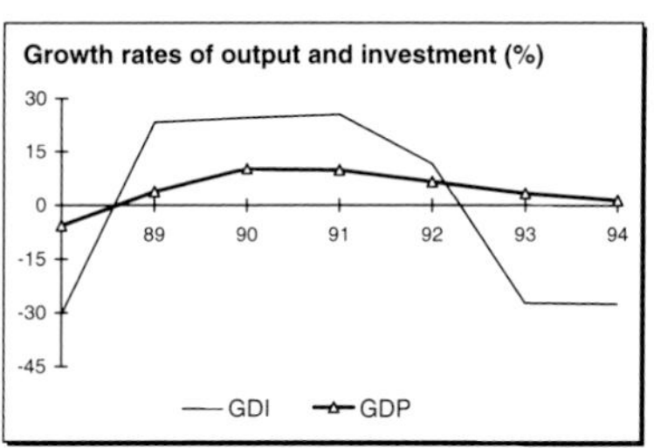

	1975-84	1985-94	1993	1994
(average annual growth)				
Agriculture	4.5	4.3	5.5	4.4
Industry	-7.2	5.6	3.0	0.0
Manufacturing	2.6	5.9	1.0	3.0
Services	2.3	0.9	7.3	4.8
Private consumption	-0.6	3.4	2.4	3.1
General government consumption	-2.7	0.2	17.3	7.3
Gross domestic investment	-0.3	-2.0	-27.3	-27.6
Exports of goods and non-factor services	-15.6	11.6	16.1	-1.7
Imports of goods and non-factor services	-4.1	1.9	-16.3	-38.7
Gross national product	-1.7	2.3	3.5	1.5

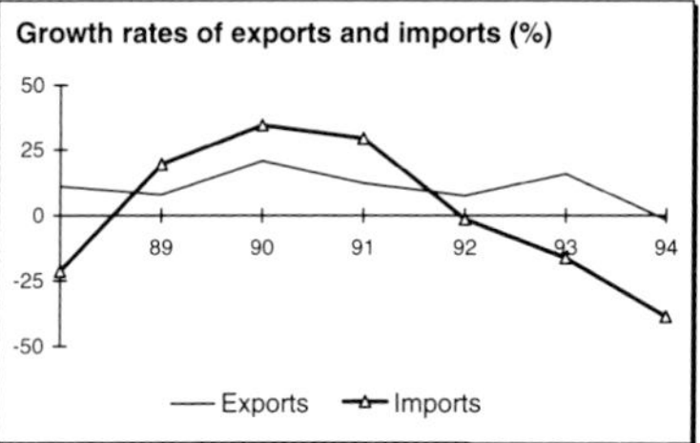

Note: 1994 data are preliminary estimates. Figures in italics are for years other than those specified. /1 Poverty is defined as spending less than one dollar per person per day (1985$ PPP).

* The diamonds show four key indicators in the country (in bold) compared with its income-group average. If data are missing, the diamond will be incomplete.

PRICES and GOVERNMENT FINANCE

	1975	1985	1993	1994
Domestic prices				
(% change)				
Consumer prices *(1995 to May: 36.2)*	12.9	4.4	22.9	35.2
Implicit GDP deflator	6.5	4.1	38.4	36.4
Government finance				
(% of GDP)				
Current revenue	..	17.4	30.9	26.0
Current budget balance	..	1.3	2.4	4.2
Overall surplus/deficit	..	-5.5	-6.3	-4.9

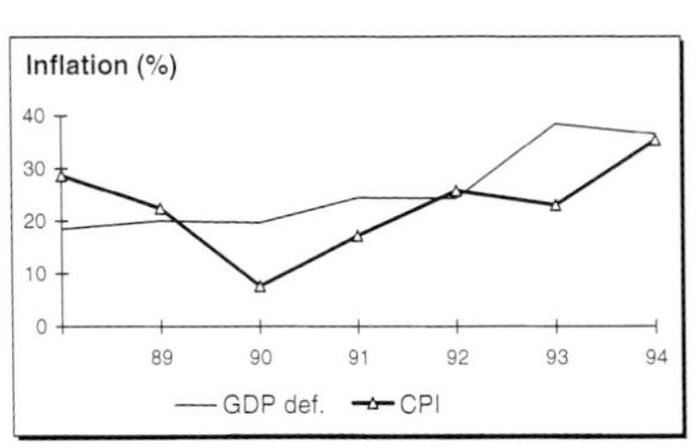

TRADE

	1975	1985	1993	1994
(millions US$)				
Total exports (fob)	..	14,175	18,080	19,054
Fuel	..	..	14,333	14,604
Textiles	..	..	1,420	..
Manufactures	..	..	1,231	..
Total imports (cif)	..	12,006	19,287	12,683
Food	..	..	2,446	643
Fuel and energy	..	..	..	..
Capital goods	..	2,421	5,085	..
Export price index *(1987=100)*	..	..	..	..
Import price index *(1987=100)*	..	..	..	..
Terms of trade *(1987=100)*	..	..	..	..

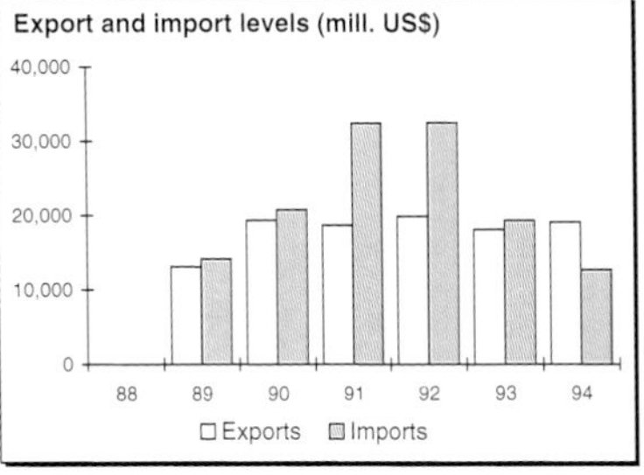

BALANCE of PAYMENTS

	1975	1985	1993	1994
(millions US$)				
Exports of goods and non-factor services	22,202	14,545	18,170	19,156
Imports of goods and non-factor services	17,470	15,314	22,298	14,052
Resource balance	4,732	-769	-4,128	5,104
Net factor income	-6	293	-1,587	-1,723
Net current transfers	-1	0	1,200	1,200
Current account balance, before official transfers	4,724	-476	-4,515	4,581
Financing items (net)	-4,657	1,093	4,594	-3,349
Changes in net reserves	-67	-617	-79	-1,232
Memo:				
Reserves including gold *(mill. US$)*	9,268	..	2,939	4,171
Conversion rate *(local/US$)*	68.2	87.7	..	..

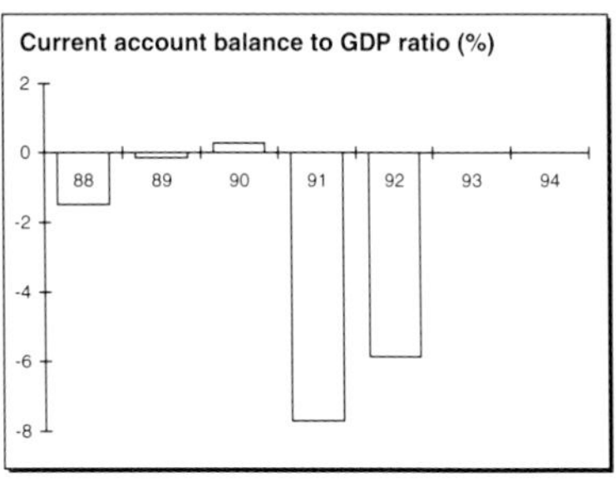

EXTERNAL DEBT and RESOURCE FLOWS

	1975	1985	1993	1994
(millions US$)				
Total debt outstanding and disbursed	..	6,057	18,603	20,637
IBRD	..	344	190	260
IDA	..	0	0	0
Total debt service	..	613	1,287	1,809
IBRD	..	71	19	24
IDA	..	0	0	0
Composition of net resource flows				
Official grants	1	8	57	65
Official creditors	..	-67	88	490
Private creditors	..	-200	1,399	1,265
Foreign direct investment	141	-38	-50	10
Portfolio equity	..	0	0	0
World Bank program				
Commitments	..	0	165	0
Disbursements	..	0	58	48
Principal repayments	..	48	7	8
Net flows	..	-48	51	40
Interest payments	..	24	12	16
Net transfers	..	-71	39	24

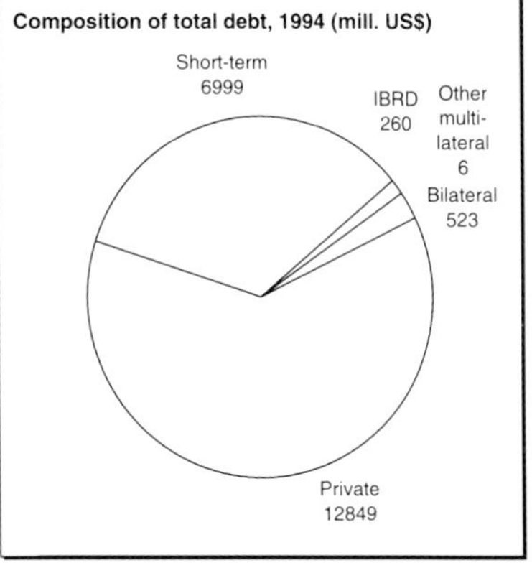

International Economics Department

Debt data are from *World Debt Tables 1994-95*.

Israel

POVERTY and SOCIAL

	Israel	M. East & North Africa	High-income
Population mid-1994 *(millions)*	5.4	268	833
GNP per capita 1994 *(US$)*	*13,920*	..	23,100
Average annual growth, 1990-94			
Population *(%)*	3.8	2.6	0.6
Labor force *(%)*	2.1	3.1	0.0
Most recent estimate *(latest year available since 1988)*			
Poverty: headcount index *(% of population)*	..	..	..
Urban population *(% of total population)*	91	55	78
Life expectancy at birth *(years)*	77	66	77
Infant mortality *(per 1,000 live births)*	9	52	7
Child malnutrition *(% of children under 5)*	..	..	..
Access to safe water *(% of population)*	100	84	..
Illiteracy *(% of population age 15+)*	..	45	..
Gross primary enrollment *(% of school-age population)*	94	97	103
Male	94	103	103
Female	94	90	103

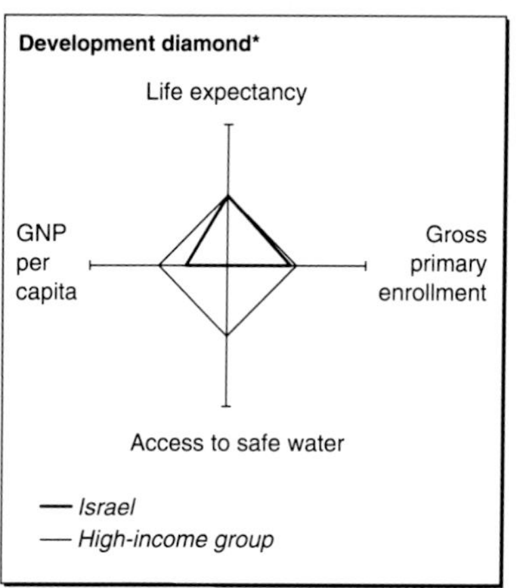

KEY ECONOMIC RATIOS and LONG-TERM TRENDS

	1975	1985	1993	1994
Gross domestic investment/GDP	29.2	17.8	22.3	..
Exports of goods and non-factor services/GDP	26.6	39.6	31.3	..
Gross domestic savings/GDP	4.9	11.3	13.7	..
Gross national savings/GDP	7.3	10.9	16.7	..
Current account balance/GDP	-23.1	-11.7	-7.6	..
Interest payments/GDP	..	..	..	..
Total debt/GDP	..	..	..	..
Total debt service/exports	..	..	..	..
Present value of debt/GDP	..	..	..	..
Present value of debt/exports	..	..	..	..

	1975-84	1985-94	1993	1994	1995-04
(average annual growth)					
GDP	4.0	*4.9*	3.7	..	..
GNP per capita	1.8	*2.6*	0.6	..	..
Exports of goods and nfs	5.2	*4.4*	11.6	..	..

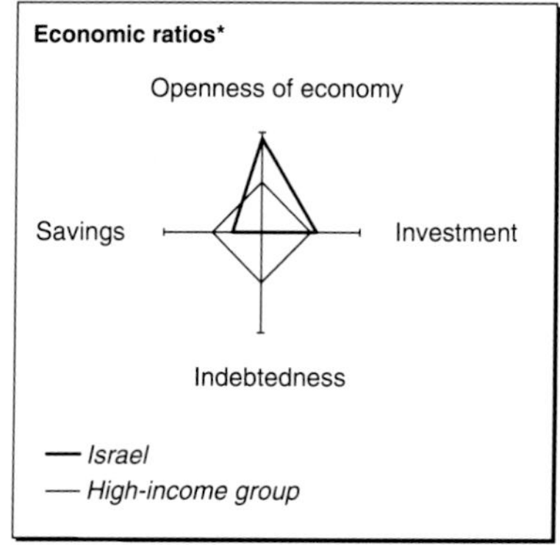

STRUCTURE of the ECONOMY

	1975	1985	1993	1994
(% of GDP)				
Agriculture	..	..	..	..
Industry	..	..	..	..
Manufacturing	..	..	..	..
Services	..	..	..	..
Private consumption	54.9	54.3	59.3	..
General government consumption	40.2	34.3	27.1	..
Gross domestic investment	29.2	17.8	22.3	..
Exports of goods and non-factor services	26.6	39.6	31.3	..
Imports of goods and non-factor services	50.9	46.2	40.0	..

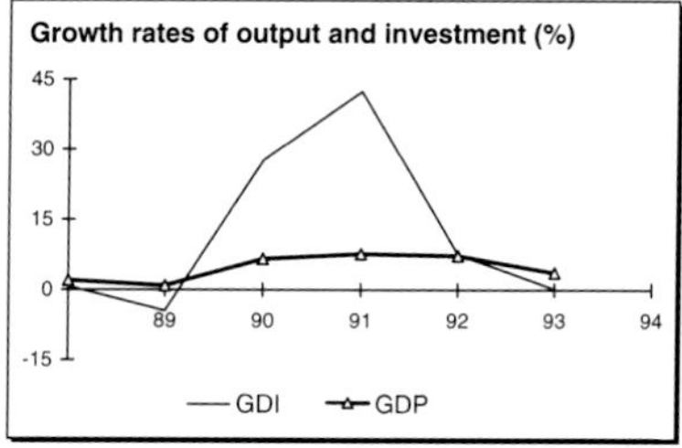

	1975-84	1985-94	1993	1994
(average annual growth)				
Agriculture	..	..	..	..
Industry	..	..	..	..
Manufacturing	..	..	..	..
Services	..	..	..	..
Private consumption	5.4	*5.9*	7.7	..
General government consumption	1.9	*1.2*	6.3	..
Gross domestic investment	-0.1	*11.2*	0.2	..
Exports of goods and non-factor services	5.2	*4.4*	11.6	..
Imports of goods and non-factor services	2.1	*6.5*	15.1	..
Gross national product	3.9	*5.2*	4.4	..

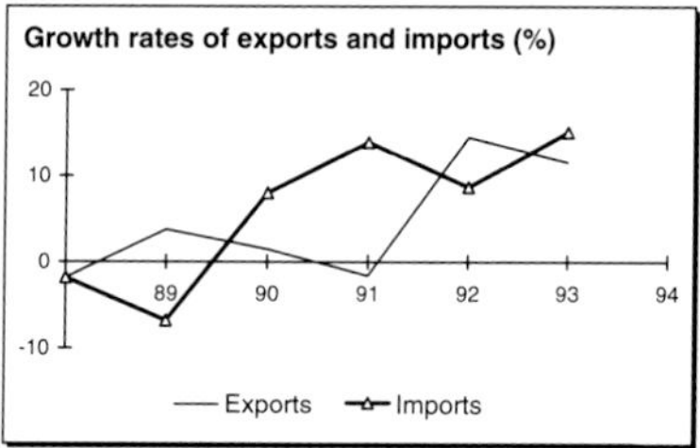

Note: 1994 data are preliminary estimates. Figures in italics are for years other than those specified.

* The diamonds show four key indicators in the country (in bold) compared with its income-group average. If data are missing, the diamond will be incomplete.

PRICES and GOVERNMENT FINANCE

	1975	1985	1993	1994
Domestic prices				
(% change)				
Consumer prices *(1995 to April: 1.2)*	39.3	304.6	10.9	12.3
Implicit GDP deflator	36.4	265.7	11.0	..
Government finance				
(% of GDP)				
Current revenue	..	..	..	..
Current budget balance	..	..	..	..
Overall surplus/deficit	..	..	..	..

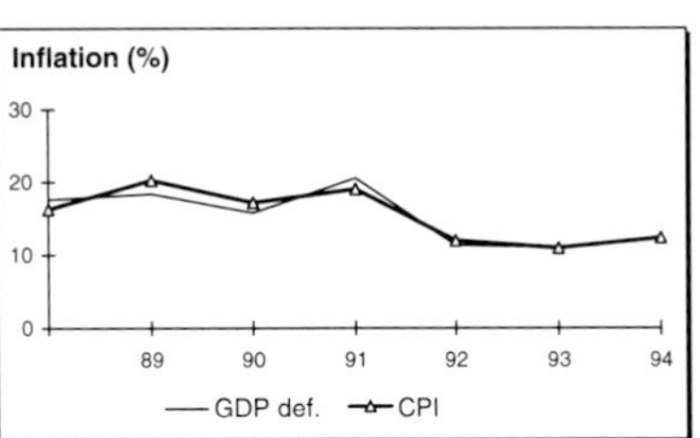

TRADE

	1975	1985	1993	1994
(millions US$)				
Total exports (fob)	..	..	..	..
n.a.	..	..	..	..
n.a.	..	..	..	..
Manufactures	..	..	..	..
Total imports (cif)	..	..	..	..
Food	..	..	..	..
Fuel and energy	..	..	..	..
Capital goods	..	..	..	..
Export price index *(1987=100)*	..	..	..	..
Import price index *(1987=100)*	..	..	..	..
Terms of trade *(1987=100)*	..	..	..	..

BALANCE of PAYMENTS

	1975	1985	1993	1994
(millions US$)				
Exports of goods and non-factor services	3,261	9,700	20,674	..
Imports of goods and non-factor services	6,599	11,644	27,164	..
Resource balance	-3,338	-1,943	-6,490	..
Net factor income	-511	-1,938	-1,630	..
Net current transfers	759	848	2,853	..
Current account balance, before official transfers	-3,090	-3,033	-5,268	..
Financing items (net)	2,934	3,432	6,749	..
Changes in net reserves	156	-399	-1,481	..
Memo:				
Reserves including gold *(mill. US$)*	1,292	4,013	6,386	6,796
Conversion rate *(local/US$)*	6.3E-04	1.2	2.8	..

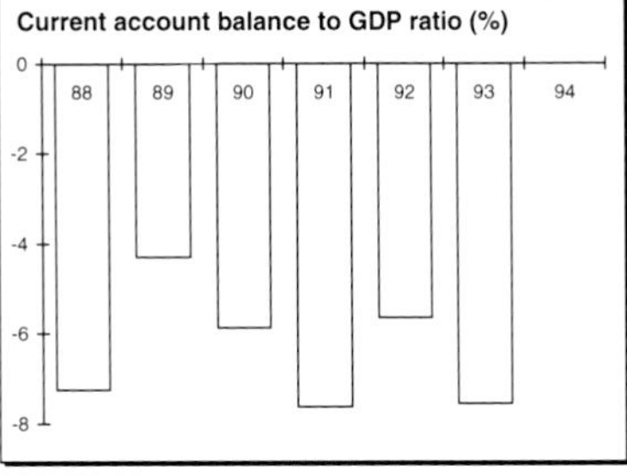

EXTERNAL DEBT and RESOURCE FLOWS

	1975	1985	1993	1994
(millions US$)				
Total debt outstanding and disbursed	..	..	..	..
IBRD	..	..	..	..
IDA	..	..	..	..
Total debt service	..	..	..	..
IBRD	..	..	..	..
IDA	..	..	..	..
Composition of net resource flows				
Official grants	424	2,973	1,284	..
Official creditors	..	..	..	..
Private creditors	..	..	..	..
Foreign direct investment	45	99	..	..
Portfolio equity	..	..	..	..
World Bank program				
Commitments	..	..	..	..
Disbursements	..	..	..	..
Principal repayments	..	..	..	..
Net flows	..	..	..	..
Interest payments	..	..	..	..
Net transfers	..	..	..	..

International Economics Department

Jordan

POVERTY and SOCIAL

	Jordan	M. East & North Africa	Lower-middle-income
Population mid-1994 *(millions)*	4.2	268	1,112
GNP per capita 1994 *(US$)*	1,390	..	1,510
Average annual growth, 1990-94			
Population *(%)*	6.3	2.6	1.5
Labor force *(%)*	..	3.1	1.7
Most recent estimate *(latest year available since 1988)*			
Poverty: headcount index *(% of population, 1992) /1*	15	..	..
Poverty: headcount index *(% of population, 1990) /2*	13		
Urban population *(% of total population)*	71	55	55
Life expectancy at birth *(years)*	70	66	67
Infant mortality *(per 1,000 live births)*	26	52	39
Child malnutrition *(% of children under 5)*	6	..	..
Access to safe water *(% of population)*	99	84	78
Illiteracy *(% of population age 15+)*	20	45	19
Gross primary enrollment *(% of school-age population)*	105	97	104
Male	105	103	103
Female	105	90	96

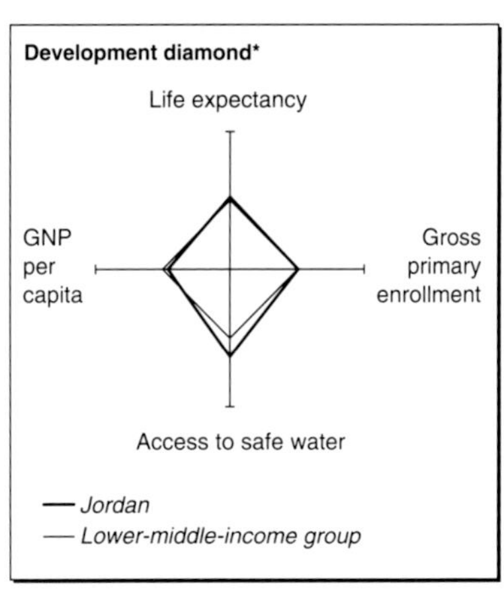

KEY ECONOMIC RATIOS and LONG-TERM TRENDS

	1975	1985	1993	1994
Gross domestic investment/GDP	..	21.7	31.8	26.4
Exports of goods and non-factor services/GDP	..	37.2	50.4	48.9
Gross domestic savings/GDP	..	-17.4	1.9	3.3
Gross national savings/GDP	..	-2.2	14.1	14.6
Current account balance/GDP	..	-19.9	-17.7	-11.8
Interest payments/GDP	..	3.8	3.7	4.3
Total debt/GDP	..	80.4	124.4	121.6
Total debt service/exports	3.7	17.1	14.4	14.8
Present value of debt/GDP	..	..	110.6	..
Present value of debt/exports	..	..	156.5	..

	1975-84	1985-94	1993	1994	1995-04
(average annual growth)					
GDP	..	-0.1	5.9	5.4	5.7
GNP per capita	..	-6.3	3.7	2.4	3.9
Exports of goods and nfs	..	8.7	7.7	1.9	5.6

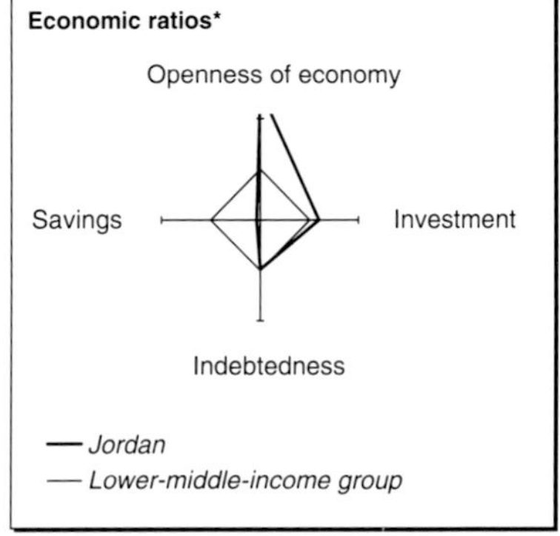

STRUCTURE of the ECONOMY

	1975	1985	1993	1994
(% of GDP)				
Agriculture	..	4.9	8.3	7.9
Industry	..	26.9	26.8	27.0
Manufacturing	..	11.9	13.7	..
Services	..	68.2	64.9	65.0
Private consumption	..	90.6	76.2	75.1
General government consumption	..	26.8	21.9	21.6
Gross domestic investment	..	21.7	31.8	26.4
Exports of goods and non-factor services	..	37.2	50.4	48.9
Imports of goods and non-factor services	..	76.3	80.3	72.0

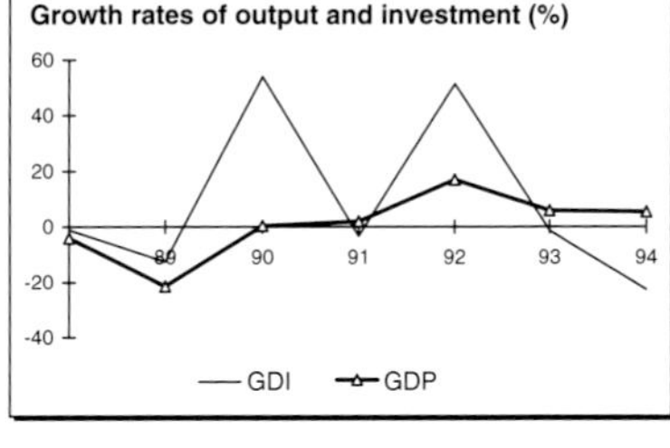

	1975-84	1985-94	1993	1994
(average annual growth)				
Agriculture	..	11.9	10.1	1.0
Industry	..	2.0	5.9	6.5
Manufacturing	..	5.3	6.0	9.3
Services	..	-3.3	5.6	5.5
Private consumption	..	-3.0	12.3	12.4
General government consumption	..	-0.9	2.9	5.5
Gross domestic investment	..	9.9	-1.3	-22.6
Exports of goods and non-factor services	..	8.7	7.7	1.9
Imports of goods and non-factor services	..	5.8	6.7	-5.1
Gross national product	..	-0.8	7.1	5.9

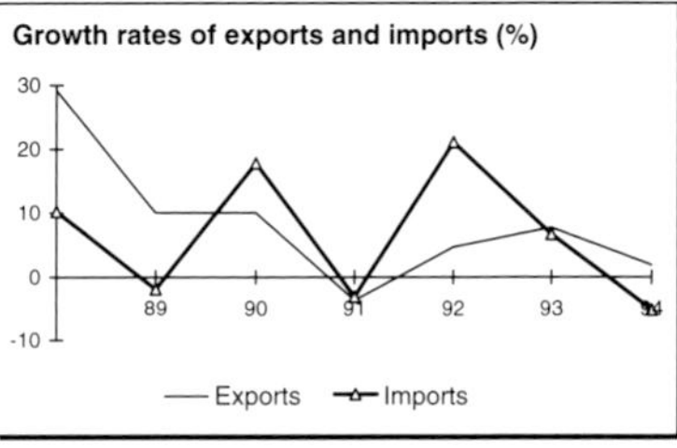

Note: 1994 data are preliminary estimates. /1 Poverty line is local. /2 Poverty is defined as spending less than one dollar per person per day (1985$, PPP).

* The diamonds show four key indicators in the country (in bold) compared with its income-group average. If data are missing, the diamond will be incomplete.

PRICES and GOVERNMENT FINANCE

	1975	1985	1993	1994
Domestic prices				
(% change)				
Consumer prices *(1995 to March: -1.6)*	12.0	3.0	4.7	3.5
Implicit GDP deflator	..	-0.3	4.9	4.3
Government finance				
(% of GDP)				
Current revenue	..	22.4	30.7	29.2
Current budget balance	..	-11.6	0.2	0.0
Overall surplus/deficit	..	-21.6	-5.7	-5.9

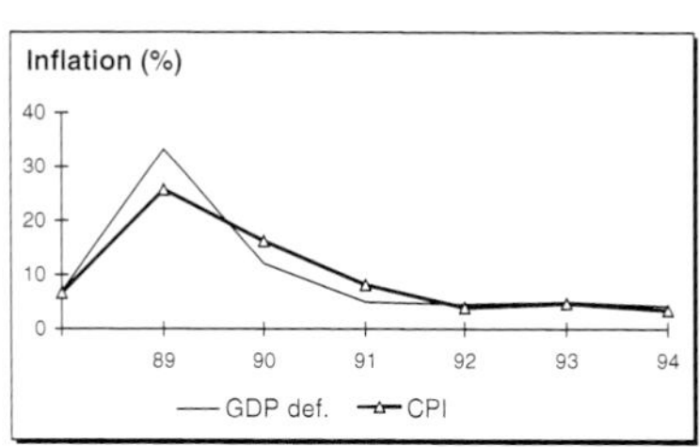

TRADE

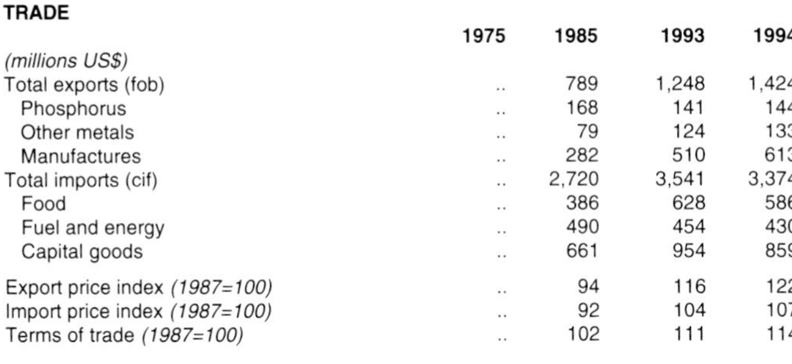

	1975	1985	1993	1994
(millions US$)				
Total exports (fob)	..	789	1,248	1,424
Phosphorus	..	168	141	144
Other metals	..	79	124	133
Manufactures	..	282	510	613
Total imports (cif)	..	2,720	3,541	3,374
Food	..	386	628	586
Fuel and energy	..	490	454	430
Capital goods	..	661	954	859
Export price index *(1987=100)*	..	94	116	122
Import price index *(1987=100)*	..	92	104	107
Terms of trade *(1987=100)*	..	102	111	114

BALANCE of PAYMENTS

	1975	1985	1993	1994
(millions US$)				
Exports of goods and non-factor services	379	1,976	2,822	2,985
Imports of goods and non-factor services	942	3,723	4,499	4,395
Resource balance	-562	-1,747	-1,677	-1,410
Net factor income	26	-89	-310	-315
Net current transfers	172	845	997	1,002
Current account balance, before official transfers	-365	-991	-990	-723
Financing items (net)	538	1,145	895	781
Changes in net reserves	-173	-154	95	-58
Memo:				
Reserves including gold *(mill. US$)*	571	770	1,946	1,997
Conversion rate *(local/US$)*	0.3	0.4	0.7	0.7

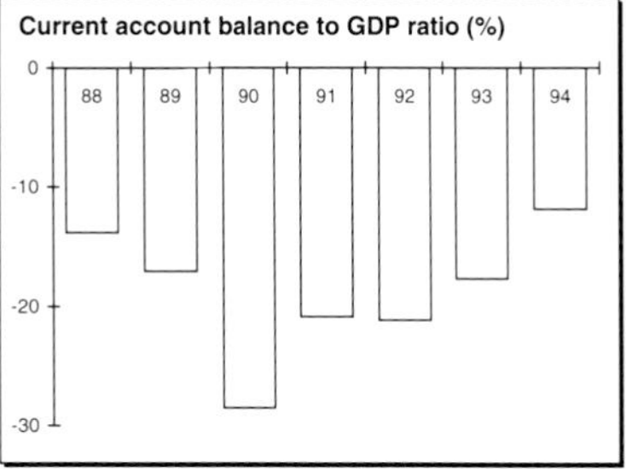

EXTERNAL DEBT and RESOURCE FLOWS

	1975	1985	1993	1994
(millions US$)				
Total debt outstanding and disbursed	348	4,012	6,972	7,421
IBRD	0	168	592	635
IDA	33	82	73	71
Total debt service	21	528	569	613
IBRD	0	21	101	102
IDA	0	2	2	3
Composition of net resource flows				
Official grants	357	453	155	200
Official creditors	71	209	42	211
Private creditors	19	187	-161	-152
Foreign direct investment	26	25	-34	-10
Portfolio equity	0	0	0	0
World Bank program				
Commitments	12	97	135	107
Disbursements	10	64	69	58
Principal repayments	0	10	59	59
Net flows	10	54	10	0
Interest payments	0	12	44	46
Net transfers	10	42	-33	-46

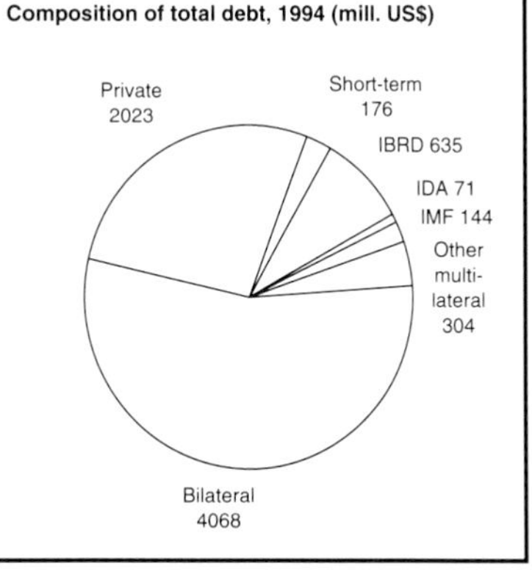

International Economics Department

Debt data are from *World Debt Tables 1994-95*.

Kuwait

POVERTY and SOCIAL	Kuwait	M. East & North Africa	High-income
Population mid-1994 *(millions)*	1.7	268	833
GNP per capita 1994 *(US$)*	*20,270*	..	23,100
Average annual growth, 1990-94			
Population *(%)*	-6.5	2.6	0.6
Labor force *(%)*	..	3.1	0.0
Most recent estimate *(latest year available since 1988)*			
Poverty: headcount index *(% of population)*	..	..	..
Urban population *(% of total population)*	97	55	78
Life expectancy at birth *(years)*	75	66	77
Infant mortality *(per 1,000 live births)*	17	52	7
Child malnutrition *(% of children under 5)*	..	..	..
Access to safe water *(% of population)*	100	84	..
Illiteracy *(% of population age 15+)*	27	45	..
Gross primary enrollment *(% of school-age population)*	61	97	103
Male	60	103	103
Female	60	90	103

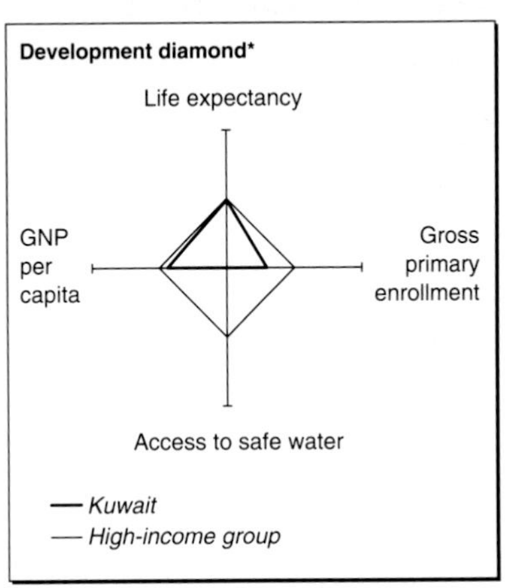

KEY ECONOMIC RATIOS and LONG-TERM TRENDS

	1975	1985	1993	1994
Gross domestic investment/GDP	12.7	18.9	13.8	10.7
Exports of goods and non-factor services/GDP	80.5	53.7	49.7	55.2
Gross domestic savings/GDP	67.2	29.8	18.8	22.4
Gross national savings/GDP	71.3	46.4	29.7	..
Current account balance/GDP	55.9	26.9	27.0	..
Interest payments/GDP	..	..	..	..
Total debt/GDP	..	..	..	..
Total debt service/exports	..	..	..	..
Present value of debt/GDP	..	..	..	..
Present value of debt/exports	..	..	..	..

(average annual growth)	1975-84	1985-94	1993	1994	1995-04
GDP	-4.4	..	..	..	..
GNP per capita	-7.7	*-4.5*	48.1	..	..
Exports of goods and nfs	-8.4	..	..	..	..

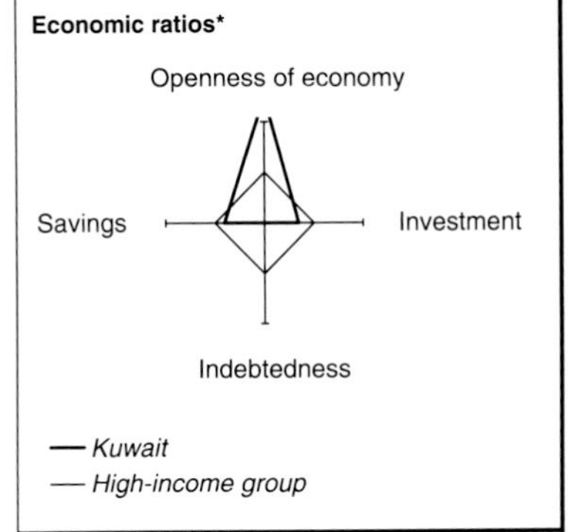

STRUCTURE of the ECONOMY

(% of GDP)	1975	1985	1993	1994
Agriculture	0.3	0.6	0.3	0.3
Industry	78.2	57.0	53.2	52.9
Manufacturing	5.7	5.9	9.0	10.6
Services	21.5	42.4	46.5	46.8
Private consumption	21.8	47.8	44.9	40.9
General government consumption	11.1	22.4	36.4	36.7
Gross domestic investment	12.7	18.9	13.8	10.7
Exports of goods and non-factor services	80.5	53.7	49.7	55.2
Imports of goods and non-factor services	26.0	42.7	44.8	43.4

(average annual growth)	1975-84	1985-94	1993	1994
Agriculture	13.4	..	..	..
Industry	-8.2	..	..	..
Manufacturing	*1.5*	..	..	..
Services	0.5	..	..	..
Private consumption	8.6	..	..	..
General government consumption	6.5	..	..	..
Gross domestic investment	6.8	..	..	..
Exports of goods and non-factor services	-8.4	..	..	..
Imports of goods and non-factor services	14.1	..	..	..
Gross national product	-2.5	*-3.8*	38.8	..

Note: 1994 data are preliminary estimates. Figures in italics are for years other than those specified.
* The diamonds show four key indicators in the country (in bold) compared with its income-group average. If data are missing, the diamond will be incomplete.

PRICES and GOVERNMENT FINANCE

	1975	1985	1993	1994
Domestic prices				
(% change)				
Consumer prices	8.4	1.5	-1.2	4.7
Implicit GDP deflator	0.1	3.7	0.8	..
Government finance				
(% of GDP)				
Current revenue	..	..	..	..
Current budget balance	..	..	..	..
Overall surplus/deficit	..	..	..	..

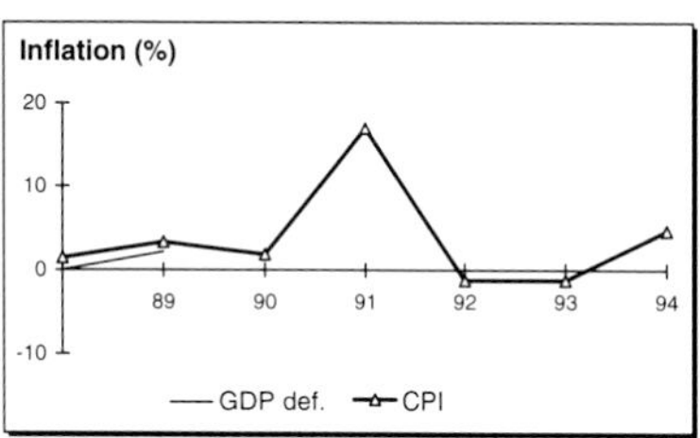

TRADE

	1975	1985	1993	1994
(millions US$)				
Total exports (fob)	..	..	..	..
Petroleum	8,595	10,378	9,647	10,354
n.a.	..	..	..	..
Manufactures	..	..	..	..
Total imports (cif)	2,390	5,732	6,967	6,652
Food	..	..	..	..
Fuel and energy	..	..	..	..
Capital goods	..	..	..	..
Export price index *(1987=100)*	..	..	..	..
Import price index *(1987=100)*	..	..	..	..
Terms of trade *(1987=100)*	..	..	..	..

BALANCE of PAYMENTS

	1975	1985	1993	1994
(millions US$)				
Exports of goods and non-factor services	9,006	11,511	11,758	..
Imports of goods and non-factor services	3,158	9,343	10,747	..
Resource balance	5,848	2,168	1,010	..
Net factor income	1,152	4,655	4,141	..
Net current transfers	-276	-1,044	-1,229	-1,441
Current account balance, before official transfers	6,723	5,779	3,922	3,712
Financing items (net)	-6,408	-5,234	-5,407	..
Changes in net reserves	-315	-545	1,485	..
Memo:				
Reserves including gold *(mill. US$)*	2,051	6,301	5,206	4,474
Conversion rate *(local/US$)*	0.3	0.3	0.3	..

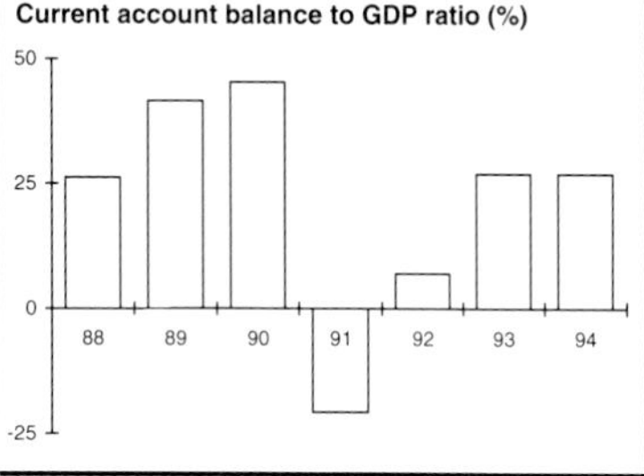

EXTERNAL DEBT and RESOURCE FLOWS

	1975	1985	1993	1994
(millions US$)				
Total debt outstanding and disbursed	..	..	..	..
IBRD	..	..	..	..
IDA	..	..	..	..
Total debt service	..	..	..	..
IBRD	..	..	..	..
IDA	..	..	..	..
Composition of net resource flows				
Official grants	..	..	..	..
Official creditors	..	..	..	..
Private creditors	..	..	..	..
Foreign direct investment	..	..	..	..
Portfolio equity	..	..	..	..
World Bank program				
Commitments	..	..	..	..
Disbursements	..	..	..	..
Principal repayments	..	..	..	..
Net flows	..	..	..	..
Interest payments	..	..	..	..
Net transfers	..	..	..	..

International Economics Department

Lebanon

POVERTY and SOCIAL	Lebanon	M. East & North Africa	Lower-middle-income
Population mid-1994 *(millions)*	3.9	268	1,112
GNP per capita 1994 *(US$)*	..	..	1,510
Average annual growth, 1990-94			
Population *(%)*	2.0	2.6	1.5
Labor force *(%)*	2.7	3.1	1.7
Most recent estimate *(latest year available since 1988)*			
Poverty: headcount index *(% of population)*	..	..	..
Urban population *(% of total population)*	87	55	55
Life expectancy at birth *(years)*	69	66	67
Infant mortality *(per 1,000 live births)*	33	52	39
Child malnutrition *(% of children under 5)*	..	..	..
Access to safe water *(% of population)*	..	84	78
Illiteracy *(% of population age 15+)*	20	45	19
Gross primary enrollment *(% of school-age population)*	111	97	104
Male	113	103	103
Female	109	90	96

Development diamond*

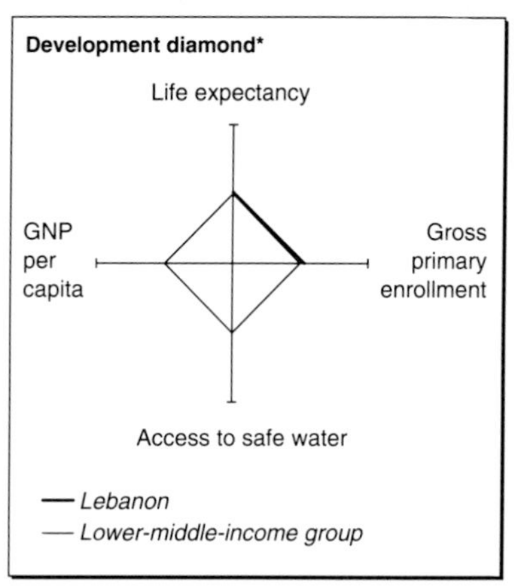

KEY ECONOMIC RATIOS and LONG-TERM TRENDS

	1975	1985	1993	1994
Gross domestic investment/GDP	..	..	24.0	28.3
Exports of goods and non-factor services/GDP	..	..	9.7	9.6
Gross domestic savings/GDP	..	..	-27.9	-21.5
Gross national savings/GDP	..	..	-21.3	-14.8
Current account balance/GDP	..	..	-45.3	-42.7
Interest payments/GDP	..	..	0.3	0.3
Total debt/GDP	..	..	18.0	15.1
Total debt service/exports	..	..	10.2	10.9
Present value of debt/GDP	..	..	17.6	..
Present value of debt/exports	..	..	100.0	..

	1975-84	1985-94	1993	1994	1995-04
(average annual growth)					
GDP	..	..	..	..	8.0
GNP per capita	..	..	..	..	..
Exports of goods and nfs	..	..	..	..	9.1

Economic ratios*

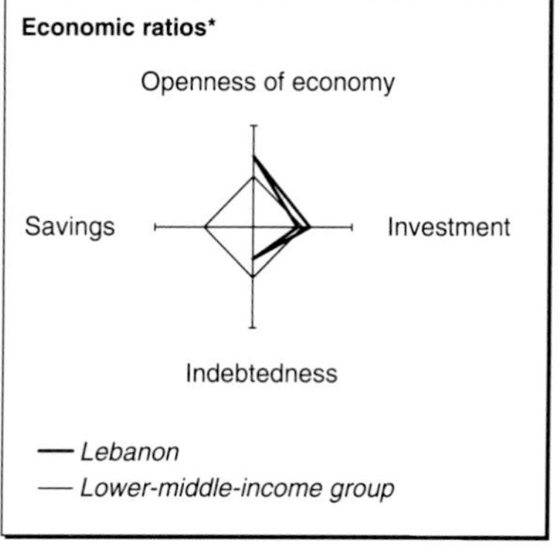

STRUCTURE of the ECONOMY

	1975	1985	1993	1994
(% of GDP)				
Agriculture	..	..	..	..
Industry	..	..	..	..
Manufacturing	..	..	..	..
Services	..	..	..	..
Private consumption	..	..	118.3	109.9
General government consumption	..	..	9.6	11.6
Gross domestic investment	..	..	24.0	28.3
Exports of goods and non-factor services	..	..	9.7	9.6
Imports of goods and non-factor services	..	..	61.6	59.4

	1975-84	1985-94	1993	1994
(average annual growth)				
Agriculture	..	..	..	..
Industry	..	..	..	..
Manufacturing	..	..	..	..
Services	..	..	..	..
Private consumption	..	..	..	..
General government consumption	..	..	..	..
Gross domestic investment	..	..	..	..
Exports of goods and non-factor services	..	..	..	..
Imports of goods and non-factor services	..	..	..	..
Gross national product	..	..	..	..

Note: 1994 data are preliminary estimates.

* The diamonds show four key indicators in the country (in bold) compared with its income-group average. If data are missing, the diamond will be incomplete.

PRICES and GOVERNMENT FINANCE

	1975	1985	1993	1994
Domestic prices				
(% change)				
Consumer prices	..	54.5	15.7	6.8
Implicit GDP deflator	..	..	..	..
Government finance				
(% of GDP)				
Current revenue	..	..	14.1	16.7
Current budget balance	..	..	-6.9	-8.5
Overall surplus/deficit	..	..	-8.4	-18.7

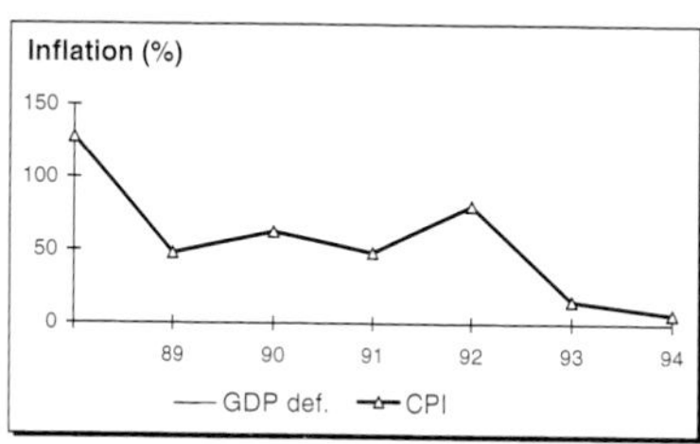

TRADE

	1975	1985	1993	1994
(millions US$)				
Total exports (fob)	..	..	686	825
Other agriculture	..	..	..	..
Fuel	..	..	..	..
Manufactures	..	..	..	..
Total imports (cif)	..	..	4,222	5,039
Food	..	..	..	..
Fuel and energy	..	..	..	..
Capital goods	..	..	..	..
Export price index *(1987=100)*	..	..	..	..
Import price index *(1987=100)*	..	..	..	..
Terms of trade *(1987=100)*	..	..	..	..

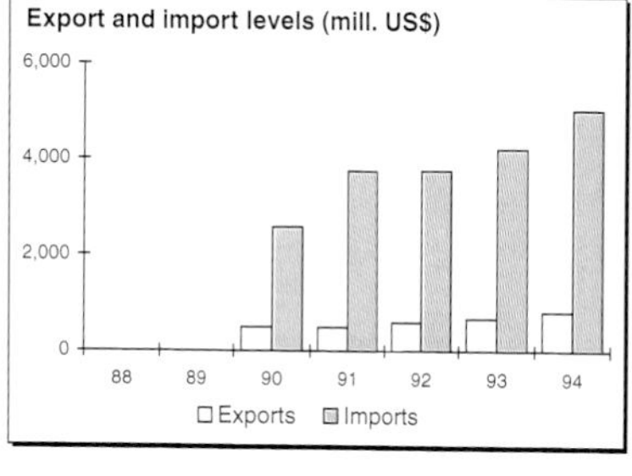

BALANCE of PAYMENTS

	1975	1985	1993	1994
(millions US$)				
Exports of goods and non-factor services	..	..	731	880
Imports of goods and non-factor services	..	..	4,644	5,442
Resource balance	..	..	-3,913	-4,562
Net factor income	..	..	196	298
Net current transfers	..	..	300	320
Current account balance, before official transfers	..	..	-3,417	-3,944
Financing items (net)	..	..	3,873	4,934
Changes in net reserves	..	..	-456	-990
Memo:				
Reserves including gold *(mill. US$)*	2,494	4,089	5,863	7,419
Conversion rate *(local/US$)*	..	..	1,741.4	1,680.1

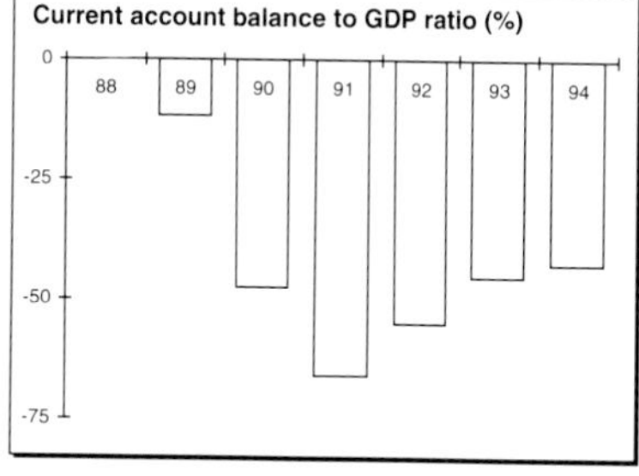

EXTERNAL DEBT and RESOURCE FLOWS

	1975	1985	1993	1994
(millions US$)				
Total debt outstanding and disbursed	46	860	1,356	1,397
IBRD	16	36	39	64
IDA	0	0	0	0
Total debt service	11	125	135	167
IBRD	3	7	6	8
IDA	0	0	0	0
Composition of net resource flows				
Official grants	9	-946	65	60
Official creditors	-3	7	16	26
Private creditors	0	-30	-6	0
Foreign direct investment	0	7	6	7
Portfolio equity	0	0	0	218
World Bank program				
Commitments	0	0	175	77
Disbursements	5	4	22	27
Principal repayments	2	4	5	4
Net flows	4	0	17	23
Interest payments	1	3	2	4
Net transfers	3	-2	16	19

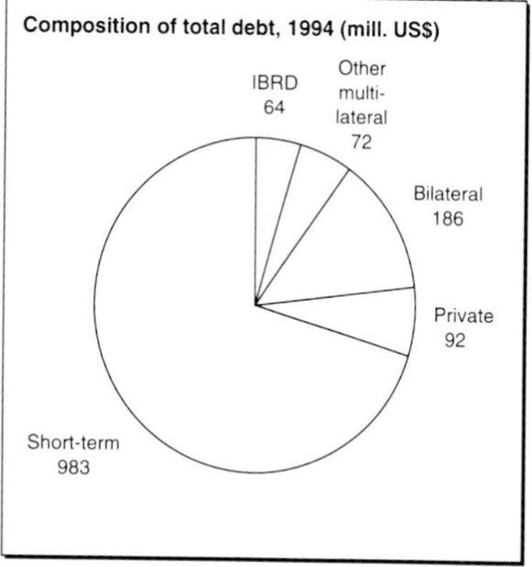

International Economics Department

Debt data are from *World Debt Tables 1994-95*.

Morocco

POVERTY and SOCIAL	Morocco	M. East & North Africa	Lower-middle-income
Population mid-1994 *(millions)*	26.5	268	1,112
GNP per capita 1994 *(US$)*	1,150	..	1,510
Average annual growth, 1990-94			
Population *(%)*	2.1	2.6	1.5
Labor force *(%)*	3.0	3.1	1.7
Most recent estimate *(latest year available since 1988)*			
Poverty: headcount index *(% of population, 1990) /1*	13	..	..
Poverty: headcount index *(% of population, 1990) /2*	2		
Urban population *(% of total population)*	48	55	55
Life expectancy at birth *(years)*	64	66	67
Infant mortality *(per 1,000 live births)*	66	52	39
Child malnutrition *(% of children under 5)*	9	..	..
Access to safe water *(% of population)*	73	84	78
Illiteracy *(% of population age 15+)*	51	45	19
Gross primary enrollment *(% of school-age population)*	69	97	104
Male	80	103	103
Female	57	90	96

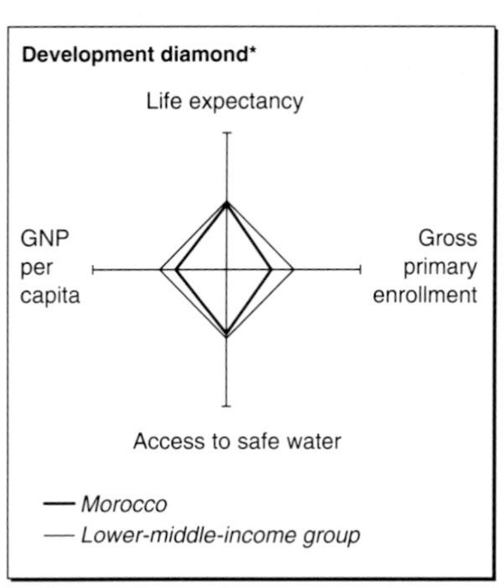

KEY ECONOMIC RATIOS and LONG-TERM TRENDS

	1975	1985	1993	1994
Gross domestic investment/GDP	25.2	27.1	21.2	21.0
Exports of goods and non-factor services/GDP	22.5	24.7	23.3	21.7
Gross domestic savings/GDP	14.3	18.1	15.7	16.0
Gross national savings/GDP	18.7	20.4	19.1	18.6
Current account balance/GDP	-6.1	-9.3	-2.1	-1.9
Interest payments/GDP	0.6	3.8	3.8	3.5
Total debt/GDP	21.0	128.4	80.5	68.3
Total debt service/exports	6.3	35.3	30.4	32.5
Present value of debt/GDP	..	..	71.7	..
Present value of debt/exports	..	..	225.0	..

	1975-84	1985-94	1993	1994	1995-04
(average annual growth)					
GDP	4.4	3.3	-1.1	11.5	5.6
GNP per capita	1.7	1.1	-3.1	9.4	3.8
Exports of goods and nfs	4.2	4.8	4.8	5.1	7.5

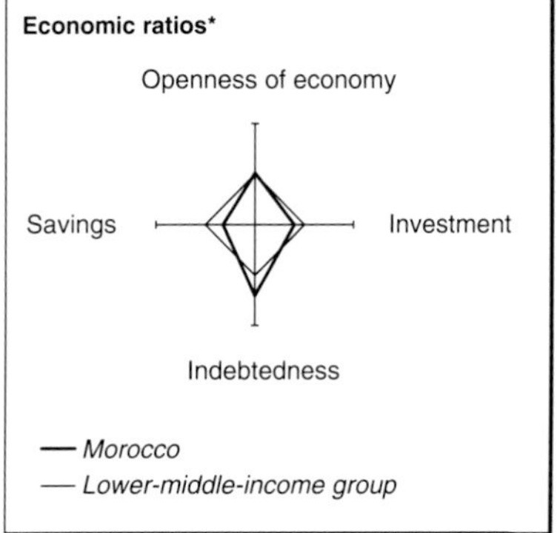

STRUCTURE of the ECONOMY

	1975	1985	1993	1994
(% of GDP)				
Agriculture	17.3	16.6	14.3	21.1
Industry	34.7	33.4	32.4	30.1
Manufacturing	16.6	18.6	18.0	16.7
Services	48.0	50.0	53.3	48.8
Private consumption	69.4	66.0	66.1	67.4
General government consumption	16.3	15.8	18.2	16.7
Gross domestic investment	25.2	27.1	21.2	21.0
Exports of goods and non-factor services	22.5	24.7	23.3	21.7
Imports of goods and non-factor services	33.4	33.7	28.8	26.8

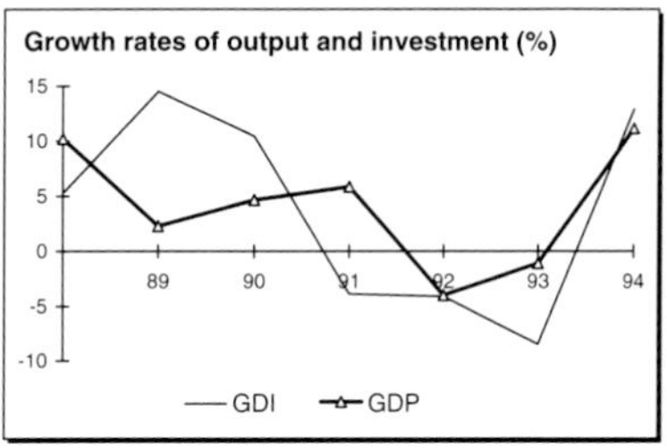

	1975-84	1985-94	1993	1994
(average annual growth)				
Agriculture	1.4	1.8	-6.2	63.0
Industry	3.0	2.5	-2.0	2.3
Manufacturing	..	3.3	-1.5	2.0
Services	6.4	4.2	0.7	4.3
Private consumption	3.8	4.5	-1.7	14.0
General government consumption	5.7	3.4	6.4	2.4
Gross domestic investment	-0.1	1.9	-8.4	10.5
Exports of goods and non-factor services	4.2	4.8	4.8	5.1
Imports of goods and non-factor services	-0.6	6.5	0.4	4.8
Gross national product	4.1	3.3	-2.7	11.5

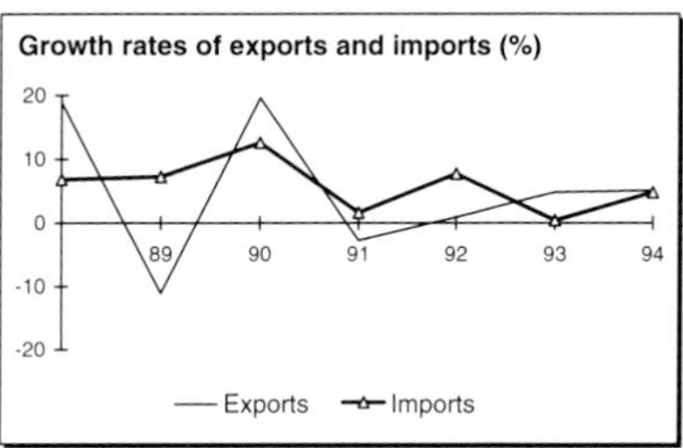

Note: 1994 data are preliminary estimates. /1 Poverty line is local. /2 Poverty is defined as spending less than one dollar per person per day (1985$, PPP).

* The diamonds show four key indicators in the country (in bold) compared with its income-group average. If data are missing, the diamond will be incomplete.

PRICES and GOVERNMENT FINANCE

	1975	1985	1993	1994
Domestic prices				
(% change)				
Consumer prices *(1995 to March:* 4.7*)*	7.9	7.8	5.2	5.1
Implicit GDP deflator	1.5	8.4	3.6	2.7
Government finance				
(% of GDP)				
Current revenue	..	20.7	26.7	23.4
Current budget balance	..	-2.4	4.6	2.9
Overall surplus/deficit	..	-9.6	-3.3	-3.8

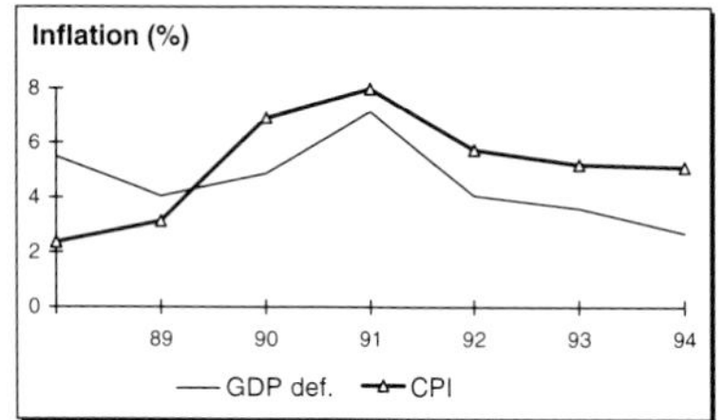

TRADE

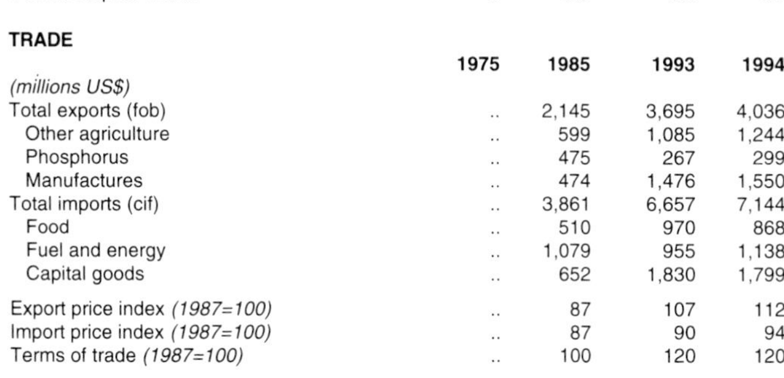

	1975	1985	1993	1994
(millions US$)				
Total exports (fob)	..	2,145	3,695	4,036
Other agriculture	..	599	1,085	1,244
Phosphorus	..	475	267	299
Manufactures	..	474	1,476	1,550
Total imports (cif)	..	3,861	6,657	7,144
Food	..	510	970	868
Fuel and energy	..	1,079	955	1,138
Capital goods	..	652	1,830	1,799
Export price index *(1987=100)*	..	87	107	112
Import price index *(1987=100)*	..	87	90	94
Terms of trade *(1987=100)*	..	100	120	120

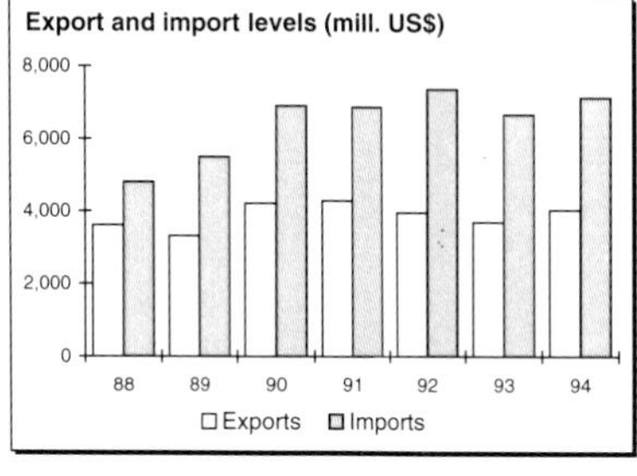

BALANCE of PAYMENTS

	1975	1985	1993	1994
(millions US$)				
Exports of goods and non-factor services	1,997	3,185	6,205	6,696
Imports of goods and non-factor services	2,939	4,341	7,671	8,265
Resource balance	-942	-1,156	-1,466	-1,569
Net factor income	-88	-766	-1,326	-1,295
Net current transfers	482	1,063	2,251	2,158
Current account balance, before official transfers	-548	-859	-542	-706
Financing items (net)	520	877	1,026	1,320
Changes in net reserves	27	-19	-484	-614
Memo:				
Reserves including gold *(mill. US$)*	438	345	3,942	4,377
Conversion rate *(local/US$)*	4.1	10.1	9.3	9.2

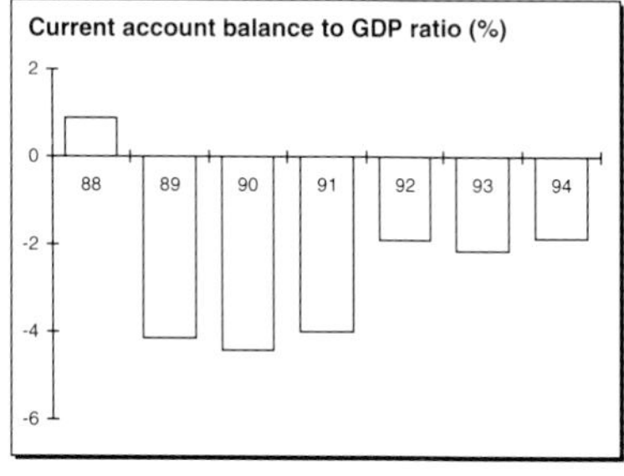

EXTERNAL DEBT and RESOURCE FLOWS

	1975	1985	1993	1994
(millions US$)				
Total debt outstanding and disbursed	1,889	16,526	21,430	22,096
IBRD	244	1,288	3,559	3,746
IDA	31	43	36	35
Total debt service	163	1,372	2,614	2,965
IBRD	33	167	552	572
IDA	0	1	2	2
Composition of net resource flows				
Official grants	26	416	179	151
Official creditors	232	428	-91	-265
Private creditors	283	153	274	a
Foreign direct investment	0	20	522	776
Portfolio equity	0	0	0	0
World Bank program				
Commitments	33	379	809	127
Disbursements	111	307	377	246
Principal repayments	18	87	294	302
Net flows	93	220	83	-56
Interest payments	15	81	260	271
Net transfers	78	139	-177	-327

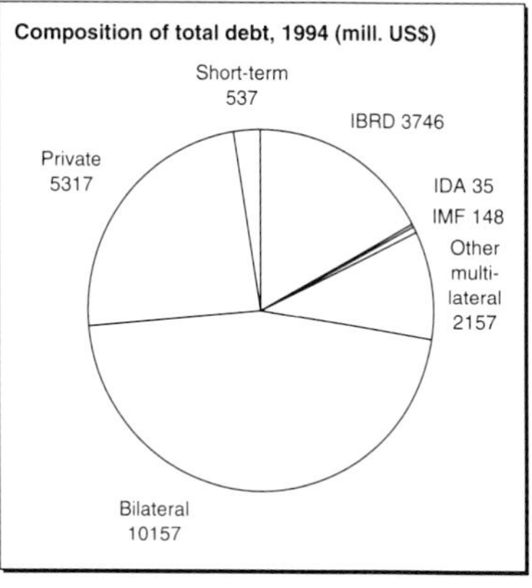

International Economics Department

Debt data are from *World Debt Tables 1994-95,* except for composition of net resource flows, 1994 (COD).
a. Private creditor net resource flows for 1994 are included in official creditors.

Oman

POVERTY and SOCIAL	Oman	M. East & North Africa	Upper-middle-income
Population mid-1994 *(millions)*	2.1	268	510
GNP per capita 1994 *(US$)*	5,200	..	4,760
Average annual growth, 1990-94			
Population *(%)*	4.2	2.6	1.7
Labor force *(%)*	2.7	3.1	2.2
Most recent estimate *(latest year available since 1988)*			
Poverty: headcount index *(% of population)*	..	..	..
Urban population *(% of total population)*	13	55	71
Life expectancy at birth *(years)*	70	66	69
Infant mortality *(per 1,000 live births)*	29	52	36
Child malnutrition *(% of children under 5)*	..	..	..
Access to safe water *(% of population)*	57	84	87
Illiteracy *(% of population age 15+)*	..	45	14
Gross primary enrollment *(% of school-age population)*	100	97	105
Male	104	103	105
Female	96	90	105

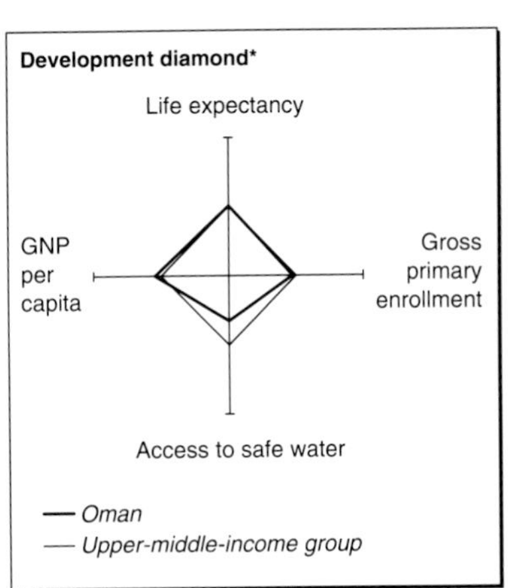

KEY ECONOMIC RATIOS and LONG-TERM TRENDS

	1975	1985	1993	1994
Gross domestic investment/GDP	35.6	27.6	..	..
Exports of goods and non-factor services/GDP	67.6	49.8	..	..
Gross domestic savings/GDP	52.5	40.2	..	..
Gross national savings/GDP	23.9	21.3	..	..
Current account balance/GDP	-17.0	2.2	-9.6	..
Interest payments/GDP	0.3	1.1	1.4	1.1
Total debt/GDP	17.4	23.3	23.4	23.6
Total debt service/exports	..	5.4	10.4	..
Present value of debt/GDP	..	..	22.3	..
Present value of debt/exports	..	..	43.5	..

(average annual growth)	1975-84	1985-94	1993	1994	1995-04
GDP	7.6	5.1	6.5	4.0	..
GNP per capita	2.9	0.6	1.8	-0.6	..
Exports of goods and nfs	..	..	..	..	..

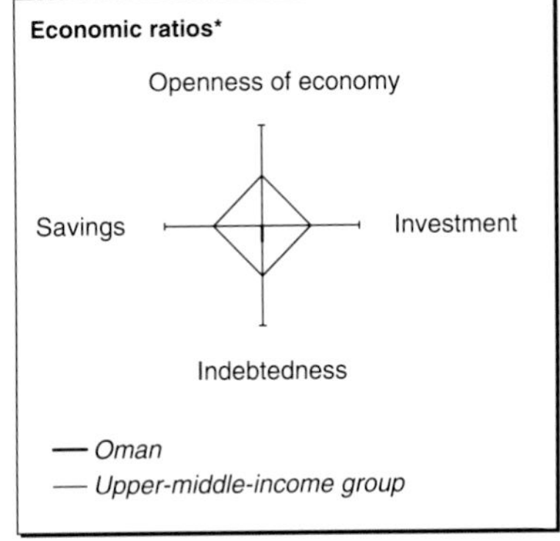

STRUCTURE of the ECONOMY

(% of GDP)	1975	1985	1993	1994
Agriculture	2.8	2.8	..	..
Industry	77.5	59.3	..	..
Manufacturing	0.3	2.4	..	..
Services	19.7	37.9	..	..
Private consumption	15.9	32.6	..	..
General government consumption	31.6	27.1	..	..
Gross domestic investment	35.6	27.6	..	..
Exports of goods and non-factor services	67.6	49.8	..	..
Imports of goods and non-factor services	50.7	37.2	..	..

(average annual growth)	1975-84	1985-94	1993	1994
Agriculture	*13.3*	*4.4*	..	..
Industry	*9.8*	*5.1*	..	..
Manufacturing	*43.8*	*5.4*	..	..
Services	*13.4*	*3.8*	..	..
Private consumption	..	..	..	..
General government consumption	..	..	..	..
Gross domestic investment	..	..	..	..
Exports of goods and non-factor services	..	..	..	..
Imports of goods and non-factor services	..	..	..	..
Gross national product	8.2	5.1	6.2	3.7

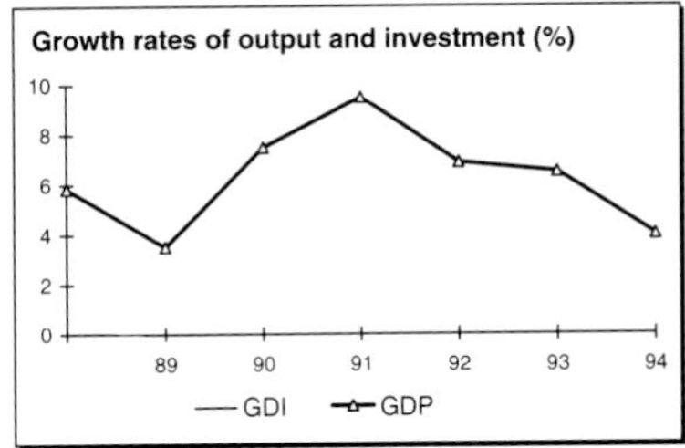

Note: 1994 data are preliminary estimates. Figures in italics are for years other than those specified.

* The diamonds show four key indicators in the country (in bold) compared with its income-group average. If data are missing, the diamond will be incomplete.

PRICES and GOVERNMENT FINANCE

	1975	1985	1993	1994
Domestic prices				
(% change)				
Consumer prices	..	..	..	..
Implicit GDP deflator	2.4	-0.3	-7.1	-1.7
Government finance				
(% of GDP)				
Current revenue	..	..	..	..
Current budget balance	..	..	..	..
Overall surplus/deficit	..	..	..	..

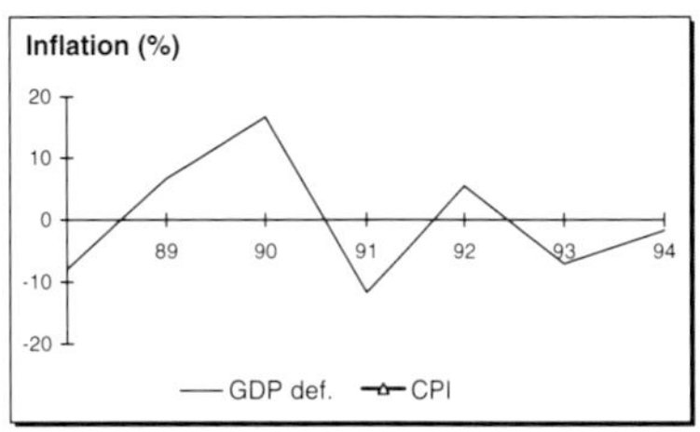

TRADE

	1975	1985	1993	1994
(millions US$)				
Total exports (fob)	..	..	..	..
n.a.	..	..	..	..
n.a.	..	..	..	..
Manufactures	..	..	..	..
Total imports (cif)	..	3,153	..	..
Food	..	391	..	..
Fuel and energy	..	..	..	..
Capital goods	..	824	..	..
Export price index *(1987=100)*	..	..	..	..
Import price index *(1987=100)*	..	..	..	..
Terms of trade *(1987=100)*	..	..	..	..

BALANCE of PAYMENTS

	1975	1985	1993	1994
(millions US$)				
Exports of goods and non-factor services	..	4,986	5,378	..
Imports of goods and non-factor services	..	3,778	4,926	..
Resource balance	..	1,207	453	..
Net factor income	..	-252	-211	..
Net current transfers	-208	-732	-1,329	..
Current account balance, before official transfers	-357	223	-1,087	..
Financing items (net)	..	-127	29	..
Changes in net reserves	..	-96	1,058	1
Memo:				
Reserves including gold *(mill. US$)*	166	1,185	1,021	1,090
Conversion rate *(local/US$)*	0.3	0.3	0.4	0.4

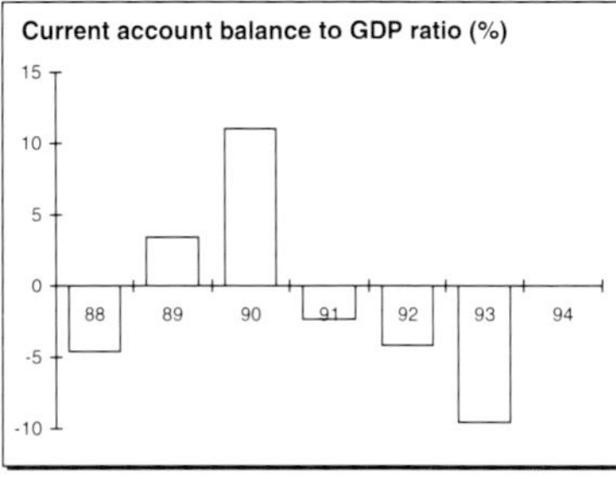

EXTERNAL DEBT and RESOURCE FLOWS

	1975	1985	1993	1994
(millions US$)				
Total debt outstanding and disbursed	364	2,330	2,661	2,740
IBRD	0	43	46	33
IDA	0	0	0	0
Total debt service	28	289	607	525
IBRD	0	10	17	20
IDA	0	0	0	0
Composition of net resource flows				
Official grants	29	41	10	5
Official creditors	15	19	64	55
Private creditors	106	501	-118	-44
Foreign direct investment	106	161	99	130
Portfolio equity	0	0	0	0
World Bank program				
Commitments	0	23	0	0
Disbursements	0	9	6	0
Principal repayments	0	6	13	17
Net flows	0	2	-8	-16
Interest payments	0	3	4	4
Net transfers	0	-1	-12	-20

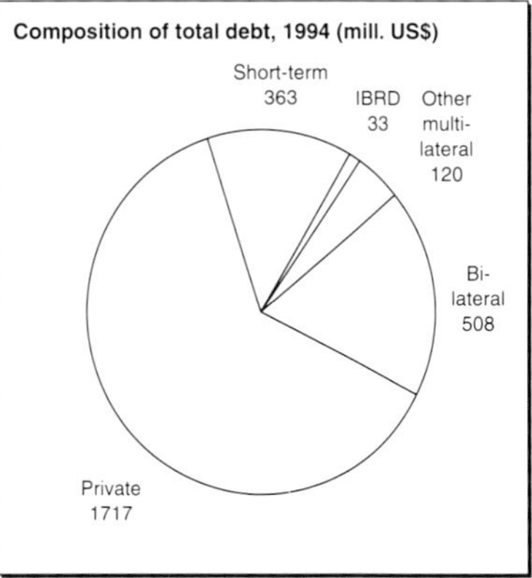

International Economics Department

Debt data are from *World Debt Tables 1994-95*.

Republic of Yemen

POVERTY and SOCIAL	Yemen	M. East & North Africa	Low-income
Population mid-1994 *(millions)*	13.9	268	3,092
GNP per capita 1994 *(US$)*	280	..	390
Average annual growth, 1990-94			
Population *(%)*	5.1	2.6	1.9
Labor force *(%)*	..	3.1	1.8
Most recent estimate *(latest year available since 1988)*			
Poverty: headcount index *(% of population)*	..	..	19
Urban population *(% of total population)*	33	55	28
Life expectancy at birth *(years)*	51	66	62
Infant mortality *(per 1,000 live births)*	117	52	63
Child malnutrition *(% of children under 5)*	30	..	40
Access to safe water *(% of population)*	..	84	67
Illiteracy *(% of population age 15+)*	62	45	41
Gross primary enrollment *(% of school-age population)*	76	97	108
Male	112	103	116
Female	37	90	101

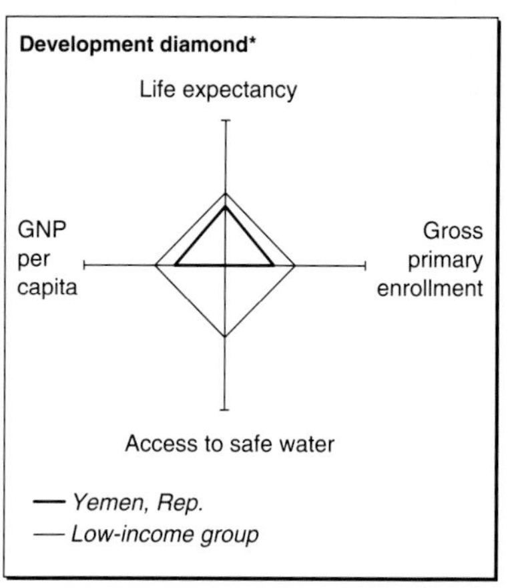

KEY ECONOMIC RATIOS and LONG-TERM TRENDS

	1975	1985	1993	1994
Gross domestic investment/GDP	..	..	15.0	11.9
Exports of goods and non-factor services/GDP	..	..	31.4	47.9
Gross domestic savings/GDP	..	..	-13.9	4.4
Gross national savings/GDP	..	..	-32.5	-10.7
Current account balance/GDP	..	..	-30.8	-2.7
Interest payments/GDP	..	..	0.5	0.8
Total debt/GDP	..	..	139.2	130.6
Total debt service/exports	..	..	4.9	5.8
Present value of debt/GDP	..	..	111.2	..
Present value of debt/exports	..	..	194.4	..

	1975-84	1985-94	1993	1994	1995-04
(average annual growth)					
GDP	..	..	5.9	6.0	4.4
GNP per capita	..	..	-3.1	5.9	2.4
Exports of goods and nfs	..	..	17.8	56.3	0.8

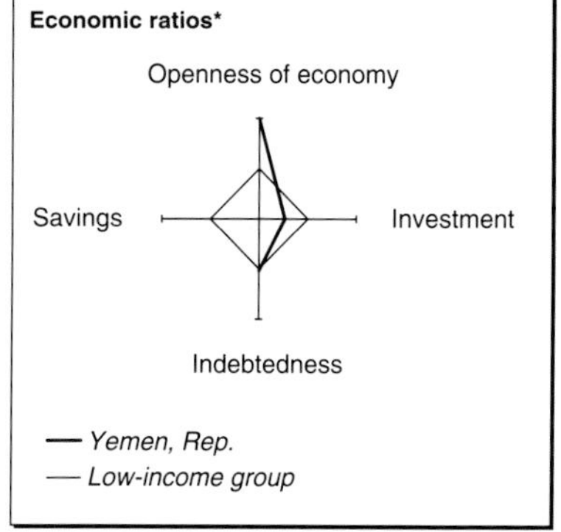

STRUCTURE of the ECONOMY

	1975	1985	1993	1994
(% of GDP)				
Agriculture	..	..	18.9	18.8
Industry	..	..	25.1	27.4
Manufacturing	..	..	12.3	13.2
Services	..	..	56.0	53.9
Private consumption	..	..	86.5	68.1
General government consumption	..	..	27.4	27.4
Gross domestic investment	..	..	15.0	11.9
Exports of goods and non-factor services	..	..	31.4	47.9
Imports of goods and non-factor services	..	..	60.4	55.4

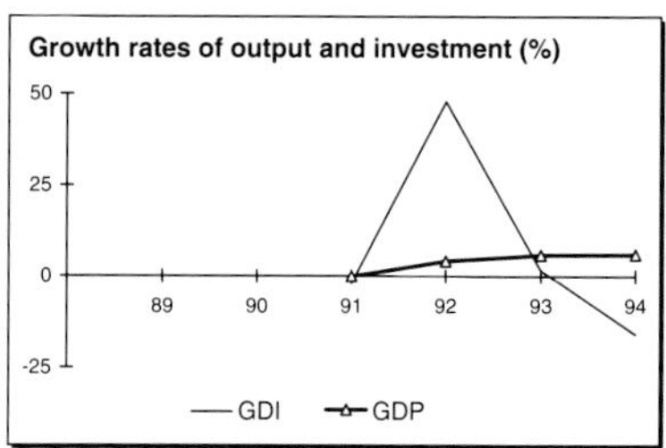

	1975-84	1985-94	1993	1994
(average annual growth)				
Agriculture	..	..	2.2	-1.5
Industry	..	..	12.1	28.8
Manufacturing	..	..	3.0	..
Services	..	..	2.9	-3.6
Private consumption	..	..	6.4	-14.6
General government consumption	..	..	4.4	6.0
Gross domestic investment	..	..	1.6	-15.9
Exports of goods and non-factor services	..	..	17.8	56.3
Imports of goods and non-factor services	..	..	10.7	-12.0
Gross national product	..	..	2.4	11.4

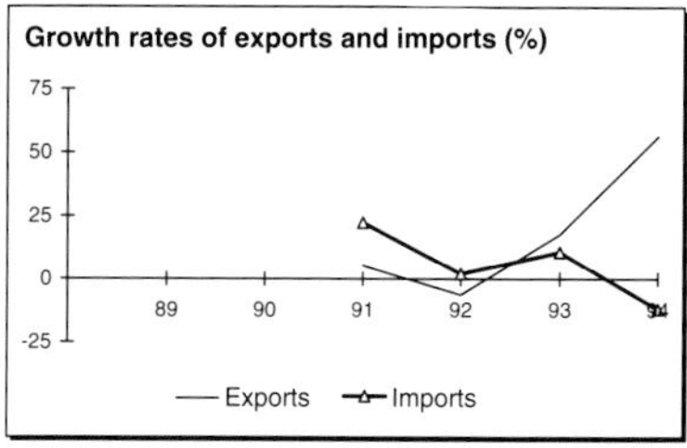

Note: 1994 data are preliminary estimates.

* The diamonds show four key indicators in the country (in bold) compared with its income-group average. If data are missing, the diamond will be incomplete.

PRICES and GOVERNMENT FINANCE

	1975	1985	1993	1994
Domestic prices				
(% change)				
Consumer prices	..	..	..	..
Implicit GDP deflator	..	..	19.1	21.3
Government finance				
(% of GDP)				
Current revenue	..	..	20.4	17.0
Current budget balance	..	..	-14.4	-18.4
Overall surplus/deficit	..	..	-18.1	-21.5

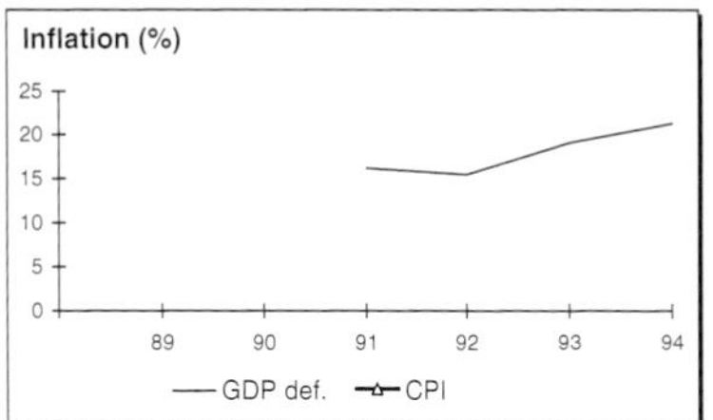

TRADE

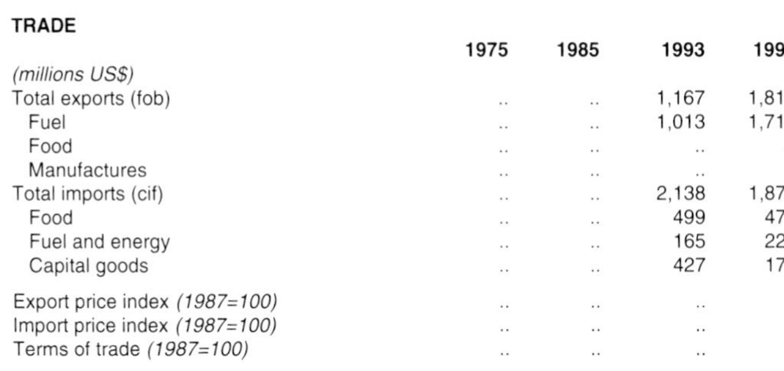

	1975	1985	1993	1994
(millions US$)				
Total exports (fob)	..	..	1,167	1,811
Fuel	..	..	1,013	1,715
Food	..	..	..	..
Manufactures	..	..	..	..
Total imports (cif)	..	..	2,138	1,876
Food	..	..	499	476
Fuel and energy	..	..	165	228
Capital goods	..	..	427	173
Export price index *(1987=100)*	..	..	..	..
Import price index *(1987=100)*	..	..	..	..
Terms of trade *(1987=100)*	..	..	..	..

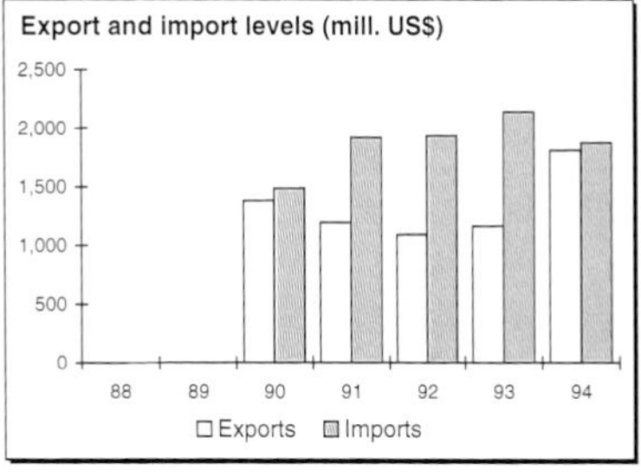

BALANCE of PAYMENTS

	1975	1985	1993	1994
(millions US$)				
Exports of goods and non-factor services	..	..	1,337	1,976
Imports of goods and non-factor services	..	..	2,568	2,284
Resource balance	..	..	-1,231	-308
Net factor income	..	..	-1,094	-860
Net current transfers	..	..	1,014	1,044
Current account balance, before official transfers	..	..	-1,311	-124
Financing items (net)	..	..	1,174	250
Changes in net reserves	..	..	137	-126
Memo:				
Reserves including gold *(mill. US$)*	..	..	165	..
Conversion rate *(local/US$)*	4.6	..	39.9	46.9

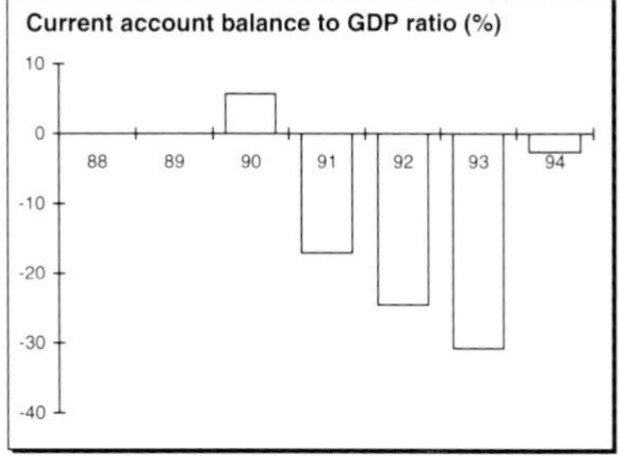

EXTERNAL DEBT and RESOURCE FLOWS

	1975	1985	1993	1994
(millions US$)				
Total debt outstanding and disbursed	440	3,339	5,923	6,077
IBRD	0	0	0	0
IDA	12	348	726	780
Total debt service	6	131	120	177
IBRD	0	0	0	0
IDA	0	4	11	13
Composition of net resource flows				
Official grants	185	208	100	200
Official creditors	55	202	48	67
Private creditors	0	6	10	1
Foreign direct investment	0	3	0	0
Portfolio equity	0	0	0	0
World Bank program				
Commitments	47	44	27	33
Disbursements	8	45	46	37
Principal repayments	0	1	6	7
Net flows	8	44	41	30
Interest payments	0	3	5	6
Net transfers	8	41	36	24

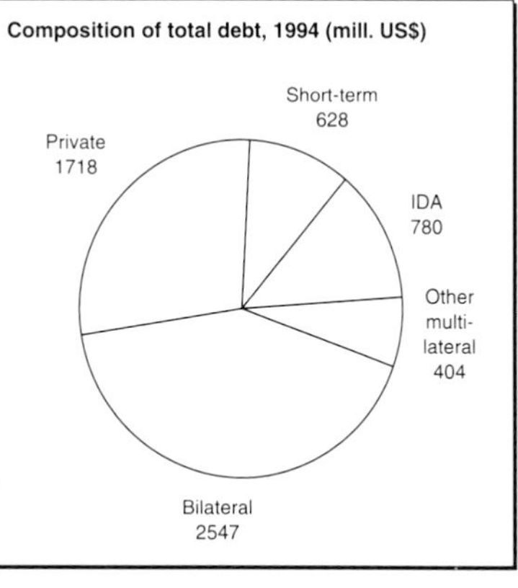

International Economics Department

Data before 1990 are from Yemen Arab Republic and the People's Democratic Republic of Yemen, which were unified in 1990. Foreign oil companies' shares are not included in exports. Debt data are from *World Debt Tables 1994-95*.

Saudi Arabia

POVERTY and SOCIAL	Saudi Arabia	M. East & North Africa	Upper-middle-income
Population mid-1994 *(millions)*	17.5	268	510
GNP per capita 1994 *(US$)*	*7,860*	..	4,760
Average annual growth, 1990-94			
Population *(%)*	2.2	2.6	1.7
Labor force *(%)*	..	3.1	2.2
Most recent estimate *(latest year available since 1988)*			
Poverty: headcount index *(% of population)*	..	..	..
Urban population *(% of total population)*	80	55	71
Life expectancy at birth *(years)*	70	66	69
Infant mortality *(per 1,000 live births)*	28	52	36
Child malnutrition *(% of children under 5)*	..	..	..
Access to safe water *(% of population)*	95	84	87
Illiteracy *(% of population age 15+)*	38	45	14
Gross primary enrollment *(% of school-age population)*	78	97	105
Male	81	103	105
Female	75	90	105

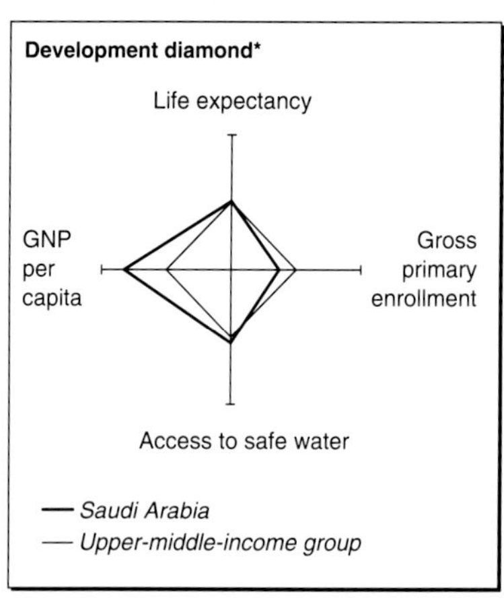

KEY ECONOMIC RATIOS and LONG-TERM TRENDS

	1975	1985	1993	1994
Gross domestic investment/GDP	20.9	20.9	..	..
Exports of goods and non-factor services/GDP	73.1	36.0	..	..
Gross domestic savings/GDP	67.9	13.0	..	..
Gross national savings/GDP	66.1	19.4	..	..
Current account balance/GDP	37.4	-11.2	..	..
Interest payments/GDP	..	..	..	..
Total debt/GDP	..	..	..	..
Total debt service/exports	..	..	..	..
Present value of debt/GDP	..	..	..	..
Present value of debt/exports	..	..	..	..

	1975-84	1985-94	1993	1994	1995-04
(average annual growth)					
GDP	1.1	*4.4*	..	..	..
GNP per capita	-3.0	*-1.1*	..	..	..
Exports of goods and nfs	..	..	..	..	..

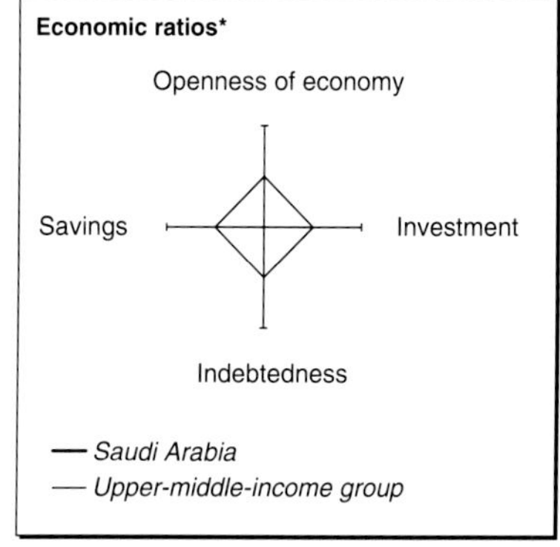

STRUCTURE of the ECONOMY

	1975	1985	1993	1994
(% of GDP)				
Agriculture	1.0	4.4	..	..
Industry	81.6	48.9	..	..
Manufacturing	5.0	7.8	..	..
Services	17.4	46.7	..	..
Private consumption	14.5	50.5	..	..
General government consumption	17.6	36.4	..	..
Gross domestic investment	20.9	20.9	..	..
Exports of goods and non-factor services	73.1	36.0	..	..
Imports of goods and non-factor services	26.1	43.9	..	..

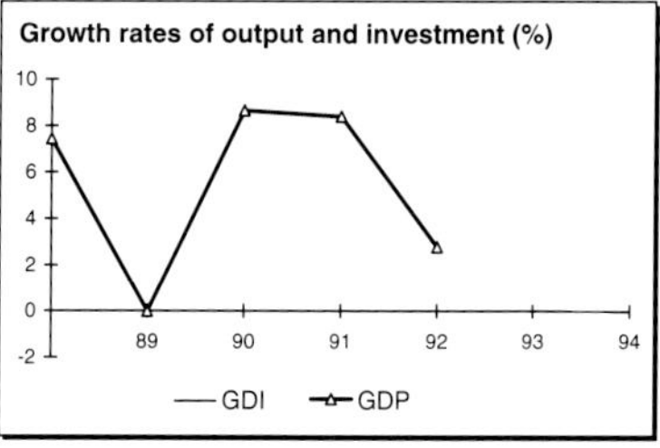

	1975-84	1985-94	1993	1994
(average annual growth)				
Agriculture	8.4	*11.2*	..	..
Industry	-1.7	*6.2*	..	..
Manufacturing	9.0	*5.3*	..	..
Services	4.0	*0.0*	..	..
Private consumption	..	..	..	..
General government consumption	..	..	..	..
Gross domestic investment	..	..	..	..
Exports of goods and non-factor services	..	..	..	..
Imports of goods and non-factor services	..	..	..	..
Gross national product	2.6	*3.2*	..	..

Note: 1994 data are preliminary estimates. Figures in italics are for years other than those specified.

* The diamonds show four key indicators in the country (in bold) compared with its income-group average. If data are missing, the diamond will be incomplete.

PRICES and GOVERNMENT FINANCE

	1975	1985	1993	1994
Domestic prices				
(% change)				
Consumer prices *(1995 to May: 4.7)*	34.6	-3.1	1.1	0.6
Implicit GDP deflator	10.1	-6.6	..	..
Government finance				
(% of GDP)				
Current revenue	..	..	34.2	30.4
Current budget balance	..	..	-3.6	-2.7
Overall surplus/deficit	..	..	-10.3	-7.5

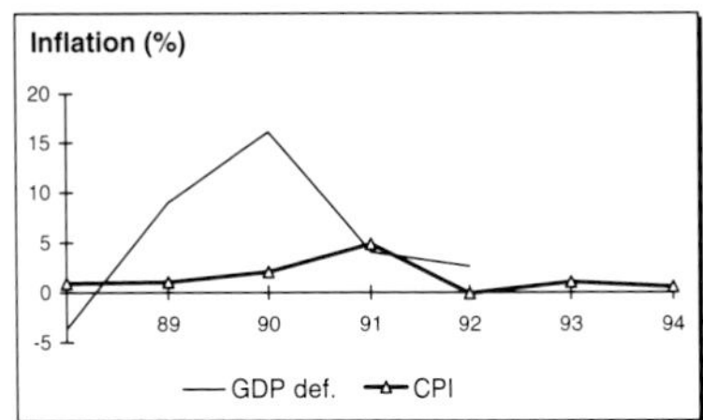

TRADE

	1975	1985	1993	1994
(millions US$)				
Total exports (fob)	..	..	..	..
Oil	..	..	41,100	37,400
n.a.	..	..	..	..
Manufactures	..	..	..	..
Total imports (cif)	..	..	..	..
Food	..	..	..	..
Fuel and energy	..	..	..	..
Capital goods	..	..	..	..
Export price index *(1987=100)*	..	..	..	..
Import price index *(1987=100)*	..	..	..	..
Terms of trade *(1987=100)*	..	..	..	..

BALANCE of PAYMENTS

	1975	1985	1993	1994
(millions US$)				
Exports of goods and non-factor services	28,730	31,040	48,444	..
Imports of goods and non-factor services	10,379	46,185	50,208	..
Resource balance	18,351	-15,146	-1,764	..
Net factor income	-284	10,662	4,203	..
Net current transfers	-554	-5,199	-15,717	..
Current account balance, before official transfers	17,512	-9,682	-13,278	..
Financing items (net)	-8,453	8,973	14,774	..
Changes in net reserves	-9,059	709	-1,496	351
Memo:				
Reserves including gold *(mill. US$)*	23,625	26,507	9,224	9,139
Conversion rate *(local/US$)*	3.5	3.6	3.7	3.7

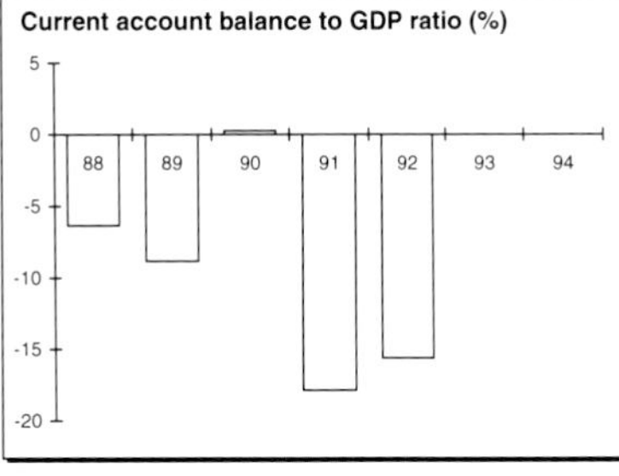

EXTERNAL DEBT and RESOURCE FLOWS

	1975	1985	1993	1994
(millions US$)				
Total debt outstanding and disbursed	..	..	..	..
IBRD	..	..	..	..
IDA	..	..	..	..
Total debt service	..	..	..	..
IBRD	..	..	..	..
IDA	..	..	..	..
Composition of net resource flows				
Official grants	0	0	5	0
Official creditors	..	..	..	..
Private creditors	..	..	..	..
Foreign direct investment	1,865	251	200	350
Portfolio equity	..	..	..	..
World Bank program				
Commitments	..	..	..	..
Disbursements	..	..	..	..
Principal repayments	..	..	..	..
Net flows	..	..	..	..
Interest payments	..	..	..	..
Net transfers	..	..	..	..

International Economics Department

Syrian Arab Republic

POVERTY and SOCIAL	Syrian Arab Republic	M. East & North Africa	Lower-middle-income
Population mid-1994 *(millions)*	14.2	268	1,112
GNP per capita 1994 *(US$)*	..	..	1,510
Average annual growth, 1990-94			
Population *(%)*	3.4	2.6	1.5
Labor force *(%)*	3.9	3.1	1.7
Most recent estimate *(latest year available since 1988)*			
Poverty: headcount index *(% of population)*	..	..	..
Urban population *(% of total population)*	52	55	55
Life expectancy at birth *(years)*	68	66	67
Infant mortality *(per 1,000 live births)*	38	52	39
Child malnutrition *(% of children under 5)*	..	..	..
Access to safe water *(% of population)*	79	84	78
Illiteracy *(% of population age 15+)*	36	45	19
Gross primary enrollment *(% of school-age population)*	107	97	104
Male	113	103	103
Female	101	90	96

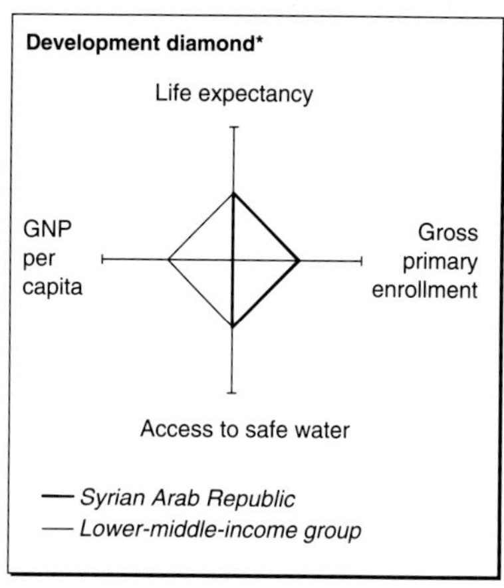

KEY ECONOMIC RATIOS and LONG-TERM TRENDS

	1975	1985	1993	1994
Gross domestic investment/GDP	25.0	23.8	..	..
Exports of goods and non-factor services/GDP	21.4	12.3	..	..
Gross domestic savings/GDP	12.5	11.2	..	..
Gross national savings/GDP	13.6	12.2	..	..
Current account balance/GDP	-8.2	-13.2	..	..
Interest payments/GDP	0.3	0.4	..	..
Total debt/GDP	11.5	66.1	..	..
Total debt service/exports	8.1	12.3	5.3	..
Present value of debt/GDP	..	..	..	..
Present value of debt/exports	..	..	315.3	..

	1975-84	1985-94	1993	1994	1995-04
(average annual growth)					
GDP	5.3	*2.4*	..	..	..
GNP per capita	1.8	*-2.4*	..	..	..
Exports of goods and nfs	0.1	*2.2*	..	..	..

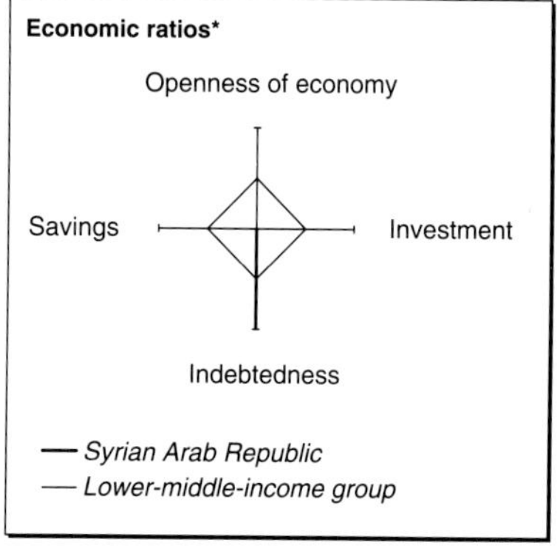

STRUCTURE of the ECONOMY

	1975	1985	1993	1994
(% of GDP)				
Agriculture	18.0	21.0	..	..
Industry	24.2	21.9	..	..
Manufacturing	..	..	..	..
Services	57.9	57.1	..	..
Private consumption	66.4	65.1	..	..
General government consumption	21.1	23.8	..	..
Gross domestic investment	25.0	23.8	..	..
Exports of goods and non-factor services	21.4	12.3	..	..
Imports of goods and non-factor services	34.0	24.9	..	..

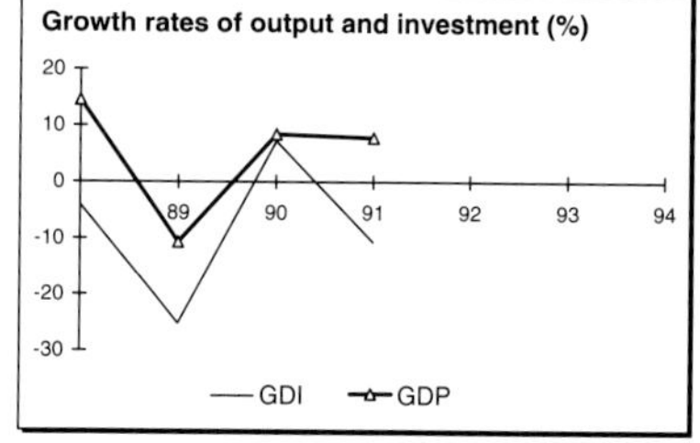

	1975-84	1985-94	1993	1994
(average annual growth)				
Agriculture	4.8	*0.0*	..	..
Industry	3.3	*12.8*	..	..
Manufacturing	..	..	..	..
Services	6.3	*-1.2*	..	..
Private consumption	2.4	*6.3*	..	..
General government consumption	7.6	*-3.2*	..	..
Gross domestic investment	5.7	*-14.1*	..	..
Exports of goods and non-factor services	0.1	*2.2*	..	..
Imports of goods and non-factor services	-0.8	*-4.7*	..	..
Gross national product	5.2	*1.1*	..	..

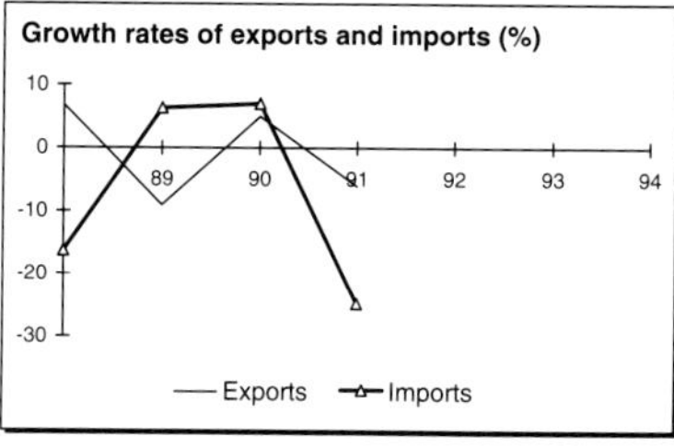

Note: 1994 data are preliminary estimates. Figures in italics are for years other than those specified.

* The diamonds show four key indicators in the country (in bold) compared with its income-group average. If data are missing, the diamond will be incomplete.

PRICES and GOVERNMENT FINANCE

	1975	1985	1993	1994
Domestic prices				
(% change)				
Consumer prices	11.5	17.3	11.8	..
Implicit GDP deflator	8.0	4.1	..	..
Government finance				
(% of GDP)				
Current revenue	..	..	..	..
Current budget balance	..	..	..	..
Overall surplus/deficit	..	..	..	..

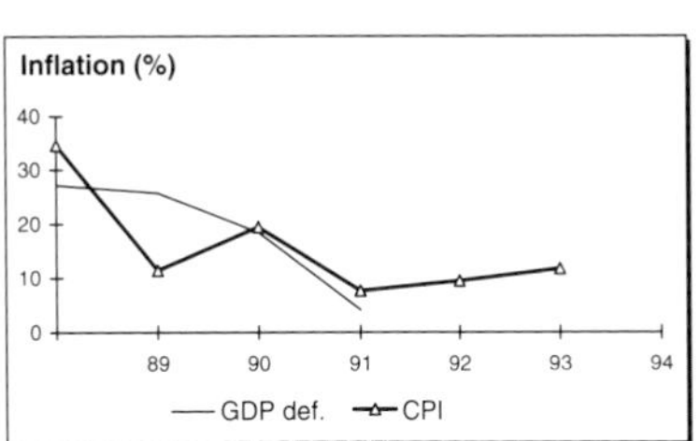

TRADE

	1975	1985	1993	1994
(millions US$)				
Total exports (fob)	..	..	..	..
n.a.	..	..	..	..
n.a.	..	..	..	..
Manufactures	..	..	..	..
Total imports (cif)	..	..	..	..
Food	..	..	..	..
Fuel and energy	..	..	..	..
Capital goods	..	..	..	..
Export price index *(1987=100)*	..	..	..	..
Import price index *(1987=100)*	..	..	..	..
Terms of trade *(1987=100)*	..	..	..	..

BALANCE of PAYMENTS

	1975	1985	1993	1994
(millions US$)				
Exports of goods and non-factor services	1,265	2,512	4,651	..
Imports of goods and non-factor services	1,892	4,920	4,703	..
Resource balance	-627	-2,409	-52	..
Net factor income	13	-110	-1,196	..
Net current transfers	52	350	600	..
Current account balance, before official transfers	-561	-2,169	-647	..
Financing items (net)	804	1,984	711	..
Changes in net reserves	-243	186	-64	..
Memo:				
Reserves including gold *(mill. US$)*	813	355	..	..
Conversion rate *(local/US$)*	3.0	5.1	..	..

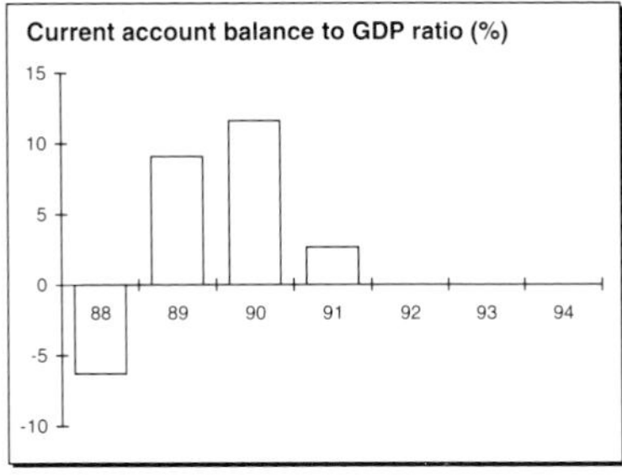

EXTERNAL DEBT and RESOURCE FLOWS

	1975	1985	1993	1994
(millions US$)				
Total debt outstanding and disbursed	786	10,843	19,975	20,444
IBRD	4	311	419	405
IDA	9	46	44	44
Total debt service	111	356	283	492
IBRD	1	38	39	107
IDA	0	1	0	1
Composition of net resource flows				
Official grants	540	616	77	80
Official creditors	139	1,737	150	168
Private creditors	52	85	-28	-28
Foreign direct investment	0	37	70	72
Portfolio equity	0	0	0	0
World Bank program				
Commitments	81	8	0	0
Disbursements	5	22	0	0
Principal repayments	0	19	19	50
Net flows	5	3	-19	-50
Interest payments	1	21	20	59
Net transfers	4	-17	-39	-108

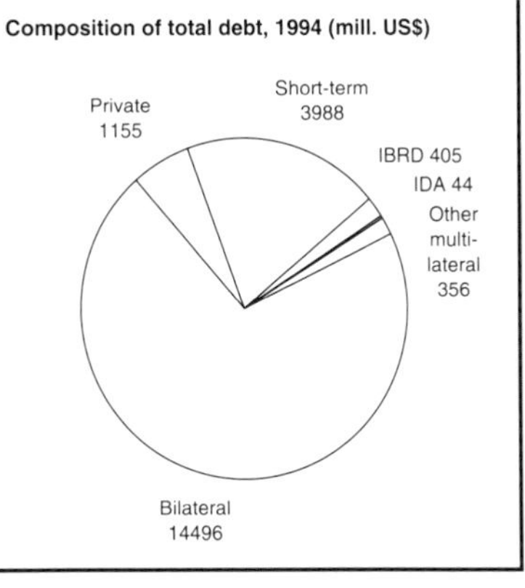

International Economics Department

Debt data are from *World Debt Tables 1994-95*.

Tunisia

POVERTY and SOCIAL	Tunisia	M. East & North Africa	Lower-middle-income
Population mid-1994 *(millions)*	8.8	268	1,112
GNP per capita 1994 *(US$)*	1,800	..	1,510
Average annual growth, 1990-94			
Population *(%)*	2.2	2.6	1.5
Labor force *(%)*	2.8	3.1	1.7
Most recent estimate *(latest year available since 1988)*			
Poverty: headcount index *(% of population, 1990) /1*	7	..	..
Poverty: headcount index *(% of population, 1990) /2*	3		
Urban population *(% of total population)*	57	55	55
Life expectancy at birth *(years)*	68	66	67
Infant mortality *(per 1,000 live births)*	42	52	39
Child malnutrition *(% of children under 5)*	8	..	..
Access to safe water *(% of population)*	67	84	78
Illiteracy *(% of population age 15+)*	32	45	19
Gross primary enrollment *(% of school-age population)*	120	97	104
Male	125	103	103
Female	115	90	96

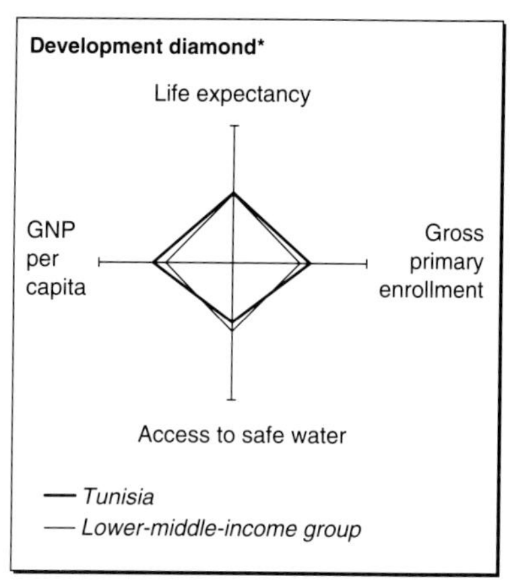

KEY ECONOMIC RATIOS and LONG-TERM TRENDS

	1975	1985	1993	1994
Gross domestic investment/GDP	28.0	26.6	29.2	24.3
Exports of goods and non-factor services/GDP	31.0	32.6	40.8	44.9
Gross domestic savings/GDP	23.2	20.4	22.0	22.0
Gross national savings/GDP	23.5	19.4	22.6	22.8
Current account balance/GDP	-4.9	-7.1	-8.0	-2.6
Interest payments/GDP	0.8	3.0	2.9	2.9
Total debt/GDP	25.6	59.0	59.4	60.2
Total debt service/exports	7.0	24.7	20.7	19.3
Present value of debt/GDP	..	..	52.0	..
Present value of debt/exports	..	..	117.0	..

(average annual growth)	1975-84	1985-94	1993	1994	1995-04
GDP	5.2	4.0	2.3	3.5	5.6
GNP per capita	2.6	1.8	-0.3	1.7	3.9
Exports of goods and nfs	5.2	7.5	3.6	13.7	7.7

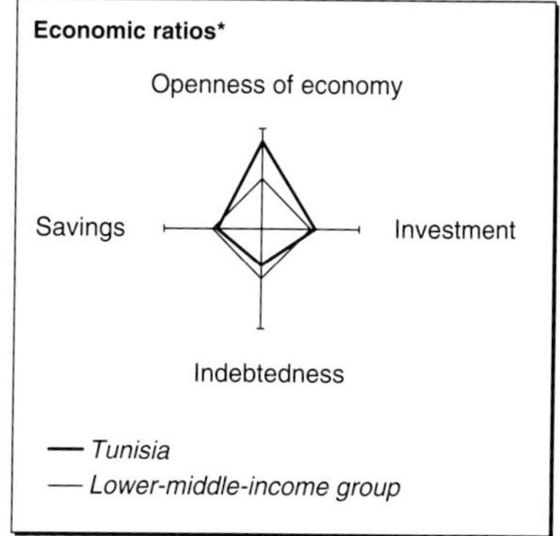

STRUCTURE of the ECONOMY

(% of GDP)	1975	1985	1993	1994
Agriculture	21.0	17.3	16.9	15.0
Industry	29.4	34.1	31.7	32.3
Manufacturing	10.3	13.5	19.8	20.5
Services	49.7	48.6	51.3	52.7
Private consumption	62.2	63.0	61.9	61.9
General government consumption	14.6	16.5	16.1	16.1
Gross domestic investment	28.0	26.6	29.2	24.3
Exports of goods and non-factor services	31.0	32.6	40.8	44.9
Imports of goods and non-factor services	35.8	38.7	48.0	47.2

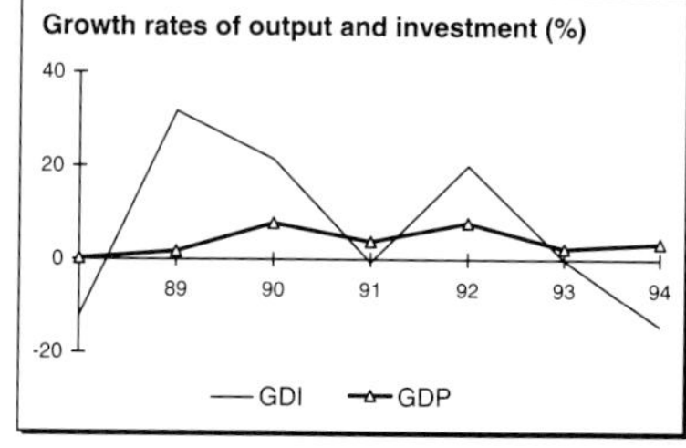

(average annual growth)	1975-84	1985-94	1993	1994
Agriculture	1.1	4.4	-5.3	-9.9
Industry	7.0	4.3	0.9	4.9
Manufacturing	9.7	7.8	3.3	7.6
Services	5.8	3.6	5.8	5.5
Private consumption	6.7	3.1	3.4	3.9
General government consumption	6.5	3.2	3.1	3.7
Gross domestic investment	5.4	5.5	-0.1	-14.2
Exports of goods and non-factor services	5.2	7.5	3.6	13.7
Imports of goods and non-factor services	8.0	6.2	3.6	2.7
Gross national product	5.2	4.2	2.1	3.5

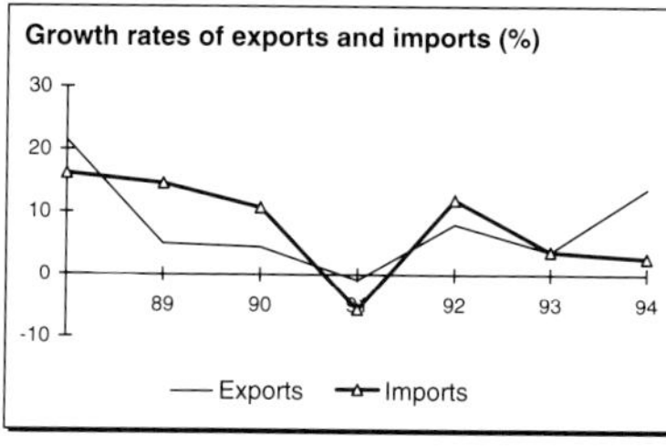

Note: 1994 data are preliminary estimates. /1 Poverty line is local. /2 Poverty is defined as spending less than one dollar per person per day (1985$, PPP).

* The diamonds show four key indicators in the country (in bold) compared with its income-group average. If data are missing, the diamond will be incomplete.

PRICES and GOVERNMENT FINANCE

	1975	1985	1993	1994
Domestic prices				
(% change)				
Consumer prices *(1995 to May: 2.4)*	..	7.3	4.0	4.7
Implicit GDP deflator	5.1	4.9	4.5	5.0
Government finance				
(% of GDP)				
Current revenue	..	31.3	26.5	27.2
Current budget balance	..	6.6	3.4	3.9
Overall surplus/deficit	..	-4.9	-2.2	-2.7

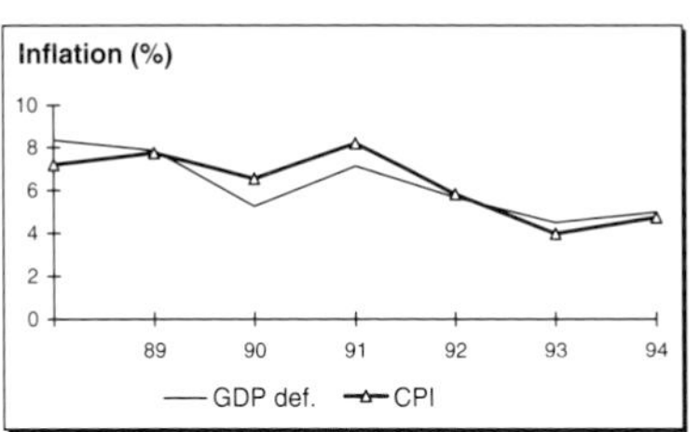

TRADE

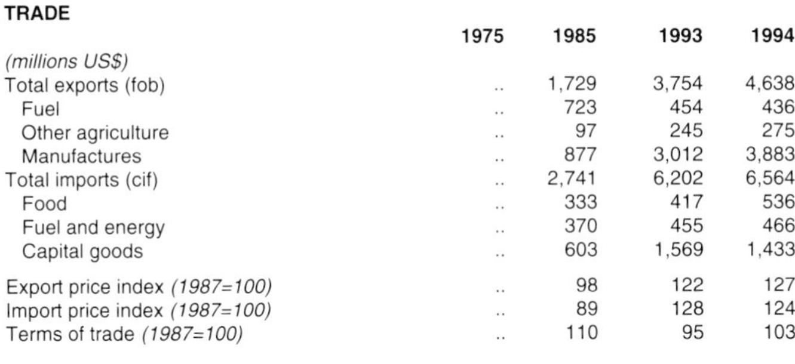

	1975	1985	1993	1994
(millions US$)				
Total exports (fob)	..	1,729	3,754	4,638
Fuel	..	723	454	436
Other agriculture	..	97	245	275
Manufactures	..	877	3,012	3,883
Total imports (cif)	..	2,741	6,202	6,564
Food	..	333	417	536
Fuel and energy	..	370	455	466
Capital goods	..	603	1,569	1,433
Export price index *(1987=100)*	..	98	122	127
Import price index *(1987=100)*	..	89	128	124
Terms of trade *(1987=100)*	..	110	95	103

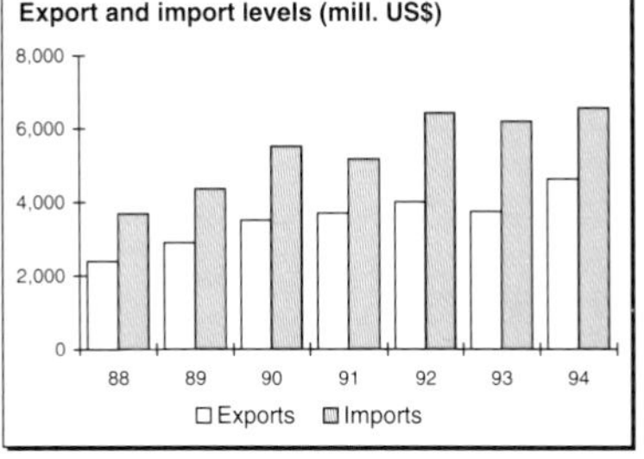

BALANCE of PAYMENTS

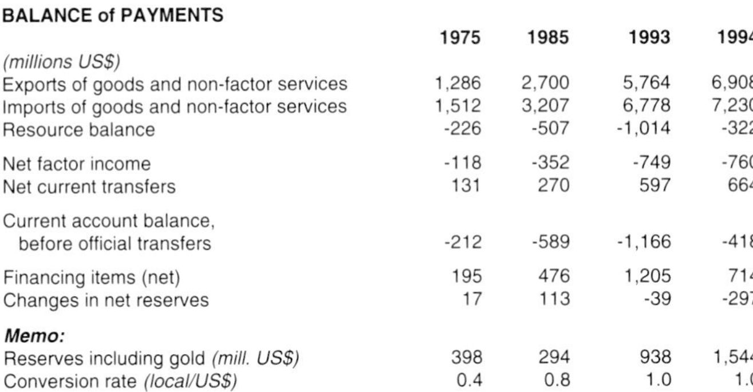

	1975	1985	1993	1994
(millions US$)				
Exports of goods and non-factor services	1,286	2,700	5,764	6,908
Imports of goods and non-factor services	1,512	3,207	6,778	7,230
Resource balance	-226	-507	-1,014	-322
Net factor income	-118	-352	-749	-760
Net current transfers	131	270	597	664
Current account balance, before official transfers	-212	-589	-1,166	-418
Financing items (net)	195	476	1,205	714
Changes in net reserves	17	113	-39	-297
Memo:				
Reserves including gold *(mill. US$)*	398	294	938	1,544
Conversion rate *(local/US$)*	0.4	0.8	1.0	1.0

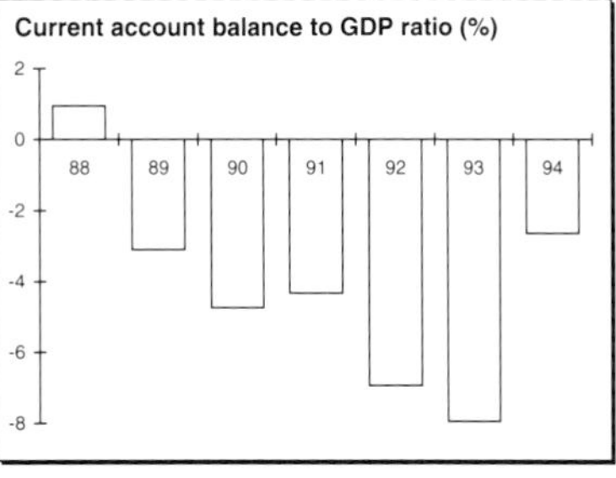

EXTERNAL DEBT and RESOURCE FLOWS

	1975	1985	1993	1994
(millions US$)				
Total debt outstanding and disbursed	1,109	4,884	8,701	9,495
IBRD	110	558	1,595	1,715
IDA	55	65	54	52
Total debt service	103	746	1,350	1,489
IBRD	15	88	263	297
IDA	1	1	2	3
Composition of net resource flows				
Official grants	49	30	135	148
Official creditors	104	210	375	255
Private creditors	20	109	-99	283
Foreign direct investment	45	108	239	275
Portfolio equity	0	0	0	66
World Bank program				
Commitments	37	169	189	304
Disbursements	40	109	248	189
Principal repayments	7	48	149	175
Net flows	32	61	99	13
Interest payments	8	41	117	124
Net transfers	24	20	-18	-111

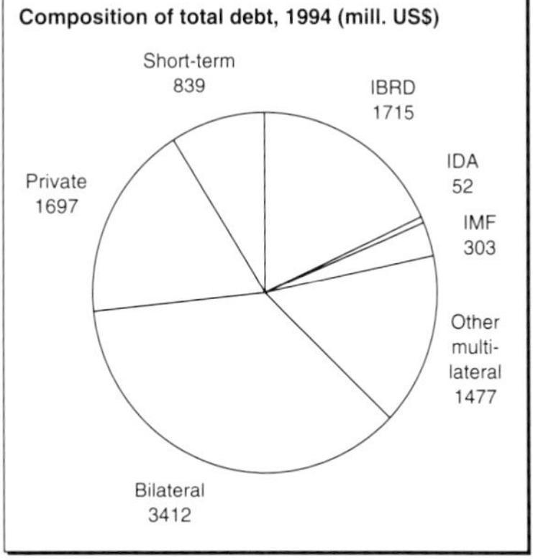

International Economics Department

Debt data are from *World Debt Tables 1994-95*.

United Arab Emirates

POVERTY and SOCIAL	United Arab Emirates	M. East & North Africa	High-income
Population mid-1994 *(millions)*	1.9	268	833
GNP per capita 1994 *(US$)*	*21,430*	..	23,100
Average annual growth, 1990-94			
Population *(%)*	2.6	2.6	0.6
Labor force *(%)*	1.9	3.1	0.0
Most recent estimate *(latest year available since 1988)*			
Poverty: headcount index *(% of population)*	..	..	..
Urban population *(% of total population)*	83	55	78
Life expectancy at birth *(years)*	74	66	77
Infant mortality *(per 1,000 live births)*	18	52	7
Child malnutrition *(% of children under 5)*	..	..	..
Access to safe water *(% of population)*	100	84	..
Illiteracy *(% of population age 15+)*	..	45	..
Gross primary enrollment *(% of school-age population)*	118	97	103
Male	119	103	103
Female	117	90	103

Development diamond*

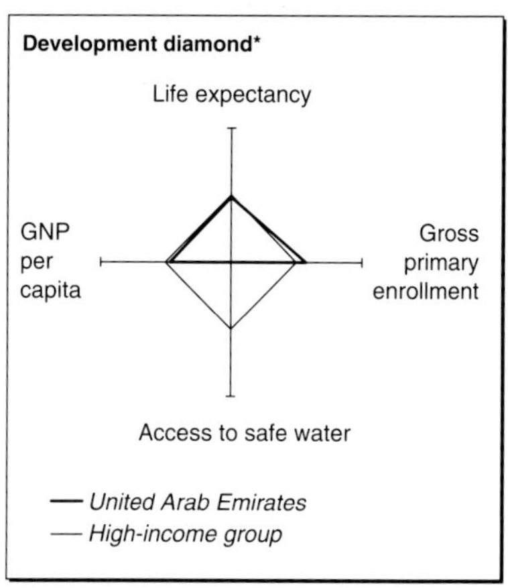

KEY ECONOMIC RATIOS and LONG-TERM TRENDS

	1975	1985	1993	1994
Gross domestic investment/GDP	30.7	25.1	24.6	24.9
Exports of goods and non-factor services/GDP	74.2	58.7	67.7	69.3
Gross domestic savings/GDP	75.9	53.0	33.4	27.0
Gross national savings/GDP	69.4	52.6	..	..
Current account balance/GDP	39.5	26.3	..	..
Interest payments/GDP	..	..	..	..
Total debt/GDP	..	..	..	..
Total debt service/exports	..	..	..	..
Present value of debt/GDP	..	..	..	..
Present value of debt/exports	..	..	..	..

	1975-84	1985-94	1993	1994	1995-04
(average annual growth)					
GDP	8.5	*3.1*	-1.4	1.1	..
GNP per capita	-1.9	*0.2*	-3.9	-1.5	..
Exports of goods and nfs	4.6	..	-2.6	6.9	..

Economic ratios*

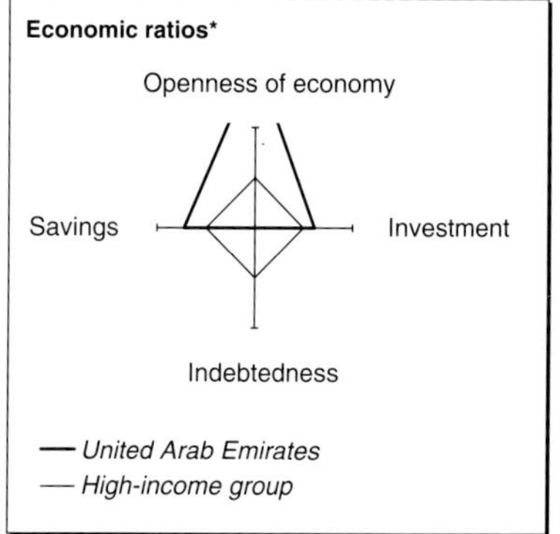

STRUCTURE of the ECONOMY

	1975	1985	1993	1994
(% of GDP)				
Agriculture	0.8	1.4	2.2	2.8
Industry	79.1	64.0	57.5	54.6
Manufacturing	0.9	9.1	8.5	8.6
Services	20.1	34.5	40.3	42.6
Private consumption	15.8	27.4	48.6	53.8
General government consumption	8.3	19.6	18.0	19.2
Gross domestic investment	30.7	25.1	24.6	24.9
Exports of goods and non-factor services	74.2	58.7	67.7	69.3
Imports of goods and non-factor services	29.0	30.9	58.8	67.2

	1975-84	1985-94	1993	1994
(average annual growth)				
Agriculture	15.2	*8.8*	3.5	4.5
Industry	6.9	*4.1*	-2.4	-2.1
Manufacturing	41.5	*2.0*	1.5	0.7
Services	11.9	*3.7*	4.6	5.2
Private consumption	8.0	..	..	4.5
General government consumption	17.7	..	..	-2.1
Gross domestic investment	5.6	..	..	0.7
Exports of goods and non-factor services	4.6	..	-2.6	6.9
Imports of goods and non-factor services	4.8	..	..	..
Gross national product	9.1	*3.7*	2.6	..

Note: 1994 data are preliminary estimates. Figures in italics are for years other than those specified.

* The diamonds show four key indicators in the country (in bold) compared with its income-group average. If data are missing, the diamond will be incomplete.

PRICES and GOVERNMENT FINANCE

	1975	1985	1993	1994
Domestic prices				
(% change)				
Consumer prices	..	..	4.7	4.6
Implicit GDP deflator	19.0	4.4	1.1	1.2
Government finance				
(% of GDP)				
Current revenue	..	..	..	..
Current budget balance	..	..	..	..
Overall surplus/deficit	..	..	..	..

TRADE

	1975	1985	1993	1994
(millions US$)				
Total exports (fob)	..	..	23,645	25,280
n.a.	..	..	..	..
n.a.	..	..	..	..
Manufactures	..	..	..	..
Total imports (cif)	..	..	19,613	21,792
Food	..	..	..	..
Fuel and energy	..	..	..	..
Capital goods	..	..	..	..
Export price index *(1987=100)*	..	..	..	..
Import price index *(1987=100)*	..	..	..	..
Terms of trade *(1987=100)*	..	..	..	..

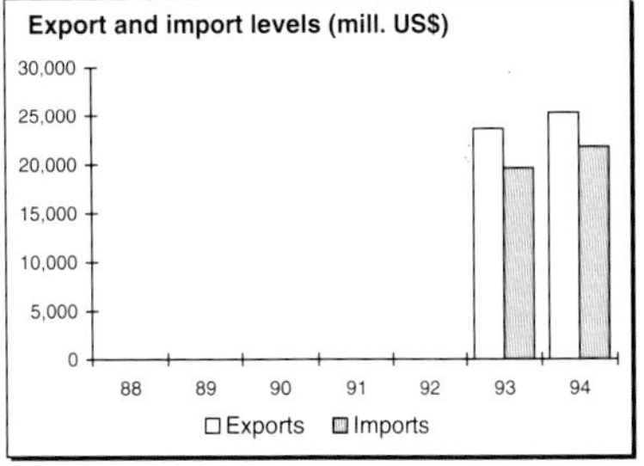

BALANCE of PAYMENTS

	1975	1985	1993	1994
(millions US$)				
Exports of goods and non-factor services	7,600	15,880	..	..
Imports of goods and non-factor services	3,040	8,680	..	..
Resource balance	4,560	7,200	..	..
Net factor income	70	1,500	..	..
Net current transfers	-710	-1,600	..	..
Current account balance, before official transfers	3,920	7,100	..	..
Financing items (net)	-2,410	-5,800	..	..
Changes in net reserves	-1,510	-1,300	..	..
Memo:				
Reserves including gold *(mill. US$)*	988	3,471	6,415	6,964
Conversion rate *(local/US$)*	4.0	3.7	3.7	..

EXTERNAL DEBT and RESOURCE FLOWS

	1975	1985	1993	1994
(millions US$)				
Total debt outstanding and disbursed	..	..	..	..
IBRD	..	..	..	..
IDA	..	..	..	..
Total debt service	..	..	..	..
IBRD	..	..	..	..
IDA	..	..	..	..
Composition of net resource flows				
Official grants	..	..	..	..
Official creditors	..	..	..	..
Private creditors	..	..	..	..
Foreign direct investment	..	..	..	..
Portfolio equity	..	..	..	..
World Bank program				
Commitments	..	..	..	..
Disbursements	..	..	..	..
Principal repayments	..	..	..	..
Net flows	..	..	..	..
Interest payments	..	..	..	..
Net transfers	..	..	..	..

International Economics Department